THE CHALLENGE OF SIMULTANEOUS ECONOMIC RELATIONS WITH EAST AND WEST

Also by Michael Marrese

SOVIET SUBSIDIZATION OF TRADE WITH EASTERN EUROPE:
A Soviet Perspective (*with Jan Vanous*)

The Challenge of Simultaneous Economic Relations with East and West

Edited by

Michael Marrese
Associate Professor of Economics
Northwestern University, Evanston, Illinois

and

Sándor Richter
Research Fellow
Hungarian Academy of Sciences, Budapest

MACMILLAN

© Michael Marrese and Sándor Richter 1990
Softcover reprint of the hardcover 1st edition 1990
All rights reserved. No reproduction, copy or transmission
of this publication may be made without written permission.

No paragraph of this publication may be reproduced, copied or
transmitted save with written permission or in accordance with
the provisions of the Copyright, Designs and Patents Act 1988,
or under the terms of any licence permitting limited copying
issued by the Copyright Licensing Agency, 33–4 Alfred Place,
London WC1E 7DP.

Any person who does any unauthorised act in relation to
this publication may be liable to criminal prosecution and
civil claims for damages.

First published 1990

Published by
THE MACMILLAN PRESS LTD
Houndmills, Basingstoke, Hampshire RG21 2XS
and London
Companies and representatives
throughout the world

British Library Cataloguing in Publication Data
The challenge of simultaneous economic relations with East
and West.
1. Eastern Europe. Economic relations with Western Europe
2. Western Europe. Economic relations with Eastern Europe
I. Marrese, Michael, *1950–* II. Richter, Sándor, *1953–*
337.4074
ISBN 978-1-349-11411-5   ISBN 978-1-349-11409-2 (eBook)
DOI 10.1007/978-1-349-11409-2

Contents

List of Tables	vii
List of Figures	ix
Preface	x
Acknowledgements	xv
Notes on the Contributors	xvi

1. Introduction
   Friedrich Levcik — 1

2. Hard Currency Settlement of Payments or Bilateralism and Clearing: how long will the dilemma remain?
   Sándor Richter — 5

3. Hungarian Foreign Trade: Failure to Reform
   Michael Marrese — 23

4. *Perestroika* in the Soviet Union: The Domestic and International Dimensions
   Nikolay Shmelev — 58

5. A new situation in Hungarian-Soviet trade: What is to be done?
   András Köves — 64

6. Economic Policy and Foreign Trade in Austria: Relations with West and East
   Jan Stankovsky — 80

   Appendix Austria's East–West Trade: A Descriptive Background Survey
   Friedrich Levcik and Jan Stankovsky — 95

7. Internal Regulation of Foreign Trade with Respect to Socialist Trading Partners: a comparison of the Finnish and the Hungarian systems
   Gábor Oblath — 109

8. Effects of Trade with Centrally Planned Economies on exchange rates and prices in Market Economies
   Yrjänä Tolonen — 126

Contents

9 An Appearance of Dual Attachment in the Soviet Union's Imports: Variations in Imports from the West in relation to Imports from CMEA Countries
   Urpo Kivikari 140

10 Dual Systems of International Settlements: an analysis of Yugoslavia's experience and some proposals for more efficient alternative settlement systems
   Ante Cicin-Sain 157

11 Some specific features of Inflation in a heavily-indebted Socialist country
   Neven Mates 174

12 The Foreign Policy conditions affecting economic relations between the smaller European states
   Peter Knirsch 192

13 Problems and Prospects of East–West Transfer of Technology
   Stanislav Simanovsky 194

14 Towards a comprehensive economic reform? A pessi-optimistic view
   László Szamuely 195

15 Reflections on enterprise-level currency conversion in Foreign Trade: The case of Hungary
   Ádám Török 197

16 Joint ventures between East and West
   Tauno Tiusanen 200

17 The involvement of the CMEA countries in the international trade in services: can they be competitive?
   Marie Lavigne 202

18 Money as a means of Communication and Reforms in Eastern Europe: Some Propositions
   Raimund Dietz 204

19 Summary Remarks
   Tamás Földi 207

Index 211

List of Tables

3.1	Relative Hungarian macroeconomic performance, 1970–86	30
3.2	Foreign-trade performance of CMEA and Yugoslavia, 1981–6	31
3.3	International comparison of changes in terms of trade, 1974–6	34
3.4	Pattern of Hungarian trade for 1974–86, by commodity categories and trade partners	36
3.5	Measures of trade instability for 1974–86, by commodity categories and trade partners	42
6.1a	Austria's foreign trade by region: exports	84
6.1b	Austria's foreign trade by region: imports	86
6.2	Commodity structure of Austrian foreign trade with the East, the EC-12, and total in 1987	88
6.3	Commodity structure of foreign trade with the East, and total of Austria, Germany, and Switzerland in 1987	89
8.1	Effects of a shift in ME1 from ME2 importables to CPE importables on ME1's output, Y, on its real Exchange rate, p, and on ME2's output, Y*, when the exchange rate between MEs is flexible	130
8.2	Effects of a shift in ME1 from ME2 importables to CPE importables when the ME exchange rate is fixed	132
9.1	Annual percentage changes in the Soviet Union's foreign trade in 1965–83	144
9.2	Annual percentage changes in the Soviet Union's imports from the West (X) and the CMEA 6 (X') in 1963–83	145
9.3	Regression results for annual variations (1971–83) in the Soviet Union's imports of grain from the West	149
9.4	Regression results for annual variations (1965–78) in the Soviet Union's imports of soap and cleansing and polishing preparations from the West	150
9.5	Regression results for annual variations (1971–83) in the Soviet Union's imports of textile and food-processing machines from the West	151

9.6	Regression results for annual variations (1965–83) in the Soviet Union's imports of paper and paperboard from the West (excluding Finland)	152
9.7	Regression results for annual variations (1965–83) in the Soviet Union's imports of paper and paperboard from Finland	152
9.8	Regression results for annual variations (1965–83) in the Soviet Union's imports of footwear from the West (excluding Finland)	154
9.9	Regression results for annual variations (1966–83) in the Soviet Union's imports of footwear from Finland	155
10.1	Socialist countries' share in Yugoslavia's merchandise trade 1976–87	160
10.2	Yugoslavia's trade with socialist countries	163
10.3	Monetary effects of bilateral credit balances realised in Yugoslavia's trade with CMEA clearing countries	169
11.1	Balance of the central banking system	180

List of Figures

8.1 Effects of a shift from ME2 importables to CPE importables on ME1s exports to the CPE, X^c, output Y, and exchange rate P 133

9.1 The linkage of Soviet imports from the West with the realisation of production plans and the purchasing power on Western markets   141

10.1 Yugoslavia's merchandise trade balance with two groups of socialist countries   163

Preface

In 1982 the Economic Information Unit of the Hungarian Academy of Sciences began to co-ordinate an international research project entitled *The Economic Relations of Austria, Finland, Yugoslavia and Hungary with the Soviet Union: Comparative Analysis*. The co-ordinator of the research project was the Economic Information Unit of the Hungarian Academy of Sciences. Other contributing institutions included the Hungarian Institute for Economic and Market Research and Informatics and the Vienna Institute for Comparative Economic Studies. Individually, Hungarian, Austrian, Finnish and Soviet researchers took part in the writing, revising, and preparation of the research papers. In the course of completing the country studies, it became apparent that a bilateral 'small country–Soviet Union' approach to the problems of the above mentioned four countries was too limiting. Economic relations with the Soviet Union should be analysed in a broader context, namely together with the problems of the economic relations of the concerned countries with the West and the other East European countries. This perception gave birth to the idea of organising the conference 'The Challenge of Simultaneous Economic Relations with East and West' that took place in March 1988 at the Rockefeller Foundation's Bellagio Conference Center. This volume is a product of that conference and we thank the Rockefeller Foundation for their generous support.

Austria, Finland, Hungary, and Yugoslavia belong to those European countries that maintain economic relations of vital importance with both the West (OECD countries) and the East (CMEA countries) simultaneously. Due to their different historical, political and social background, the solutions these countries found to problems deriving from their 'double attachment' have varied.

The objective of the conference was to identify the kinds of institutions, methods of settling payments, trade patterns, and so forth that have emerged in these four countries that have 'double attachment' to the OECD and the CMEA. Moreover, the comparison was to serve as a device to understand whether, why, and how much these four countries benefited from 'double attachment'.

Preface xi

Although the basic idea of the conference was a detailed discussion of the four countries concerned, the organisers intended to place the issues discussed into a broader international context. For this reason, besides scholars from Finland, Austria, Yugoslavia, and Hungary, outstanding experts of East–West economic relations were invited from France, Germany, Poland, the Soviet Union and the USA. This carefully planned composition of participants contributed to the unique atmosphere that characterised those four days of the conference in Bellagio. Certainly this atmosphere was primarily due to the interesting conference papers and the lively but tolerant discussion style of the participants.

In this volume approximately two-thirds of the conference papers are published in full, while a brief summary of the remaining third appears near the end of this volume. In Chapter 1, Friedrich Levcik suggests that the dilemma of dual attachment is more of a dilemma for Hungary than for Austria, Finland, or Yugoslavia. He then contrasts changes in the world economy with changes within the CMEA. Finally, he concludes that genuine economic reform within most CMEA countries is a precondition for more effective intra-CMEA economic relations and the integration of the CMEA in the world economy.

Sándor Richter (Chapter 2) focuses on the methods of settling payments utilised by Austria, Finland, Hungary, and Yugoslavia. In doing so, he supplies an overview of the nature of dual attachment. He goes on to discuss the tradeoffs involved in maintaining both hard currency payments and bilateral clearing; the ability of a country to abandon bilateral clearing; and the possible economic consequences to Eastern Europe if clearing were abolished in intra-CMEA trade.

Michael Marrese (Chapter 3) argues that Hungary has had three rather than two attachments: to the Soviet Union, to the rest of the CMEA, and to the West. He then demonstrates that the distinct manner and short-term orientation with which Hungary has addressed each of its attachments have been major factors behind Hungary's foreign-trade failures and the generally poor performance of the Hungarian economy. For an open economy such as Hungary's, economic reform and foreign-trade reform should have been implemented simultaneously in order to reinforce one another rather than in a piecemeal, sequential manner.

Nikolay Shmelev (Chapter 4) addresses the domestic and international dimensions of *perestroika* in the Soviet Union. After providing a broad overview of the progress and hopes of domestic transformation, Shmelev outlines possible ways by which the Soviet Union could become more integrated into the world economy. He points out the pitfalls of the reform process but is generally confident in the Soviet Union's future. Shmelev's long-term view of the reform process signals a warning sign to East European countries that the pace of the Soviet reform may be too slow to counteract the economic dangers that Eastern Europe faces.

András Köves (Chapter 5) implicitly acknowledges the difference in pressure on Eastern Europe and on the Soviet Union. He suggests that Hungary act alone, if necessary, to integrate itself into the world economy. This possibility has arisen because Hungarian terms of trade vis-à-vis the Soviet Union have been improving and will continue to improve. Thus Hungary has three choices: lend to the Union, obtain more imports from the Soviet Union in exchange for the current level of exports, or reduce the volume of exports to the Soviet Union and redirect those flows to the West. Köves sees the third choice as the only one consistent with Hungary's long-term interests.

Jan Stankovsky (Chapter 6) examines Austria's economic policies and foreign trade with the West and East. An appendix written by Friedrich Levcik and Jan Stankovsky provides a detailed description of the evolution of Austrian foreign economic policy. In the body of the paper, Stankovsky shows how Austria has attempted to exploit its dual attachment, yet is being drawn to closer and stronger economic ties with the West.

Gábor Oblath (Chapter 7) compares Hungarian financial regulation of trade with CMEA countries to Finnish regulation of its trade with the Soviet Union. Finland relies exclusively on administrative policy tools to regulate, on the macro level, Fino–Soviet trade, but makes no attempt to utilise either exchange rate policy or to manipulate individual trade prices. Hungary, however, while also avoiding the use of the exchange rate as a policy instrument, actively differentiates the bilateral trade prices that emerge from Hungarian–Soviet trade negotiations from the prices that Hungarian firms pay for imports and receive for exports. In summary, Oblath emphasises that the mechanisms of Fino–Soviet trade are based on a compromise of economic philosophies, while intra-CMEA trade is built upon traditional directive central planning.

Yrjänä Tolonen (Chapter 8) adopts a theoretical trade approach to point out that whether an increase in a market economy's (ME) trade with a centrally planned economy (CPE) is beneficial to the ME depends on the ME's initial share of CPE trade, the type of exchange rate between MEs (flexible or fixed), and the time horizon under consideration. The lower an ME's initial share of CPE trade, the presence of flexible exchange rates, and the longer the time horizon, the less likely it is that an increase in an ME's trade with a CPE will be beneficial for the ME.

Urpo Kivikari (Chapter 9) empirically demonstrates that the Soviet Union has dual attachment with respect to imports. For instance, the stability of Soviet imports for specific products is high whenever one partner (either the West or the CMEA) supplies the overwhelming portion of Soviet needs, rather than Soviet import stability being based on allegiance considerations (the CMEA) or on quality considerations (the West). Another result is that purchasing power considerations have not influenced Soviet imports of high priority items such as grain and machinery.

Ante Cicin-Sain (Chapter 10) begins by explaining the basic characteristics and problems arising out of Yugoslavia's internal economic development. Cicin-Sain concludes his contribution by outlining an alternative settlement system in which CMEA currencies could be upgraded and limited convertibility could be implemented.

Neven Mates (Chapter 11) investigates an overlooked area of dual dependence, namely the domestic financial system's simultaneous debt to the West and balance of trade surplus with the East. He starts by analysing the specific sources of inflation in Yugoslavia, then shifts to the institutionally built-in pressure to generate negative real interest rates. Next, Mates explains how hard currency exchange losses are accumulated within the banking system, resulting in losses for households but net capital gains for the productive sector. The Yugoslav government, on the whole, does not receive seignorage due to inflation. Finally, Mates examines the impact of contact with the East on Yugoslavia's domestic financial system.

Chapters 12 through 18 contain brief summaries of seven conference contributions: *The Foreign Policy Conditions Affecting Economic Relations Between the Smaller European States*, Peter Knirsch; *Problems and Prospects of East–West Transfer of Technology*, Stanislav Simanovsky; *Towards a Comprehensive Economic Reform? A Pessi-Optimistic View*, László Szamuely; *Reflections On Enterprise-Level Currency Conversion in Foreign Trade: The Case of Hungary*, Ádám Török; *Joint Ventures Between East and West*, Tauno Tiusanen; *The Involvement of the CMEA Countries in the International Trade in Services: Can They Be Competitive?*, Marie Lavigne; and

Money as a means of Communication and Reforms in Eastern Europe: Some propositions, Raimund Dietz.

Tamás Földi (Chapter 19), in his summary remarks, concentrates on the political and institutional framework which determines the overall form and content of East–West and East–East economic relations. He points out that the almost exclusive role of the government bureaucracies of CMEA countries in shaping foreign economic relations has led to the contradiction between the domestic needs of a centrally planned economy and the prerequisites necessary for competitiveness in the international sphere. Földi also discusses the minimum conditions needed to achieve progress in economic reform, which leads to his final remarks on the relationship between politics and the success of economic reform.

MICHAEL MARRESE
SÁNDOR RICHTER

Acknowledgements

The editors wish to express their deep gratitude to two sets of individuals at Northwestern University. Gregory Moerschel, Jeffrey Squire, Caryn Franklin, Scott Johnson, Thomas Maycock, Cindy Skach and Lauren Wittenberg provided proof-reading and editorial assistance on all the contributions to this volume. In effect, they helped to transform various versions of Euro–English into a more standard variety. Paula Nielsen and Karen Bandusch typed and retyped many versions of this manuscript, with attentive care and intelligent scrutiny. Their good humour and keen dedication have been deeply appreciated by the editors.

M. M.
S. R.

Notes on the Contributors

Ante Cicin-Sain is a professor at the Institute of Economics, Zagreb, Yugoslavia. Professor Cicin-Sain is a specialist in exchange rates and has conducted a number of studies on the disparity between Yugoslav internal trade prices and the effective economic exchange Yugoslavia has with bilateral-clearing countries.

Raimund Dietz is a senior researcher at the Vienna Institute for Comparative Economic Studies. Dr Dietz's research has included studies on CMEA trade patterns, intra-CMEA trade-related transfers, and the political economy of CMEA countries.

Tamás Földi is Head of Department at the Institute of Economics of the Hungarian Academy of Sciences. Professor Földi is a specialist on the role of economic theory in the shaping of economic policy in Hungary. His work has been notable for taking into account international trends in the determination of Hungary's foreign economic policy.

Urpo Kivikari is Director at the Institute of East–West Trade, Turku, Finland. Dr Kivikari has studied East–West trade from both an institutional and an econometric point of view. For instance, in his research on the Soviet Union, he has paid attention to the deviation between actual values and the corresponding plan targets.

Peter Knirsch is a professor in the Department of Economics of the Free University of Berlin. Professor Knirsch's work has been in the fields of political economy and foreign policy, particularly with respect to East–West relations.

András Köves is the Deputy Director of the Institute for Economic and Market Research in Budapest. Dr Köves is a foreign-trade specialist who has published numerous articles on the CMEA, including energy policy within the CMEA, and on Hungary's future foreign trade policies.

Marie Lavigne is a professor of economics at the University of Paris, Panthéon-Sorbonne. Professor Lavigne's research has covered all aspects of the East European and Soviet economies. Her current research concentrates on intra-CMEA trade in services and the convertibility of CMEA currencies.

Friedrich Levcik is currently a consultant to the Vienna Institute for Comparative Economic Studies, an organisation for which he served as director. Dr Levcik is most renowned as a specialist on the Czechoslovak economy, but has also conducted research on Eastern Europe as a whole and on Austria.

Michael Marrese is an associate professor in the Department of Economics at Northwestern University in the United States. Dr Marrese has written on Soviet trade subsidisation of Eastern Europe, on the political economy of the CMEA, and on various aspects of the Hungarian economy.

Neven Mates is a senior researcher at the Institute of Economics, Zagreb, Yugoslavia. Dr Mates is a macro economist who has written extensively on the interaction and impact of financial markets, large public-sector deficits, and inflation.

Gábor Oblath is Head of Department at the Institute for Economic and Market Research in Budapest. Dr Oblath directs research projects that involve short- and medium-term forecasts of socialist countries and the world economy. His publications have focused on the economics of exchange rates and on Finland's and Hungary's trade with the Soviet Union.

Sándor Richter is a senior research economist at the Economic Information Unit of the Hungarian Academy of Sciences and Managing Director of a consultancy that specialises in the economies of Eastern Europe. Dr Richter has specialised in the many forms of financial relations among CMEA countries. He has written articles on Hungarian–Soviet, Hungarian–CMEA, and Austrian–Soviet economic relations.

Nikolay Shmelev is a senior researcher at the Institute of the USA and Canada of the USSR Academy of Sciences. Dr Shmelev's wide-ranging articles in both the popular press and economic journals demonstrate his belief that only radical shifts in Soviet economic management can prepare the Soviet Union for the next century.

Stanislav Simanovsky is a senior researcher at the Institute of Economics of the World Social System of the USSR Academy of Sciences. Dr Simanovsky's primary research deals with the measurement of innovation and the spread of new technology, both for the Soviet Union and internationally.

Jan Stankovsky is a senior research economist at the Austrian Institute for Economic Research in Vienna. Dr Stanovsky's specialty is the Austrian economy, but he has also written on East–West economic relations and on industrial co-operation.

László Szamuely is a scientific adviser at the Institute for Economic and Market Research in Budapest. Dr Szamuely is a specialist on the process of economic reform and his research has been directed at both Hungary and the Soviet Union.

Tauno Tiusanen is the Managing Director of a Finnish consultancy that specialises in East–West joint ventures. Mr Tiusanen's decades of experience in negotiating joint ventures have served as the basis of his publications.

Yrjänä Tolonen is an assistant professor at the Turku School of Economics and Business Administration in Finland. Dr Tolonen's research involves the formal modelling of the microeconomic consequences for market economies of trade with centrally planned economies.

Ádám Török is Deputy Director of the Research Institute of Industrial Economics at the Hungarian Academy of Sciences. Dr Török's publications deal with the detailed domestic macroeconomic consequences of international trade and finance.

1 Introduction
Friedrich Levcik

It is a great pleasure for me to act as chairman of this interesting conference which brings together over twenty outstanding economists and experts from ten different countries. On behalf of all participants I should like to express my thanks to the Rockefeller Foundation for the kind invitation to use the magnificent facilities of its Study and Conference Center at Bellagio. We have here scholars from three European CMEA member countries, from a non-aligned socialist country, from the USA, from three European countries that are members of the European Communities, and lastly, from two neutral European market economies. This seems to be suitable territorial mix for discussing the complex problem of the so-called 'dual attachment' to both East and West.

In my opinion, it is no chance occurrence that some three years ago the research on this topic was initiated by our Hungarian partners who also shaped the orientation and scope of the conference. It is especially Hungary, which in the course of its already twenty-year economic reform, is trying to integrate itself more effectively into the world economy and at the same time – as a member country of the CMEA – to comply to the specifics of intra-CMEA trade. To a lesser extent, this may also apply to non-aligned Yugoslavia. The other two countries included into the group of economies with 'dual attachment', namely Austria and Finland, seem to have few problems in trading simultaneously with developed market economies, with developing countries and also with CMEA countries. The only distinguishing feature for these two countries is a relatively larger trade share with CMEA countries than the standard share for OECD countries. Insofar as Finland is still trading with the Soviet Union on the basis of clearing, this is, in my opinion, a matter of expediency but not one of necessity for Finland.

Some three or four years ago Hungary was the only CMEA country striving for economic reform not only in its domestic economy, but also in its external economic relations. To compare Hungary's problems and experiences with those of others which have already mastered the path to multilateral and essentially unified trade, or with those which are well set on this way may yield some valuable insight for Hungarian policy makers.

Since then the problem of 'dual attachment', in the sense of having to cope with two completely different trading regimes with all the adverse consequences, has become a burning issue for the other CMEA countries that are moving toward radical economic reform. Furthermore, it becomes not only a matter of how an individual CMEA country could overcome the fetters of this 'dual attachment', but increasingly a matter of changing the entire mechanism of intra-CMEA co-operation and integration. This may be still a long way off. But a majority of the European CMEA countries has at least voiced its intention to work towards such a solution. Taking into account the impact which the successful solution of reaching a multilateral trading system with convertible currencies within the CMEA could have for overcoming the long-lasting division between Western and Eastern Europe, it may be worthwhile to include an issue not taken up – at least to my knowledge – in any of the papers presented at this conference.

Let me say a few words as to why the matter of a far-reaching economic reform and especially of its impact on international trade and international economic and financial relations has already become a matter of urgency. The deep and ongoing changes in economic and industrial structures which we can observe in the world and especially in the developed market economies are caused – among other factors – to a large extent by the internationalisation of economic life, or to speak in the parlance of the CMEA countries – by a deepening of the international division of labour. This internationalisation can be documented, namely by the growing dependency of domestic markets on international manufacturing industries and of domestic producers of manufactured goods on components and technology from abroad. Between the 1960s and the middle of the 1980s, exports and imports of manufactured goods in the developed industrial countries grew dramatically in relation to the domestic production of manufacturing industries. At the same time the economies of the Newly Industrialised Countries (NICs) have grown even more rapidly on an export-led path to the point where they now have captured a twenty per cent market share of the imports of the developed market economies relative to only a five percent share at the beginning of the 1970s. Add to this the dynamic growth of trade in high-technology products, parts and components of technologically comprehensive products and financial services, and a clear picture of growing interdependence emerges in which a specific role is being played by the transnationals which are integrating research and development, manufacturing, supply of intermediary goods and marketing on a global scale. In this way, the entire chain of the production process is drawn into the internationalisation of the economy with the aim to lower costs and to gain new markets.

All these developments have somehow bypassed the CMEA countries. Since the middle of the 1970s, East–West trade has developed much more slowly than other regional trade flows and the CMEA countries have suffered extensive market share losses in the West. In view of the balance of payment difficulties, the CMEA countries have had to adopt severe import restrictions, especially for manufactured goods and investment goods from the West. A process of loosening the ties of the CMEA with the world economy has begun.

But equally, in intra-CMEA trade one cannot observe a similar process of internationalisation similar to that seen in the economies of the West. In trade between the six East European countries there was never a trend towards stronger mutual integration and since the mid-1970s a process of disintegration has developed. In the relation of the East–European countries to the Soviet Union, the originally high trade turnover in mutual trade decreased from the early 1960s through the mid-1970s. An opposite trend developed up to the mid-1980s, but the growing share of mutual trade was only due to the exploding oil and fuel prices and not to deeper economic and industrial integration. Mutual trade between Eastern Europe and the Soviet Union kept its original complementary feature, exchanging mainly Soviet fuels and raw materials for East European industrial goods.

Other developments which I have briefly mentioned above as being the dominating trends in world trade are at best contained in various documents of the CMEA as 'declarations of intent' but were hardly introduced in real economic intercourse among CMEA countries. Trade is still being transacted on a strictly bilateral basis and in essence with clearing settlements of mutual deliveries of a set of goods bartered between government negotiators. Programmatic intentions to include other instruments of co-operation contained in the Comprehensive Programme of the early 1970s on paper.

Only one lesson seems to have been learned. The majority of CMEA countries realise that one cannot expect genuine commodity-money relations to develop between CMEA economies if they are not unequivocally applied in the domestic economy. Therefore, a deep and ongoing reform within each or most of the CMEA countries is an indispensable precondition for applying instruments such as meaningful exchange rates, flexible prices, credits, and other financial instruments to intra-CMEA trade. This is certainly a drawn-out and often painful process. But without following this path, the CMEA countries will not be able to reap the benefits of an efficient international division of labour.

2 Hard Currency Settlement of Payments or Bilateralism and Clearing: How Long will the Dilemma Remain?
Sándor Richter

INTRODUCTION

Ever since the completion of the liberalisation of external trade in the 1950s, the mutual trade of the OECD countries has been characterised by some evident features: transactions are settled in convertible currency; trade balances do not exert influence on the development of trade, except in cases of extraordinary imbalance; state influence on trade is mostly indirect, and its means are financial ones; trading activity of enterprises is supported by a wide range of financial institutions; and a substantial part of the trade is related to international co-operation between enterprises or inside individual enterprises with production sites in different countries. Approximately 70 per cent of world trade falls to the mutual trade of the OECD countries and in this trade the above-mentioned characteristics of trading practice are predominant.[1] Since the trading practice of Newly Industrialised Countries (NICs), which occupy an ever growing segment of world trade, tends to correspond to the above conditions, it is no exaggeration to say that these conditions reflect the requirements of the contemporary world economy or, in less normative wording, they characterise the great majority of contemporary world trade.

As I write, in the middle of the 1980s, approximately eight or nine per cent of world trade falls to the CMEA countries. The mutual trade of these countries has a less than five per cent share in world trade.[2] In this 'pocket' of world trade, a special trade system has prevailed – its main features unchanged – since the early 1960s. This system reminds the observer partly of the protectionism of the 1930s and partly of the conditions in Western Europe in the late 1940s; yet this system finds its deepest roots in the traditional practice of central planning. Some of these practices are:

1. The settlement of payments is conducted via clearing in transferable roubles, where the unit of payment can neither be converted to convertible currencies nor be transferred from or to other bilateral CMEA trade relations. Trade balances in bilateral relations are of outstanding significance from the point of view of further developments in the given bilateral relation.

2. The state exerts dominant influence on the quantity, choice and price of commodities exchanged in bilateral relations. Producers of exported, and users of imported, commodities have not been allowed to make contracts without state intervention at certain points of the contract negotiations. Concerning the means of state intervention, it is clear that individual, quantitative ones, expressed in physical terms, are preferred to normative, financial instruments.

3. Currently trade is not supplemented by sophisticated financial instruments. Although a legal framework exists, the level of financial relations lags far behind the level that corresponds to the requirements of trade relations. The same is true for industrial co-operation between enterprises of the CMEA member states.

Restricting the analysis to Europe, it is obvious that the trade of the European OECD countries with each other, with overseas OECD countries, and with NICs can best be described by the trade system mentioned first (see page 00), while the trade of the CMEA countries with each other is characterised by the latter (see page 00). Certainly trade is not constrained to intra-bloc relations, thus East–West trade brings about the opportunity for the confrontation of two characteristically different types of foreign trade systems. This confrontation is indirect since bilateral relations between the European CMEA countries and West European countries are based, in the overwhelming majority of cases, on the trade system mentioned first (although the validity of this statement concerning state influence, financial institutions, and enterprise level co-operation is limited). Confrontation of the two different systems of trade emerges first of all *inside* the economy of those countries which, on the one hand, maintain significant economic relations with that part of the world economy where the first trade system is dominant, and, on the other hand, with those CMEA countries with which clearing – the most important element of the second trade system – has been preserved either in a form that corresponds to intra-CMEA conditions or in more or less different variants.

Which economies have been described above? The group of countries concerned comprises the East European states:[3] Bulgaria, Czechoslovakia, GDR, Hungary, Poland and Romania which together form one sub-group. Besides these are Yugoslavia, Finland and Austria. This entire group is quite heterogeneous in several aspects. In the group there are members of the Warsaw Treaty, one non-aligned and two neutral states. The economic systems of the countries in the group range from market economies to classical centrally planned economies. The level of economic development differs substantially between the two extremes, namely between Finland and Austria, and the East European countries of the Balkan peninsula.

The simultaneous existence of the two different trade systems can be best observed in the case of the East European countries. Although the figure varies with different countries, between one-third (Romania) and three-quarters (Bulgaria) of their total trade falls to CMEA partners where clearing settlement of payments prevails, moreover, in a specific, very rigid form. Parallel to that, in these countries' trade with the OECD area and with most of the NICs and LDCs, hard currency payments are applied, and equilibrium in *bilateral* relations is not of major importance. This part of their foreign trade, albeit with certain reservations, corresponds to the trade system predominant in the contemporary world economy.

In Yugoslavia's trade with the OECD countries, the first trade system is applied, with the reservation that the standard of enterprise level co-operation and trade-supporting financial institutions lag behind that of the level generally found in the intra-OECD trade. Yugoslavia's trade with the CMEA countries is split in this aspect. Hard currency settlement of payments is applied in economic relations with Hungary, Bulgaria, Romania and Poland, while the clearing has been preserved in trade with the Soviet Union, Czechoslovakia and the GDR. However, a bilateral approach to economic relations has not disappeared entirely in trade with the former group of CMEA countries where the clearing is already abolished. Enterprise level co-operation and trade-supporting financial institutions are even less frequent here than in trade with the OECD countries.

Finland has mostly hard currency settlement of payments in trade with the East European CMEA countries, but in Finland's extremely important connection to the East, in trade with the Soviet Union, clearing has been preserved. In Finland's economic relations with its OECD partners and with the NICs, the first trade system is applied with all characteristics described earlier in this chapter.

Up to this point, I have been dealing with the simultaneous manifestation of two different trade systems in the external economic relations of some small, open European countries. While describing these two systems and their place in the foreign trade of the countries concerned, values were not attached directly to these trade systems, neither were they evaluated explicitly as 'good' or 'bad'. Although such an evaluation is a challenging task, the topic of this chapter deals with something else. I think that the negative impacts of bilateralism and clearing on international economic relations have already been thoroughly analysed and described in the relevant literature, mainly in literature concerning problems of trade inside the CMEA. While the postwar history of West European trade can be described as a sequence of steps to eliminate bilateralism, in Eastern Europe bilateralism has survived; yet it has grown more and more anachronistic parallel to the predominating tendency for internationalisation in the contemporary world economy.

In a couple of CMEA countries the necessity for economic reforms has already been acknowledged. The position of the traditional central planning, which has been the most important explanatory factor for the long survival of the second trade system, has been weakened. This raises the question of how much longer a situation can be preserved in which several countries – CMEA member East European states – and other, non-CMEA member European countries – with substantial relations with the CMEA – maintain two characteristically different trade systems. How long can clearing in Europe survive?

Certainly this question cannot be answered here. But two problems, closely related to the answer, can be analysed.

These include first the *intention* and second the *ability* of the governments in the countries concerned to eliminate the co-existence of the two different trade systems, making hard currency settlement of payments the only trade system in economic relations with both the East and West. This is the topic of this chapter.

INTENTION

The question which asks whether the government of a country wishes to maintain the duality manifested in two different types of foreign trade systems, depends on various factors. I mention here three factors that may be of outstanding importance in relation to this question.

Domestic Economy

Countries of dual attachment differ according to their economic system. Austria and Finland are market economies where a clearing-type system of foreign trade does not fit either the system of domestic economy or the system of foreign trade with major partners. The abolition of the clearing had no influence (in the case of Austria) or would have no influence (in case of Finland) on the system of domestic economy. However, the opposite is true for the group of the East European countries where the intra-CMEA practice of foreign trade organically fits the domestic system of a traditional centrally planned economy. No government in Eastern Europe can seriously attempt to eliminate clearing without the simultaneous introduction of major elements of the market in the domestic economy. Most likely it was the correspondence of traditional central planning to intra-CMEA clearing that served as grounds for the ideology that hailed the consequent settlement of payments (based on the transferable rouble) as the only really socialist form of foreign trade. Thus, it refuted theoretical criticism with a simultaneous denial of the existence of hard currency settlement inside the CMEA, although such settlement had emerged as a consequence of the unsolved problems of clearing. In the case of Hungary and Poland, where steps toward the implementation of market-oriented reforms have already been taken, the above mentioned 'correspondence' between the domestic economy and the intra-CMEA system of foreign trade has been loosening, according to the extent to which the functioning of market forces has been allowed. These two countries, exclusively from the point of view of the system of the domestic economy, may agree with the idea of introducing market-type foreign trade practice in intra-CMEA trade. As for Yugoslavia, although its domestic economy is based on self-management, it can hardly be described in terms of the market or non-market economy. It may be stated that a market-type foreign trade system (based on sovereign decisions at the micro level) fits better the decentralised Yugoslav economy than the system involving clearing, where central decisions are much more important.

The Foreign Policy Factor: The Intentions of the Partners

Changing the foreign trade system is a decision of great importance. Although one-sided decisions cannot be excluded theoretically, they would seriously endanger the maintenance of the prevailing volume of trade, and they could diminish the chances for further development. This is why the governments in the countries under consideration, in order to change the given system of foreign trade or to preserve it depend to a great extent upon the standpoint of the partner countries. The group of countries of dual attachment are divided on this question as well. In case of an East European country, not only does the attitude of individual partners need to be considered but also the fact that the present foreign trade system is a 'sacred' product of the mutually-created and accepted CMEA co-operation. In such circumstances a one-sided step would obviously meet with rejection, and it seems that this will be the case in the foreseeable future, as well. The acceleration of reform processes in some CMEA countries, above all in the Soviet Union, may create a new situation in which a majority opinion, favouring a change by collective decision, emerges among CMEA members; yet if this does not happen, perhaps a tolerant attitude may develop on the side of the majority towards a group of countries with the intention of abandoning the present system in their trade with other CMEA partners.

The other countries of dual attachment do not confront constraints as formidable as the collective will of an integrated bloc. Austria decided to change at the beginning of the 1960s and again in the early 1970s. Its East European partners' attitudes toward this change were either neutral or positive. The Soviet Union explicitly expressed its preference for hard currency settlements in trade with Austria. Finland abolished clearing with most of its small East European partners while preserving it in trade with the Soviet Union. It is unlikely that the Soviet Union would have rejected attempts from Finland to change the system of trade. Yugoslavia conducts foreign trade with some East European countries in hard currency while clearing was preserved in trade with the Soviet Union and some other East European countries. It is unlikely that the intention to change the system of trade would have been rejected by those partners where the clearing system prevailed.

Pondering on the Pros and Cons

The intention to abolish clearing depends to a great extent upon the domestic economy and on the intentions of the other partners involved in the system of clearing trade. However, the most important factor influencing this intention is the confrontation of the pros and cons of trade without clearing, with those of the prevailing trading practice. The most obvious handicap of bilateralism and clearing, namely the constraints on the expansion of the turnover due to the demand for close to zero trade balances every year, is well known. Less evident is the judgement of that effect of clearing that is manifested in the isolation from the mainstream of world trade, the creation of special prices for commodities, special relative prices (price proportions) and trade patterns. Benefits from participation in the (relatively) free world trade, from competition on the world market and from immediate adjustment to impulses arriving continuously from this source, can hardly be matched with facts such as the sheltered position of a safe market, export prices which are higher than on markets without the 'umbrella' of clearing, less strict expectations for quality, and the presence of markets for commodities that are not saleable on any other markets. An improved ability to adjust the economy to the needs of the contemporary world economy, that will pay off only in the long run and that cannot be translated directly in money terms, can again hardly be confronted with the impressive facts of apparent sales and purchases, and with the short-run interests of enterprises engaged in the markets of the clearing partners. As an example, I mention here the crude oil trade between the Soviet Union and the small East European countries. It is a fact that on the basis of the Bucharest price formation principle the Soviet Union delivered crude oil to her East European partners at a price lower than the actual world price over ten years from the mid-1970s to the mid-1980s. It is also true that for the East European countries this arrangement meant definite advantages compared to imports from other sources. However, the 'lower than actual world market prices' transmitted disorientating signals, and these led to the postponement of structural transformation; the failure to decrease specific energy consumption; and the justification of false investment decisions. While the extent of the advantages deriving from lower import prices can be calculated exactly (see the literature on implicit subsidies), the consequences of delayed adjustment cannot be quantified.

Coming back to the main question of this section, it is important to point out that the intention to abolish clearing is not directly connected to pondering the pros and cons of the two different foreign trade systems. Recognition and acknowledgement that a market-type foreign trade system is a more advantageous one in the long run, compared to clearing, does not necessarily result in an explicit intention to change the prevailing system. Fear of immediate losses, emerging as a consequence of the abolition of clearing, will surely make the governments of the countries concerned think twice before introducing a market-type foreign trade system in those bilateral relations where the clearing has prevailed. These losses may derive from the shrinking of market position which were earlier sheltered, from the disappearance of artificially favourable prices, from a drastic, unfavourable modification of trade patterns and from the poor performance of a series of enterprises suddenly confronted with the hard conditions of immediate competition in the world market.

The more explicit the difference between conditions in the clearing trade and those in the world market, the higher the share of clearing in total trade, and finally the less market-type the domestic economic system is, the more justified are the fears of the government of the given country. This explains why acknowledgement of the benefits to be obtained from trade without clearing may be very far from the declaration of the intention to change to that system of trade. This problem leads us to another issue in which we move from the question: 'What is it that decides whether a government *intends* to abolish clearing?' to the question: 'What decides whether a country is *able* to abolish clearing?'

ABILITY

In the group of countries with clearing trade, Austria is a member only by right of its experiences in the past. At the beginning of the 1960s and again in the early 1970s clearing was abolished in Austria's trade with the East. Austria intended to change, and it was able to implement this change. Abolition of clearing did not shock the domestic economy and did not set back the development of trade with former clearing partners.

The changeover in Austria's trade with the East deserves attention from different perspectives. Above all, special attention should be given to the time of the change. It took place in the 'peaceful years' just before the oil price explosion, when the expansion of world trade was dynamic, and the framework for an agreement between the EEC and EFTA to eliminate customs on most industrial products had already been elaborated. The economy of Austria was characterised by a high growth rate and a low level of unemployment and, significantly, the share of the CMEA countries in its total trade was relatively low, at approximately ten per cent. East European countries and the Soviet Union did not object to the change. Moreover, the Soviet Union explicitly expressed its preference for a hard currency settlement of payments in bilateral trade with Austria. The IMF also urged Austria to abolish clearing since it objected to the system of multiple exchange rates. To sum up, there was an optimal constellation of domestic and international conditions. In spite of this, Austria was divided on the decision concerning the abolishment of the clearing. According to some experts' opinion, written before the abolition of clearing, no more than 25–50 per cent of the Austrian exports to the East were regarded as competitive on the world market. Nonetheless, the abolition of clearing, despite the pessimistic voices, took place without major difficulties.

Since Austria has already abolished clearing in trade with the East, what can be said about the ability of the other countries to take this step?

Finland has preserved clearing settlement in its trade with the Soviet Union but this sole bilateral trade relation represents a much higher share in Finland's total trade than the share of all CMEA countries in Austria's total trade. This means that a rather wide sector of the Finnish economy would be influenced by a change in the settlement of payments with the Soviet Union. In Finland's trade with the OECD, significantly different trade patterns can be observed as compared with trade with the Soviet Union. This arrangement makes it likely that a possible setback of trade with the Soviet Union might lead to difficulties in the sales of certain sectors of industry, namely, ship-building and light industry. Products of the Finnish light industry would most likely face very keen competition from alternative imports from Newly Industrialised Countries, which have much lower wage costs than those in Finnish industry. On the other hand, the global performance of the Finnish economy and its balanced and dynamic expansion have been impressive; in addition, these facts compare most favourably with other OECD countries. 'Eurosklerosis' is a phenomenon that has nothing to do with the Finnish economy. In foreign trade with the OECD there are no major problems. Apart from problems in the bilateral relation itself, there are no domestic or international constraints in the way of a change towards the hard currency settlement of payments with the Soviet Union. Exceptionally good political relations with the Soviet Union may be regarded as some kind of a guarantee that such a step would not involve an immediate decline in Soviet imports from Finland. Most probably a process of rearrangement would start, however. Those products and enterprises that have been competitive on the Soviet market due mainly to their sheltered position under the 'umbrella' of clearing would either disappear or would have to improve their competitiveness in order to retain their former position.

I must make a remark here. Since Finland's domestic economy is prospering and its relations with the OECD are excellent, the change to hard currency payments in trade with the Soviet Union is not a particularly important issue at all. Paradoxically, the more feasible the accomplishment of this change is, the less significance it has. The explanation of this is the following: while the short-term benefits of the clearing system are at hand, long-term disadvantages exert their influence to a relatively small extent provided the domestic economy and trade with other partners prosper.

Yugoslavia is in a much more difficult situation as I write in 1988 regarding its ability to change the settlement of payments in trade with some CMEA countries than it was fifteen or twenty years ago. Since that time, the share (in Yugoslavia's total exports) of the Soviet Union, the most important clearing partner, grew from fourteen per cent in 1970 to approximately 30 per cent in the early 1980s.

Yugoslavia's export performance in trade with OECD region has not been too successful. Despite different agreements with the EEC, Yugoslavia has not been able to keep abreast of the dynamism of trade between West European countries since the abolition of customs in trade of most industrial commodities, following the agreement between the EEC and EFTA. Most of the traditional commodities comprising Yugoslavia's exports also have to compete with exports coming from the NICs. The domestic economy has been and still is in the grip of a severe crisis. Up to the time of writing, all stabilisation programmes have proved to be unsuccessful, and thus have failed to stop inflation and have not strengthened the function of the market in the economy. Since stability of the domestic economy and external economic relations is not in sight, it seems that the abolition of the system of clearing trade with certain CMEA countries, primarily with the Soviet Union, would involve significantly higher risks than in the cases of Finland today or Austria in the early 1960s. A possible setback of exports would have a serious impact on a wide circle of enterprises, which have already been adversely affected by the critical state of the domestic economy. Imports from the Soviet Union consist mainly of primary energy supplies. Such supplies are indispensable for the functioning of the economy, yet if clearing were abolished these supplies would have to be imported against hard currency, either from the Soviet Union or from other sources. Parallel to the obligations deriving from indebtedness to the West, a Soviet decision to decrease imports from Yugoslavia after a change to hard currency settlements would be regarded as an extremely serious additional burden. However, it is an open question whether a decrease of Soviet imports from Yugoslavia would necessarily follow the change to hard currency payments. It depends partly on whether the commodities traditionally delivered by Yugoslavia could stand the challenge of competition, and whether commodities losing their market shares could be substituted by new ones.

It is more likely that the difficulties of the East European countries in the case of the abolition of clearing would be of an even bigger magnitude than they would be in case of Yugoslavia (not to mention Finland). The foreign trade system of the CMEA is a special type of clearing. The Bucharest price principle that serves as the theoretical basis for price formation in trade between CMEA countries brought about nominal and relative prices that substantially differ from actual world market prices. Discrepancy may be much more significant here than in the case of Finland and Yugoslavia, although no concrete price formation is available for these two countries. Since the price formation in individual contracts is oriented to actual world market prices in the case of Finland and Yugoslavia, their commodities exported in clearing compete (even if indirectly because of the 'umbrella' of the clearing) with the commodities of countries observing the hard currency settlement of payments. Inside the CMEA, it is not actual world market prices but prices reflecting an earlier state of the world market that serve as the basis for price formation, and which can be further influenced by other circumstances typically different in individual bilateral relations. The completely different nominal and relative prices coupled with the general shortage of hard currency in the East European countries prevent competition with the commodities of the OECD countries. This also means that the consequences of a change to hard currency settlements inside the CMEA are even less predictable than in the Yugoslav or Finnish cases.

The share of clearing in total trade is bigger than in the trade of the other countries concerned. Thus abolition of clearing, even without considering the problems caused by special intra-CMEA price formation, would prove to be an extremely hard test for a very wide circle of enterprises in East European countries. Moreover, domestic and international circumstances at the moment are less than favourable. East European economies are coping with difficulties such as growth rates which are close to zero, obsolete production patterns, and heavy burdens connected with indebtedness. They try, with little success, to maintain their positions in OECD markets in competition with the supply of the much more vigorous NICs. Steps towards a more integrated West European market also impair indirectly the chances of East European countries.

Despite all these difficulties, what follows is speculation and calculation as to what would happen if clearing *were* abolished in the trade of CMEA countries with each other.

TRADE WITHOUT CLEARING: THE CONSEQUENCES IN EASTERN EUROPE

In all probability, if clearing were abolished different processes would be initiated: on the one hand, in the trade of East European countries with each other and on the other hand, in the trade of these countries with the Soviet Union. Bilateral trade of East European countries with each other has been balanced, export and import patterns being nearly identical. Expressed in CMEA terms, 'hard' goods are confronted with 'hard' goods and the same is true for 'soft' goods. After abolition of clearing, the categories of 'hardness' and 'softness' would be transformed into a question of prices. The prices of what were formerly hard goods (mostly primary energy supplies and raw materials) would immediately approach the actual world market prices. In the case of balanced mutual deliveries of hard goods, as is the case for East European countries, the change in settlement of payments would not involve substantial deficits in either bilateral relation. The problem is more complex in the case of soft goods. For energy and raw materials, prices are different inside and outside the CMEA, but the commodities themselves are the same; with soft goods, mainly manufactured products, the commodities themselves (performance, quality, package, and so forth) are also different. The lack of competitiveness of these products in other than CMEA markets has been manifested in the traditional system through a confrontation of groups of commodities – namely, in the exchange of hard goods for hard goods only, and soft goods for soft goods only. After a change to hard currency payments in intra-CMEA trade, a limited ability to compete with Western products would be manifested in lower prices; this is because, taking into consideration the direct comparison of prices in imports from CMEA countries and the OECD or NICs respectively, no previously soft goods would be able to stay on the market if their price did not correspond to their performance in comparison with competing Western imports' price/performance relation. However, it must also be considered that, on one hand, the CMEA countries think twice before paying for imports with hard currency in their present economic situation and, on the other hand, manufactured goods (soft goods) imported from other CMEA countries amount to a substantial part of the input of the economy and the consumption of the population. Shortage of hard currency and traditional imports from the CMEA may create a situation in which soft goods can be sold for hard currency, yet at a depressed price level compared to competing imports. The other side of this problem seems to be more controversial, namely that the price level where demand also appears for soft goods (even in case of hard currency payments) and which compensates for the weaker performance compared to that of competing Western imports, will most probably not cover the present costs of production. In this case, where will the supply be that matches the demand emerging in the case of prices reflecting the discrepancy in 'performance' of commodities imported from other CMEA countries and the West, respectively?

Problems arising after the abolition of clearing are somewhat different in the mutual trade of East European countries and in the bilateral relations of East European countries with the Soviet Union. In the latter case the sharp difference between the export and import patterns would bring about a new situation. The value of that part of Soviet primary energy and raw material exports, which has been counterbalanced by deliveries of manufactured products from the East European countries, would substantially exceed the respective value of these manufactured products after the introduction of hard currency payments and the establishment of actual world market prices in intra-CMEA trade.

In that part of the turnover where Soviet hard goods deliveries have been counterbalanced by similarly hard deliveries of the East European countries, and where soft goods are counterbalanced by soft goods, the same process is expected to take shape that is expected in the bilateral relations of East European countries with each other. However, it is also true for the Soviet Union that imported commodities from the CMEA countries are deeply embedded as regular inputs to the production process and in consumption. Hard currency purchases are limited, too. Excessive shortages, common in the Soviet economy, make it likely that the new prices for manufactured imports from the CMEA will be influenced not only downwards by the price/performance ratio (compared to competing Western commodities), but upwards by the efforts of the Soviet government to diminish shortages to the lowest possible level. (At constant outlays, 10 000 pairs of medium quality shoes from CMEA countries may be preferred to 5000 pairs of high quality shoes.) The main question here will again be the same, namely, is it profitable to produce and export manufactured products in the East European countries at that price?

On the one hand, a deficit would arise after the abolition of clearing in the trade of East European countries with the Soviet Union. On the other hand, commodities that have been regarded as soft in the traditional CMEA system of trade could maintain their market shares only at prices that reflect the difference in quality compared to competing imports. However, these prices would not even cover even the production costs in a substantial part of this group of commodities. As a consequence, abolition of clearing would shock the economy of the East European countries to an unknown extent. Yet if all this is true, and if this change involves such painful consequences, is there any sense in doing it? When pondering the answer, we must not forget that the clearing system at the time of writing only covers up already existing problems. It ensures the undisturbed existence of a very wide circle of uncompetitive enterprises, by blocking the natural impulses for adjustment. Equilibrium of the deliveries of soft goods is based on the mutuality of low quality. The change to hard currency settlement of payments would have serious consequences because it would influence a wide area of the concerned countries' economies. But it is exactly for this reason that clearing should be abolished, since no CMEA country can afford lasting uncompetitiveness in such a wide area of the economy, if it wants to reverse its marginalisation in the world economy.

Certainly it would be unforgivably irresponsible not to take into consideration those enormous difficulties that would affect the economy of the East European countries after the abolition of clearing. A good analogy would be that a medical operation may be successful but in vain – if the patient dies.

The painful consequences resulting from a change to hard currency payments should be eased. Appropriate means for that transformation must be found.

In the present writer's opinion, a gradual increase of hard currency settlement of payments is not the optimal solution to this problem. Such a solution has various forms. One is the 'no increment in the clearing' strategy, where all additional deliveries would be settled in hard currency. Another is the separation of trade into hard goods – which would be settled in hard currency – and soft goods – which would remain in clearing. Hungary's experiences in hard currency trade with her CMEA partners, mostly with the Soviet Union, may be instructive here. This segment of trade has remained isolated, and it has not launched a rearrangement in the turnover settled in clearing.

As I see it, the change to hard currency settlement of payments, if decided upon, should be implemented in one step and simultaneously measures should be introduced in order to diminish the immediate consequences of the new system. These measures should correspond to the requirements of a market-type foreign trade system.

Since the most serious problem would probably arise due to the very low price level of the former soft goods, the introduction of competition through imports from non-CMEA markets should be gradual. In order to hinder a shock deriving from the immediate instruction of full-scale import competition a deliberate *temporary* raising of prices for imports from non-CMEA markets seems to be expedient. This process ought to take place simultaneously with the removal of all other barriers in the way of imports from the West. It would mean a temporary discrimination of non-CMEA imports, coupled with a general liberalisation of all imports. Raising the cost of imports from non-CMEA markets could be implemented through either a joint tariff system of CMEA countries towards non-CMEA imports, or an introduction of financial instruments which would be expected to exert the same effects as tariffs. Parallel to that, no tariffs would be imposed on commodities imported from CMEA members. Joint tariffs would be relatively high for manufactured goods in the year of the abolition of the clearing but they would be reduced, according to a schedule, by a given percentage in each following year. After a transmission period of between five to ten years, the tariff level would drop to a level that would harmonise with the tariff level which the main trading partners had imposed on their imports from CMEA countries. In the transition period, producers of former soft goods could improve their efficiency and rearrange patterns of production, namely, they could become competitive.

Certainly all that is said above can be regarded only as a general framework for a solution to problems emerging after the abolition of clearing. If the actual implementation of the above construction were to become feasible, a serious analysis of its details should be initiated. This analysis should include the fixing of concrete measures concerning tariffs on individual groups of commodities, and the creation of the optimal differences between them in order to hinder undesired 'protection' in sectors where imports from the non-CMEA markets do not compete with the supply of intra-CMEA production. A solution based on good compromises must be achieved through a series of thorough talks.

The construction outlined above would certainly raise the issue of GATT-conformity in the case of those East European countries which are members of that organisation.

It can be assumed that a 'constitutionalised' schedule for the gradual elimination of discriminative tariffs, coupled with the prospects of a gradually increasing market for non-CMEA exporters, will make the initial discrimination acceptable or at least tolerable. Besides which there are also the precedents of other regional integrations.

The disappointing experiences of the reforms followed in the CMEA to date give rise to the question of whether the abolition of the clearing – with a one-sided step – would be feasible for an individual East European country. (Foreign policy aspects of this question have already been mentioned and here only economic aspects are regarded.) Economic difficulties, following a radical change in the settlement of payments, seem to be more serious in a 'one country' model. Other CMEA countries, preserving the traditional clearing in their mutual trade, would tend to export their soft goods for hard currency to the concerned East European country. However, they would try to buy all goods that were regarded earlier as soft in the supply of this country, from other CMEA countries, certainly for transferable roubles. A reallocation of imports according to sources would not demand great efforts regarding the competitive supply of manufactures of the East European countries. Another problem would be the substantial deficit in the trade with the Soviet Union after the change to hard currency settlements.

A more favourable solution could involve a small group of Eastern European countries, or indeed all of them, abolishing clearing, while in trade with the Soviet Union the traditional system of payments would prevail for a time, perhaps in a somewhat less rigid form than at present. In this set up East European countries would be saved from the likely imbalances in their bilateral trade with the Soviet Union. The similarities in trade patterns and the balanced turnover in the mutual trade of East European countries could secure a smooth transitional period to test the co-operation under the new conditions. In the case of more than one or two countries abolishing clearing in mutual trade, the joint tariff-like measures to protect non-competitive areas could also be introduced. After evaluating the experiences of the new system in practice, the group of countries trading without clearing could be enlarged by the Soviet Union and those East European countries that did not join the group earlier.

Summing up, I would like to point out that the challenge of simultaneous economic relations with East and West is substantially bigger at the time of writing than it would have been without the artificial differences created by an anachronistic practice of settlement of payments; this practice is being pursued in a substantial part of the foreign trade in most of the countries concerned by this challenge. In any given country, the more significant the trade with both East and West, the bigger the differences in practice of payments, trade patterns, nominal and relative prices in the trade with East and West, the bigger is the disadvantage and loss that derives from this duality, and the more important (and the more difficult) a unification of the major elements of trade with both regions becomes.

Notes

1. *Monthly Bulletin of Statistics*, June 1987, p. 107.
2. *Monthly Bulletin of Statistics*, July 1986, pp. 284–298.
3. In this chapter the category Eastern Europe covers the six small European CMEA members and excludes the Soviet Union.

Bibliography

S. AUSCH, *Theory and Practice of CMEA Cooperation* (Budapest: Akadémiai Kiadó, 1972) p. 279.

L. CSABA, 'Kelet-Európa a világgazdaságban: alkalmazkodás és gazdasági mechanizmus' (Eastern Europe in the World Economy: Adjustment and Economic Mechanism), *KJK*, (1984) 314. Forthcoming in English. To be jointly published by Akadémiai Kiadó and Cambridge University Press.

R. DIETZ, 'Soviet Foregone Gains in Trade with the CMEA Six: A Reappraisal', *Comparative Economic Studies*, XXVIII, No. 2 (Summer 1986) 69–93.

H. GABRISCH, 'Finnish-Soviet Economic Relations', WIIW Forschungsberichte Nr 109, Vienna (October 1985) 3–23.

U. KIVIKARI, 'Finnish-Soviet Trade in the Light Industries', WIIW Forschungsberichte Nr 109, Vienna (October 1985) 25–100.

A. KÖVES, *The CMEA Countries in the World Economy: Turning Inwards or Turning Outwards* (Budapest: Akadémiai Kiadó, 1985) p. 248.

A. KÖVES, '"Implicit Subsidies" and Some Issues of Economic Relations Within the CMEA' (Remarks on the Analyses Made by Michael Marrese and Jan Vanous) *Acta Oeconomica*, 31, No. 1–2 (1983) 112–136.

M. MARRESE and J. VANOUS, *Soviet Subsidization of Trade with Eastern Europe: A Soviet Perspective* (University of California, Berkeley: Institute of International Studies, 1983).

G. OBLÁTH and P. PETE, 'The Development, Mechanism and Institutional System of Finnish-Soviet Economic Relations', WIIW Forschungsberichte Nr 111, Vienna (January 1986) 125.

J. PÁNCSITY, 'A jugoszláv-szovjet külkereskedelem helye Jugoszlávia külgazdasági kapcsolataiban' (The Role of Yugoslav–Soviet Trade in the External Economic Relations of Yugoslavia) Külgazdaság 1986/11, 60–75.

M. RÁCZ, 'The Mechanism of Hungarian–Soviet Economic Relations', *Acta Oeconomica*, 38, No. 3–4 (1987) 323–338.

S. RICHTER, 'The Development of Hungarian–Soviet Economic Relations', *Acta Oeconomica*, 38, No. 3–4 (1987) 303–322.

S. RICHTER, 'Hungary's Foreign Trade with CMEA Partners in Convertible Currency', *Acta Oeconomica*, 25, No. 3–4 (1980) 323–336.

S. RICHTER, 'Some Aspects of Economic Relations Between Austria and the Soviet Union', WIIW Forschungsberichte Nr 101, Vienna (November 1984) 111.

3 Hungarian Foreign Trade: Failure to Reform
Michael Marrese

INTRODUCTION

In Hungary, the first steps toward decentralisation occurred in agriculture in 1965. Although this demonstrated Hungarian commitment to decreasing the role of central planning, it was not until 1968, under the rubric of the New Economic Mechanism (NEM), that most changes were introduced. The primary goal of Hungary's economic reform was to devise an economic system composed of the best features of market and planned economics. Although successes have been realised, Hungarian reform has suffered disappointing failures in its attempt to find a halfway house between plan and markets. The purpose of this chapter is to explain how overall weaknesses in the implementation of the Hungarian reform have contributed to Hungary's foreign trade failures and how foreign trade policies have hindered the speed and seriousness of Hungarian reform.

An evaluation of the overall strengths and weaknesses of the Hungarian reform appears in section two of this chapter, while section three contains a comparative analysis of Hungarian macroeconomic and foreign trade performance. In section four, the institutional obstacles to rational foreign trade decision-making are discussed. A survey of enterprise foreign trade behaviour, appearing in section five, shows that Hungary has ineffectively utilised its multiple trade attachments to the Soviet Union, the rest of the CMEA, and the West. The concluding section focuses on the extent to which the success of overall reform and the success of foreign trade decision-making are dependent on each other.

AN OVERVIEW OF THE HUNGARIAN REFORM

The argument put forward in this section is that the predominance of bureaucratic control within the state-owned section relative to that in the non-state sector and the comparison of macro failures to micro successes suggest that the more central authorities have been involved in economic decision-making, the worse have been the results from an efficiency point of view. Improvements in efficiency from that achieved under central planning require that enterprises secure both accountability and decision-making power. However, successful implementation of the reform depends on support by central authorities – the very group whose accountability and power should be diminished.

In the 1960s, Hungarians decided that the negative features of central planning could be eliminated by replacing centrally-determined plan targets and supply allocations for enterprises with a market-guided system based on profit-sharing for enterprise managers and workers. Central authorities would still play an important role in this model. They would guide the market along lines consistent with central preferences via control of so-called regulators such as taxes, subsidies, interest rates, access to credit and foreign currencies, import licenses, and foreign-exchange multipliers.

Underlying the scheme of 'central preferences → regulators → guided market' was the assumption that the implementation of central preferences via indirect regulation would lead to a higher level of efficiency than the implementation of those same preferences via detailed mandatory plan targets. Central preferences did not radically change in 1968. The economic system was still supposed to guarantee job security, stable prices, and a socially acceptable distribution of income. Previously existing institutional characteristics such as ministerial appointment of enterprise management, central control over all but minor investment decisions, restrictive wage and price regulation, profit-levelling among enterprises, and government-negotiated CMEA trade obligations remained intact. The above-mentioned assumption proved to be incorrect in practice because the attempts to adhere to the incompatible list of central preferences undermined the success of the reform.

Thus NEM was unable to achieve efficiency within the constraints imposed by central preferences. Rather, NEM initially demonstrated an unwillingness to trust markets, ignored the positive attributes of competitive pressure, tried to make the transition to the guided market system as painless as possible for bureaucrats, enterprise managers, and workers, and was overly optimistic about the efficiency generating attributes of limited enterprise independence.

In response to the efficiency inhibiting consequences of these early reform characteristics, the Hungarian reform became somewhat more market oriented than originally anticipated. However, progress has been uneven. There are various explanations for these dashed expectations. For instance, János Kornai distinguishes between the Hungarian state-owned sector (state-owned firms in industry, construction, transportation, communication, and trade plus state-owned farms) and the non-state sector (agricultural co-operatives, household farming, private farms, non-agricultural co-operatives, the formal private sector, the second economy, and combined private-state ownership). The state-owned sector, according to Kornai, operates in an atmosphere of dual dependence: depending vertically on the bureaucracy and horizontally on its suppliers and customers. Vertical dependence refers to: the rules of entry and exit; the selection of top management; and the prices, wages, credit conditions, taxes, and subsidies a state-owned firm will face. Vertical dependence dominates horizontal dependence, which refers to a state-owned firm's autonomy with respect to determination of its outputs and inputs. A firm in the non-state sector, though not free from bureaucratic control, does not rely on the paternalistic assistance of the state for growth and survival, but must pass the market test.[1]

Kornai goes on to explain how the initial version of NEM was fundamentally naive.

> The naive reformers searched for a responsible line of separation between the role of the bureaucracy and the role of the market. Many of them thought that such a separation line could be drawn like this: 'simple reproduction' (in Marxian terms) regulated by the market and 'extended reproduction' by the planners. In other words, current production controlled by the market and investment by the planner. It turned out that this separation is not viable. On the one hand, the bureaucracy is not ready to restrict its activity to the regulation of investment. On the other hand, the autonomy and profit motive of the firm become illusory, if growth and technical development are separated from the profitability and the financial position of the firm and are made dependent only on the will of higher authorities.
>
> The pioneer reformers wanted to reassure all members of the bureaucracy that there would be ample scope for their activity. Their intention is understandable. The reform is a movement from 'above', a voluntary change of behavior on the side of the controllers and not an uprising from 'below' on the side of those who are controlled. There is, therefore, a stubborn inner contradiction in the whole reform process: how to get the active participation of the very people who will lose a part of their power if the process is successful. The reassurance worked too well in the Hungarian case; the bureaucracy was not shattered.
>
> The naive reformers were concerned with the problems of the state-owned sector and did not spend much hard thought on a reconsideration of

the non-state sectors' role. It turned out, however, that up to the present time, it has been just the non-state sectors that have brought the most tangible changes into the life of the economy.[2]

Conflicts stemming from divergent interests are key to the understanding of Kornai's explanation of the discord between plan and market. These conflicts can be viewed as occurring among members of four hierarchic levels of the economy: (*i*) members of the Central Committee and the Council of Ministers; (*ii*) leading members of branch and functional ministries, banks, and economy-wide agencies and committees; (*iii*) managers of enterprises, state farms, and cooperatives along with the trade union leaders and members of local councils (organs of local government); and (*iv*) individual workers and consumers.

The problem of divergent interests with respect to reform has been seen most clearly among the two coalitions responsible for regulating the economy – one from level (*i*) and the other from level (*ii*). Each such coalition of decision makers has reflected the diverse opinions of many interest groups in society. Therefore, internal and external conflict within and between coalitions has flourished – as would be the case in any heterogeneous society. However, there has also existed a real awareness that a stable consensus concerning economic priorities should be reached in order to promote rapid and effective decision-making. The central question for economic reform is whether such consensus will lead to a distribution of resources based on 'bureaucratic rules of thumb' or on 'market outcomes'.

Clearly the existence of a national objective function and a commonly perceived set of national constraints would contribute greatly to the formation of consensuses able to accept market outcomes. However, in place of maximisation of a national objective function subject to commonly accepted constraints, we typically find that the diversity of opinion in these two coalitions yields too many national goals alongside too many constraints. More concretely, decision-makers in level (*i*) strive for growth of national income, a steady rise in per capita consumption, faster incorporation of technical progress, importation of needed technology, raw materials and consumer goods, increased labour productivity, and better investment decision-making. The constraints are no less formidable: maintenance of institutional stability within the political–economic hierarchy, equilibrium of domestic demand and supply, full employment, a relatively low inflation rate, fulfilment of CMEA obligations, and adherence to various restrictions concerning income distribution.

Maximisation of a national objective function would create clear tradeoffs among goals but it would also imply *visible priorities*. Visible priorities would subsequently create public antagonisms among branch interest groups because shifts in institutional power and prestige could no longer hide behind the veil of fuzzy propaganda. Current behind-the-scenes struggles would be brought into full societal view – certainly not an attractive prospect for a political elite sensitive to its lack of electoral accountability to the public.

The absence of a national objective function, in itself, is not fatal. If profitability, for instance, would be accepted by each interest group as the means through which conflicting priorities would be resolved, then the absence of an objective function may simply be understood as a sign of the game theoretic nature of reality. Game theory rarely specifies an overall objective function, rather it concentrates on the interaction of different individuals or groups. However, the highly monopolistic industrial structure and the tremendously complex tax and subsidy system in Hungary have prevented profitability from serving in this mediating role because Hungarian prices have not been good measures of scarcity.

The essence of a national objective function could also be resolved if each interest group would strive to move along the same development path, either because of a unifying socialist consciousness or a hierarchically consistent incentive system. Either would result in successful decentralisation and would therefore eliminate the need for maximisation of an explicit objective function. However, neither has occurred nor are likely to occur. All levels of the Hungarian hierarchy do not respond to the same incentives. Members of level (i) are concerned with the overall wellbeing of the economy and their status; members of level (ii) concentrate on the wellbeing of their own institutions and their own personal status; members of level (iii) focus on lifetime income, benefits, and security; while members of level (iv) maximise the utility gained from food, clothing, housing, travel, and other consumer goods. Status, power, and perquisites are the basis for the incentive system for levels (i) and (ii), whereas income, housing, bonuses, and perquisites hold for levels (iii) and (iv).

Inconsistencies among incentives arise because the national interest often does not coincide with branch or enterprise interests. For example, from a national point of view, every enterprise should reveal its honest anticipation of the completion time and benefit stream associated with each project for which it seeks centrally allocated investment funds. From an enterprise point of view, its productive capacity is crucial to its ability to bargain with the centre for special firm-specific treatment, hence it should obtain investment funds even at the 'cost of being overly optimistic' about its investment potential. Thus the inconsistency arises because of the actual opportunity cost of investment credit for an enterprise is much lower than the value the centre places on these credits.[3]

The widespread practice of determining firm-specific regulations for state-owned firms is directly related to the diversity of preferences on each decision-making level and to the absence of either an efficient price system or an explicit objection function. Such a situation permits the priorities of each interest group to be represented in terms of selected goals subject to selected constraints. Moreover, each interest group tends to maximise its own subset of goals relative to unique perceptions of shadow prices since no national shadow price system exists. The interaction of such divergent means of measuring tradeoffs results in a failure to evaluate national tradeoffs in any consistent manner.

Another way of analysing the Hungarian reform process is to compare the success that has occurred primarily on the micro level with the failure that has occurred mainly on the macro level.

The dimensions of micro success include:
1. The tremendous variety of activity in the legal second economy that has resulted in dramatic improvements in the food supply, privately constructed housing, services available to the population, and the assortment of consumer goods (mostly clothing).
2. A multitude of ways of encouraging the merger of first economy and second economy interests such as supportive policies for agricultural private plots and the opportunity to organise economic working groups in industrial enterprises.
3. The decision to allow agricultural co-operatives and state farms to engage in non-traditional industrial, trade, and construction activities.
4. New forms of private sector activity such as increased opportunities for private shop rental, organising restaurants on a contract basis, and encouraging the growth of small, non-agricultural co-operatives.
5. Industrial production systems (or technically operating production systems) in agriculture which have created competitive conditions that have stimulated rapid technological diffusion throughout Hungary.

6. A significant increase in work intensity and an increase in the numbers of hours worked per week.
7. The gradual pluralisation of Hungarian life – economically, culturally, and even politically.

There are three primary reasons for Hungarian micro success. First, Hungary has had no other choice than to release the full energies of its people in a much less planner manner because Hungary has had a very poor endowment of natural resources, thus it has had to rely more heavily on the world market than, say, the Soviet Union; Hungary's opportunities for extensive development were exhausted long ago; and Hungarian leaders and economists have been disillusioned with the relative advantages of a system of centralised economic management. The idea that Hungary has been forced to change is crucial because radical change generally implies a painful transition, which the Hungarians are currently experiencing. In the late 1970s, it was the continual accumulation of debt to Western countries that forced government decision-makers to introduce a new round of reform. At that time, all segments of the population were satisfied with the status quo; only Western bankers were uneasy. Second, opportunities to accumulate large, visible differences in individual income have served as a means of stimulating individual productivity. Third, substantial investment in consumer-oriented industries has provided the population with a desirable array of obtainable products.

Hungarian micro success was not achieved without its share of costs. A new managerial elite and a new entrepreneurial elite have emerged, while Marxist–Leninist ideology and the Hungarian Socialist Workers' Party have become less important. People have less leisure time and have exhibited deteriorating health, increased tension, and greater alcoholism. Finally, a much less egalitarian distribution of income and wealth has become the norm.

The dimensions of macro failure are well known:

- slow growth of national income (Table 3.1);
- large debt to the West (Table 3.2);
- inefficient domestic utilisation of energy and raw materials;
- a low level of competitiveness on world markets;
- a much weaker relative position in the world economy in 1990 than in 1970;
- poverty among pensioners; and
- inflation.

Table 3.1 Relative Hungarian macroeconomic performance, 1970–86

	1971–5	1976–80	1981–5	1986
	International comparison of average annual rates of growth of Gross Domestic Product			
Austria	3.9	3.4	1.6	2.3
Belgium	3.2	3.0	0.4	2.0
Denmark	1.9	2.8	2.1	2.8
UK	2.1	1.5	1.7	2.3
Finland	3.9	3.2	2.5	1.5
France	4.1	3.2	1.2	2.0
Greece	5.1	4.4	0.8	0.0
Holland	3.2	2.7	0.4	1.5
Hungary	6.3	3.2	1.7	1.5
FRG	2.1	3.5	1.2	2.8
Norway	4.7	4.9	2.7	4.3
Italy	2.5	3.9	1.0	2.5
Portugal	4.4	5.2	0.7	4.3
Spain	5.6	1.9	1.6	3.0
Switzerland	0.8	1.7	1.3	2.0
Sweden	2.7	1.3	1.7	2.3
Japan	4.6	5.1	3.9	2.3
USA	2.5	3.4	2.5	2.8
Canada	4.9	3.4	2.5	3.0
Australia	3.7	2.5	3.2	1.3
	Socialist comparison of average annual rates of growth of Net Material Product			
Bulgaria	7.8	6.1	3.7	5.5
Czechoslovakia	5.5	3.7	1.7	3.4
Yugoslavia	5.9	5.6	0.6	–
PRC	5.6	6.0	9.8	7.4
Poland	9.8	1.2	–0.8	5.0
Hungary	6.5	2.8	1.3	0.9
GDR	5.4	4.1	4.4	4.3
Romania	11.3	7.0	4.6	7.3
USSR	5.7	4.3	3.5	4.1

Source: Statisztikai Évkönyv (Hungarian Statistical Yearbook) 1986, p. 345.

Table 3.2 Foreign trade performance of CMEA and Yugoslavia, 1981–6

	Net $-debt, 12/31/86 in $ billions	Percent change in $-terms of trade from 12/31/80 to 12/31/86	Percent change in net $-debt from 12/31/80 to 12/31/86
Poland	32.4	0.3	41.0
USSR	20.2	−11.4	85.6
Yugoslavia	15.7	− 4.5	9.1
Hungary	10.6	−12.7	61.3
GDR	7.5	− 3.2	−38.0
Romania	5.8	9.6	−37.1
Bulgaria	3.5	12.5	24.9
Czechoslovakia	2.9	− 6.0	−20.2
	Ratio of net $-Debt to 1986 current account receipts	Ratio of net $-Debt to 1986 western GNP estimates	Net $-debt per Capita as of 12/31/86
Poland	4.07	12.3	864
USSR	0.58	1.0	72
Yugoslavia	1.03	11.5	675
Hungary	1.94	12.3	993
GDR	0.64	4.0	450
Romania	0.89	4.2	255
Bulgaria	1.10	5.6	386
Czechoslovakia	0.57	2.0	185

Source: Jan Vanous, 'A Review of Developments in Soviet and East European Hard Currency Trade, Balance of Payments, Debt, and Assets, 1980–86', PlanEcon Report, Nos. 36–37–38, 17 September 1987, pp. 5, 23, 26.

The reasons for macro failure are complicated. On one level, the macro failure is due to the soft budget constraints that enterprises face.[4] On another level, one may cite a variety of external and internal factors. The external factors include: declining terms of trade from 1973 to 1986; world market interest rates in real terms that have been much higher than Hungarians anticipated; the worldwide increase in agricultural protection and the continual implementation of the green revolution in developing countries; CMEA institutional characteristics such as inconvertibility of the transferable rouble (TR) that have inhibited intra-CMEA trade, product specialisation, and technological transfer; and Soviet import requirements that have not encouraged Hungarian development of commodities that would be competitive on the world market.[5] Internal factors centre around poor economic policy-making in areas of wage regulation, foreign trade (such as short-sighted investment credits used to stimulate exports), investment policy, and price-tax subsidy policy.[6]

The costs of macro failure are self-evident: a thoroughly dissatisfied population, emigration of some of the most talented young people, and a backward production and trade structure.

MACROECONOMIC AND FOREIGN TRADE PERFORMANCE

In this section, the comparison of Hungary's macroeconomic achievements to its foreign trade achievements provides additional evidence that the more levels (i) and (ii) of the Hungarian hierarchy have been involved in economic decision-making, the worse have been the results. The Hungarian government has had greater control over foreign trade than over the economy as a whole (section 4), yet Hungary's relative success in foreign trade has been worse than Hungary's relative macroeconomic success.

In the comparison of growth rates of gross domestic product (GDP) between Hungary and nineteen capitalist countries (table 3.1), Hungary is at the high end of the spectrum during 1971–75, in the middle during 1976–80, and at the low end during 1981–86. Relative to these countries, overall Hungarian growth has been average, but on a steadily declining trend.[7]

In the comparison of growth rates of net material product (NMP) between Hungary and eight other socialist countries (also table 3.1), Hungary does well for 1971–75 but ranks above only Poland for 1976–80 and above only Poland and Yugoslavia for 1981–86. This extremely negative picture of Hungarian economic growth may be due to variations among the socialist countries in price weights, coverage of the underlying data, and statistical methodologies. In fact, the following comparison using the uniform methodology employed by Alton *et al.* (1987) yields a more positive evaluation of Hungarian growth. Letting USA GNP per capita equal 100 in 1970 and in 1986, Hungary went from 44.1 per cent of the USA in 1970 to 45.3 per cent in 1986; Bulgaria, from 37.8 to 38.9; Czechoslovakia, from 52.3 to 52.7; the GDR, from 54.7 to 64.2; Poland, from 39.2 to 39.8; Rumania, from 25.9 to 35.1; and Eastern Europe (all of these countries), from 41.8 to 44.7.[8] Hence Hungary's growth record for

1970–86 according to the measures of Alton and his associates is similar to that of Bulgaria, Czechoslovakia and Poland.

Hungary's foreign trade performance has been worse than its uninspiring economic growth. For example, given that Hungary's most important foreign trade objective since 1979 has been the reduction of its convertible currency debt ($-debt), a useful criterion to measure the recent performance of Hungarian foreign trade is the change in Hungary's net $-debt, defined as gross $-debt minus all of Hungary's convertible currency assets in the West. Hungary, as of 31 December 1986, had the fourth highest level of net $-debt (after Poland, the Soviet Union, and Yugoslavia), but was highest in terms of net $-debt per capita, tied for first (with Poland) in terms of net $-debt per unit of GNP, and second highest (after Poland) in terms of net $-debt divided by 1986 current account receipts (Table 3.2). However, the overall trend for Hungary since 1980 is even more troubling. From the end of 1980 to the end of 1986 Hungary's net $-debt grew by 61.3 per cent, second only to the 85.6 per cent growth of Soviet net $-debt (growth the Soviets could afford) and in dramatic contrast to the substantial declines in net $-debt of the GDR (−38.0 per cent), Rumania (−37.1 per cent), and Czechoslovakia (−20.2 per cent).

The fundamental reason for the dismal $-trade performance is Hungary's 12.7 per cent decline in $-terms of trade during this period, the sharpest decrease among the eight countries investigated in Table 3.2. To put this decline in Hungary's $-terms of trade into a wider perspective, let us turn to Table 3.3, which contains a comparison of Hungary's overall (both $ and TR) terms of trade with that of nineteen other countries.

Table 3.3 shows that from 1973 to 1986, Hungary experienced the third sharpest decline in terms of trade (after Australia and Greece). Moreover, Hungary's decline is unrelenting from 1973 to 1986. This long-term decline in Hungary's terms of trade is another indication of fundamental weakness in Hungary's foreign trade decision-making.

INSTITUTIONAL OBSTACLES TO RATIONAL FOREIGN TRADE DECISION MAKING

Before Hungary's institutional obstacles to rational foreign trade decision-making are discussed, an examination of the pattern of Hungarian trade by commodity category and trade partner (Table 3.4) is helpful. This analysis indicates that Hungary has developed

Table 3.3 International comparison of changes in terms of trade, 1974–86 (1980=100, calculated in terms of each country's currency)

	Austria	Belgium & Luxemburg	Denmark	UK	Finland	France	Greece
1973	112	110	122	100	110	117	129
1974	110	106	106	89	109	101	116
1975	110	106	112	95	118	108	108
1976	107	104	112	93	113	107	105
1977	106	104	110	95	113	104	111
1978	106	102	114	101	107	108	105
1979	103	104	108	102	105	108	98
1980	100	100	100	100	100	100	100
1981	96	95	97	101	99	96	103
1982	100	95	98	100	102	97	103
1983	102	94	99	100	102	99	95
1984	100	93	99	99	102	101	99
1985	98	95	102	99	102	103	97
1986	105	102	106	103	112	–	93

	Holland	Yugoslavia	Poland	Hungary	FRG	Norway	Italy
1973	110	108	99	120	113	79	118
1974	106	98	100	112	104	82	96
1975	104	102	100	104	112	86	106
1976	104	103	102	106	111	81	102
1977	104	102	100	102	110	81	102
1978	104	105	101	101	113	82	108
1979	102	102	98	99	106	86	108
1980	100	100	100	100	100	100	100
1981	100	99	97	99	93	111	91
1982	103	103	97	97	97	111	95
1983	101	101	92	95	98	110	99
1984	102	93	91	93	96	118	98
1985	105	91	93	92	98	116	100
1986	107	–	–	88	113	87	115

	Switzerland	Sweden	Japan	USA	Canada	Australia
1973	103	110	183	139	98	135
1974	97	104	137	120	104	122
1975	104	114	129	123	100	116
1976	108	115	124	123	102	110
1977	105	108	127	117	98	101
1978	112	106	145	117	94	100
1979	109	103	127	111	99	102
1980	100	100	100	100	100	100
1981	100	99	103	103	96	100
1982	106	97	103	106	95	97
1983	107	96	106	112	97	97
1984	108	99	109	112	94	95

Table 3.3 continued

	Switzerland	Sweden	Japan	USA	Canada	Australia
1985	108	100	112	113	90	90
1986	115	109	154	119	87	82

Source: *Statisztikai Évkönyv* (Hungarian Statistical Yearbook = SE hereafter) 1978, pp. 539–540; SE 1981, pp. 390–391; SE 1987, pp. 381–382.

distinct foreign trade strategies for the Soviet Union, the rest of the CMEA [RCMEA = CMEA minus USSR], and the rest of the world [ROW = all countries minus CMEA = DCAP plus DEV, where DCAP = developed capitalist countries and DEV = developing countries].[9] (Notation for Table 3.4 includes: DCAP = ECAP + OCAP, where ECAP = European capitalist countries and OCAP = other capitalist countries, while RSOC = rest of socialist countries = Bulgaria + Mongolia + Romania + Cuba + Vietnam + Albania + Yugoslavia + PRC + North Korea.)

From a Hungarian export point of view (Table 3.4), the Soviet Union has resembled RCMEA in that machinery and equipment, industrial consumer goods, and food have been Hungary's three biggest export categories for both. DCAP differs from the Soviet Union and RCMEA because the share of machinery and equipment has been relatively low in DCAP's imports of Hungarian goods, while the shares of industrial consumer goods, fuels, and food have been relatively high. From a Hungarian import point of view, the Soviet Union, RCMEA, and DCAP have been clearly distinct. Imports from the Soviet Union have been much more heavily weighted towards fuels, ores, metals, and minerals than from any other of Hungary's trade partners, and less heavily weighted toward machinery and equipment. RCMEA (as summarised by the behavior of the GDR, Czechoslovakia, and Poland) has provided Hungary with a greater proportion of manufactured goods than any other market. DCAP has been a notable source of high quality machinery and equipment, chemicals, and non-food raw materials.

Hungary's long-term policy of maintaining separate foreign trade strategies for the Soviet Union, RCMEA, and ROW follows directly from the inherent conflict between the operating environment for trade with the Soviet Union and the operating environment for trade with ROW. The operating environment for Hungarian–Soviet trade

Table 3.4 Pattern of Hungarian trade for 1974–86, by commodity categories and trade partners

CAT	Markets							
	USSR	GDR	CZECH	POLAND	RSOC	ECAP	OCAP	DEV
	Hungarian category j exports to market m as a share of total Hungarian exports to market m							
1	46.7	55.3	45.3	44.3	41.5	7.8	18.3	38.6
2	18.1	11.0	16.8	15.6	13.6	21.2	43.4	16.0
3	0.6	0.7	1.5	1.8	3.3	11.5	0.1	1.4
4	3.8	5.8	5.1	12.3	12.3	12.5	7.8	13.0
5	4.0	1.9	3.6	4.7	12.5	10.2	5.8	8.1
6	0.8	1.0	3.5	1.0	2.2	1.4	1.0	2.9
7	0.7	2.9	1.7	3.1	4.3	9.9	1.7	2.0
8	7.4	5.6	8.8	6.7	4.4	7.4	3.5	8.2
9	14.3	9.8	11.4	7.4	5.5	17.1	16.8	9.8
10	3.6	6.1	2.3	3.1	0.5	1.0	1.6	0.0
	Hungarian category j imports from market m as a share of total Hungarian imports from market m							
1	22.3	62.0	49.3	48.2	30.3	32.8	34.4	0.8
2	2.3	14.4	16.0	12.7	19.4	8.6	9.4	7.3
3	43.5	3.9	7.3	13.0	7.4	2.2	1.5	28.8
4	14.9	2.9	7.5	9.6	7.9	9.6	5.0	5.6
5	6.4	10.3	6.3	4.8	13.5	23.7	16.8	4.0
6	0.8	1.7	5.8	3.2	3.3	3.9	1.0	0.2
7	9.1	2.6	2.9	3.3	5.3	15.2	27.6	29.1
8	0.2	0.1	0.8	0.2	3.0	1.1	3.3	19.6
9	0.3	1.3	1.0	2.7	8.4	2.4	1.0	4.6
10	0.2	0.9	3.0	2.3	1.5	0.5	0.1	0.0

Category 1	Machinery and Equipment (CTN 1)
Category 2	Industrial Consumer Goods (CTN 9)
Category 3	Fuels (CTN 20–23)
Category 4	Ores, Minerals, Metals (CTN 24–27)
Category 5	Chemicals (CTN 30–35)
Category 6	Building Materials (CTN 40–42)
Category 7	Non-food Raw Materials (CTN 50–53, 55–58)
Category 8	Animals, Cereals, and Food Raw Materials (CTN 60, 70–72)
Category 9	Food and Food Products (CTN 80–84)
Category 10	Beverages and Tobacco (CTN 85)

Source: KSE, annual volumes from 1974 to 1986, from tables dealing with Hungary's trade organised by two-digit CTN categories.

since 1974[10] has been defined to satisfy (a) the long-term Soviet preference to be independent; and (b) the short-term pressure felt by Hungary to obtain fuels and raw materials cheaply, to increase its convertible currency trade balance, and to maintain domestic stability. The Soviet preference for independence has meant as much Soviet self-sufficiency in the domestic production of fuels, raw materials, and strategic manufactured commodities as is reasonably possible; Soviet reliance on the CMEA market for items not produced in a sufficient quantity within the Soviet Union; and finally, utilisation of a variety of non-CMEA trade partners for high-tech imports and for those items not currently available on either the domestic market or the CMEA market.[11] Simultaneously, Hungary has bargained with the Soviet Union for at least several of the following: an assured supply of fuels and raw materials from the Soviet Union, purchased with TRs and at favourable foreign trade prices (*ftps*); implicit loans in the form of trade deficits that include a subsidy component in the form of below-market interest rates; Hungarian $-exports of wheat and meat at world market prices (*wmps*) to the Soviet Union; and expansion of Hungarian exports of manufactured goods to the Soviet Union. The nature of Hungarian–Soviet trade has been directly related to the Soviet Union's willingness to subsidise Hungary via low prices for its exports of fuels in exchange for Hungary's political, ideological, and military allegiance and in order to enhance Hungary's domestic stability.[12]

The operating environment for Hungarian trade with ROW (about 72–75 per cent of Hungary's ROW trade has been with DCAP) has been dominated by the Hungarian goal of reaching $-export levels that are consistent with timely repayment of Hungary's $-debt. Western aims – very different from the Soviet concern for independence – have focused on Hungary as yet another market for profit-maximising exporters and importers; a source of cheap skilled labour; and a potential gateway into the huge and largely unexploited Soviet market.

The operating environment for Hungarian trade with RCMEA has been a curious combination of the two previously mentioned operating environments. Hungary, in its dealings with RCMEA, has abided by the CMEA institutional rules (use of TRs, government-level negotiations, and so forth) mentioned below, but has had no incentive such as trade subsidies to encourage it to put a high priority on trade with RCMEA. The basis for Hungarian–RCMEA trade has been the bilateral exchange of manufactured goods, which account for over 60 per cent of all Hungarian–RCMEA trade (for example, Table 3.4, categories 1 and 2). East European countries share certain system characteristics and the legacy of a Stalinist-type development model. These factors have lead to East European production of somewhat outdated manufactured goods of average or poor quality that are no longer highly valued on the world market. Thus Hungary and RCMEA have exchanged such manufactured goods rather than deciding to phase out their production because CMEA populations have been willing to accept such products, the products themselves have become integrated into CMEA production structures, and CMEA authorities have feared that serious unemployment would follow any such change in CMEA production structures. In addition, Hungary and RCMEA have exchanged fuels, raw materials, some foods, and superior-quality manufactured goods among themselves at essentially *wmps*, whether the actual exchange has been in the form of a TR-denominated barter arrangement or a purchase with convertible currency.

One result of differences in the operating environments of the Soviet Union, RCMEA, and ROW is that Hungary has been able to develop Soviet-centric industries with economies of scale; however, these industries tended to produce traditional quality manufactured goods (section five). Since these traditional quality manufactured goods are not highly valued on DCAP markets, the economies of scale associated with Soviet-centric industries have not helped Hungary generate $-exports.

In order to understand Hungary's interaction with its various trade partners more clearly let us review six dimensions of Hungary's trade behaviour. First, export and import flows to CMEA are negotiated in the framework of five-year interstate agreements, while export and import flows to ROW are based on contracts between enterprises that reflect relatively recent supply and demand conditions. This means that Hungary generally concludes its CMEA trade commitments before it makes Western trade commitments.

Second, the majority of transactions in intra-CMEA trade are settled according to TRs, an accounting unit that cannot be converted into any other currency. Thus when Hungary has a surplus of TRs in one bilateral CMEA relationship, Hungary cannot use that surplus to pay for a deficit in any other bilateral trading relationship. This inconvertibility also means that surplus TRs cannot be used to purchase goods not covered in the annual bilateral trade agreements without additional bilateral negotiations. Thus bilateral balancing of exports and imports is the general rule for intra-CMEA trade, because no country wants to subsidise another country via the implicit loans that are associated with any TR-surplus.

Third, relative intra-CMEA *ftps* bear little resemblance to corresponding *wmps*. More specifically, once the overvaluation of the rouble *vis-à-vis* the dollar is taken into account, the intra-CMEA *ftps* of manufactured goods are higher than the corresponding *wmps*, while the intra-CMEA *ftps* of fuels, non-food raw materials, and food and raw materials for food are lower than corresponding *wmps*.[13] This has encouraged intra-CMEA bilateral negotiators to focus on the overall pattern of prices and quantities. In effect, Hungary barters its commodities for another country's commodities. Such bilateral barter during TR-trade negotiations is a direct consequence of trade based on government negotiations, inconvertibility, and *ftps* that deviate significantly from *wmps*.

Fourth, bounded rationality has implied that the balanced bilateral barter between CMEA countries has consisted of balanced barter mostly within each of a number of designated pairs of commodity groups (and rarely outside of these designated pairs) rather than of unconstrained barter of all of one country's commodities for all of another country's commodities. The decomposition of tradeable goods into pairs is called the process of establishing bilateral contingencies. A bilateral contingency refers to a pair of commodity lists, say, five types of exports from Hungary and eight types of exports from Poland, within which a balanced bilateral exchange is to take place. For example, Poland might offer automobiles on its commodity list while the corresponding Hungarian commodity list might include buses. The associated bilateral contingency indicates that Hungary can export its buses to Poland in exchange for a number of Polish automobiles (or for any other combination of goods on the Polish list) to be negotiated later. The following diagram shows how bilateral contingencies have greatly inhibited the full exploitation of potential bilateral gains from trade.

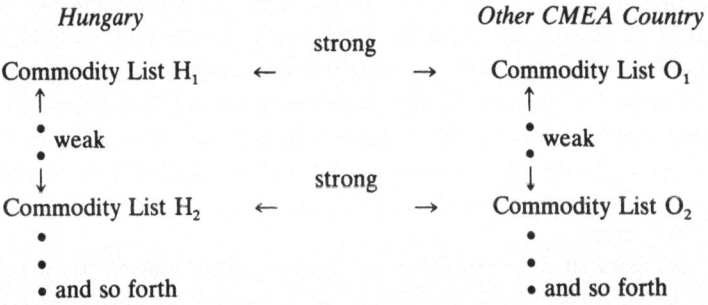

The $-trade analogue to using contingency lists in place of an overall bilateral barter process is Hungary's use of product-specific and firm-specific rationing of imports along with export incentives based on traditional export patterns and on enterprise-size to control the $-trade balance in place of a policy of adjusting Hungary's convertible currency exchange rates.

The four dimensions thus far discussed imply two radically different circumstances for Hungary: either TR-trade is negotiated between governments in an atmosphere of bilateral barter amid contingency lists or $-trade is negotiated between profit-oriented Western firms and Hungarian firms that focus on either reaching firm-specific $-export targets or spending firm-specific $-import allocations. In addition, Hungarian–Soviet trade differs from Hungarian–RCMEA trade due to the acquisition of implicit Soviet trade subsidies for a combination of Hungarian domestic stability plus Hungarian allegiance to Soviet interests.

The fifth dimension focuses on the difficulties involved in comparing trends in Hungary's major markets. For instance, is it possible to identify the trading partner that offers Hungary the best opportunities over a particular range of commodities? Unfortunately, comparisons of unit values do not contain sufficient information to answer this question. Comparison of a particular commodity's unit values is possible among DCAP trading partners (say, Hungary–France versus Hungary–FRG), but is generally impossible whenever a CMEA trading partner is involved because of the barter nature of CMEA trade and strategic game-playing by East European countries.

More specifically, comparison of unit values for manufactured goods is always an extremely risky undertaking because of the wide assortment of items often categorised under a single commodity name. However, such a comparison is even more dangerous within the context of intra-CMEA trade because of the general desire of East European countries to establish high 'reference prices' that may be utilised during trade negotiations with the Soviet Union. For example, the prices of manufactured goods in bilateral Czechoslovakian–Hungarian trade have tended to be higher than otherwise because both countries want to refer to these CMEA prices when negotiating with the Soviet Union. Such strategic behaviour on the part of Czechoslovakia and Hungary is relatively easy to accomplish in an environment of balanced bilateral barter among pairs of commodity groups.

It is easier to measure trade instability, differentiated by product category and across markets, and defined relative to a specific stable path. The stable path in Table 3.5 is an exponential time trend.[14] The instability index S_{jm} for product category j and market m is defined as the variance unexplained by the exponential time trend for the nominal value of trade in category j and market m divided by the variance unexplained by the exponential time trend for the nominal value of trade in category j over all markets. If $S_{jm}' > S_{jm}''$ then during 1974–86 an exponential time trend has explained movements of category j in market m' less completely than in market m''. Aggregation over product categories yields S_m, an average measure of trade instability for market m.

Table 3.5 indicates that the Soviet Union is the most stable market for Hungarian exports in the sense that the Soviet Union's average export instability index is the lowest among the eight markets examined and that the Soviet Union offers Hungary its most stable market for its machinery and equipment exports (47 per cent of all Hungarian exports to the Soviet Union) and a relatively stable market for industrial consumer goods exports (eighteen per cent) and for food exports (fourteen per cent). DCAP (= ECAP + OCAP) is Hungary's second most stable export market because of Hungary's high export stability to ECAP with respect to industrial consumer goods (21 per cent of all Hungarian goods to ECAP); fuels (eleven per cent); ores, minerals, and metals (twelve per cent); chemicals (ten per cent), and food (seventeen per cent) and to OCAP with respect to industrial consumer goods (43 per cent) and food (seventeen per cent). RCMEA plus OSOC are represented in Table 3.5 by the combination of GDR, Czechoslovakia, Poland and RSOC. By focusing on these four markets, one discovers substantial evidence that RCMEA is a much less stable market for Hungarian exports than the Soviet Union and DCAP. The level of instability of Hungarian exports to GDR, Czechoslovakia, Poland, and RSOC is closely connected to export instability with respect to machinery and equipment (GDR, 55 per cent; Czechoslovakia, 45 per cent; Poland, 44 per cent; RSOC, 41 per cent).

DCAP (= ECAP + OCAP) is on average a more stable market for Hungarian imports than the Soviet Union and RCMEA due to import stability with respect to machinery and equipment (33 per cent of Hungary's imports from ECAP; 34 per cent of Hungary's imports from OCAP); chemicals (ECAP, 24 per cent; OCAP, seventeen per cent); and non-food raw materials (ECAP fifteen per cent; OCAP, 28 per cent). The Soviet Union is a stable import source for

Table 3.5 Measures of trade instability for 1974–86, by commodity categories and trade partners

CAT	USSR	GDR	CZECH	POLAND	RSOC	ECAP	OCAP	DEV
				Exports				
1	1.22	13.02	3.04	3.52	7.65	6.69	4.45	6.54
2	3.77	19.59	8.22	3.20	2.19	3.60	2.35	9.57
3	0.61	4.62	5.41	6.57	2.42	1.17	3.91	0.84
4	1.21	0.34	1.72	1.44	1.63	1.77	0.85	0.91
5	0.87	4.12	7.33	15.66	4.11	1.30	4.04	2.63
6	1.93	5.33	4.64	5.34	7.10	0.83	4.87	2.10
7	3.08	2.28	3.19	7.54	1.53	2.51	4.57	3.10
8	1.06	2.14	2.98	2.78	2.27	2.87	0.45	0.98
9	2.93	5.14	2.14	4.99	1.75	1.49	1.43	4.24
10	1.51	1.69	4.37	2.53	5.18	3.45	5.81	5.16
Ave	1.93	10.32	4.01	4.01	4.70	2.54	2.61	5.02
				Imports				
1	3.01	1.59	0.51	1.22	0.69	1.35	0.44	2.04
2	25.15	13.12	1.93	9.02	2.82	1.01	4.84	6.30
3	1.36	3.50	13.20	5.09	8.85	5.72	8.59	12.08
4	1.01	0.97	1.13	1.53	1.49	0.95	1.58	1.30
5	0.53	7.93	8.55	2.50	2.14	2.40	2.82	9.01
6	3.91	2.90	2.81	6.52	2.01	1.25	1.40	3.65
7	2.40	2.63	2.65	2.13	0.20	1.17	2.61	1.44
8	0.96	0.68	1.08	0.98	1.09	0.67	0.99	0.94
9	1.58	1.33	1.48	1.37	1.17	0.99	1.47	1.56
10	1.49	1.11	2.67	1.44	3.17	0.87	2.77	5.77
Ave	2.29	4.01	2.49	3.02	2.07	1.57	2.07	5.07

Category 1	Machinery and Equipment (CTN 1)
Category 2	Industrial Consumer Goods (CTN 9)
Category 3	Fuels (CTN 20–23)
Category 4	Ores, Minerals, Metals (CTN 24–27)
Category 5	Chemicals (CTN 30–35)
Category 6	Building Materials (CTN 40–42)
Category 7	Non-food Raw Materials (CTN 50–53, 55–58)
Category 8	Animals, Cereals, and Food Raw Materials (CTN 60, 70–72)
Category 9	Food and Food Products (CTN 80–84)
Category 10	Beverages and Tobacco (CTN 85)

Table 3.5 continued

Instability Measure for Category $= S_{jm} = \dfrac{1 - \bar{R}^2_{mj}}{1 - \bar{R}^2_j}$ where
j and Market m

$\bar{R}^2_{mj}$ is the adjusted R^2 associated with fitting an exponential time trend to the data for category j in market m; and

$\bar{R}^2_j$ is the adjusted R^2 associated with fitting an exponential time trend to the data for category j in all of Hungary's markets.

Average Instability Measure $= S_m = \sum\limits_{j=1}^{10} W_{jm} S_{jm}$ where $\sum\limits_{j=1}^{m} W_{jm} = 1$;
For Market m

W_{jm} is the jth category's share of Hungarian exports (imports) with market m during 1974–86 relative to total Hungarian exports (imports).

Exports		Imports	
Category	$1 - \bar{R}^2_j$	Category	$1 - \bar{R}^2_j$
1	0.042	1	0.243
2	0.047	2	0.022
3	0.166	3	0.753
4	0.616	4	0.690
5	0.064	5	0.119
6	0.142	6	0.167
7	0.136	7	0.411
8	0.364	8	1.000
9	0.120	9	0.691
10	0.186	10	0.189

Source: *KSE*, annual volumes from 1974 to 1986, from tables dealing with Hungary's trade organised by two-digit CTN categories.

Hungary with respect to fuels (43 per cent); ores, minerals, and metals (fifteen per cent); and chemicals (six per cent). RCMEA's stability as an import source primarily comes from the stability of machinery and equipment imports from GDR (62 per cent), Czechoslovakia (49 per cent), and Poland (48 per cent).

This discussion of trade stability also suggests that Hungary's pattern of trade differs markedly among the Soviet Union, RCMEA, and DCAP, which Table 3.4 demonstrates. From a Hungarian export point of view, the Soviet Union resembles RCMEA in that machinery and equipment, industrial consumer goods, and food are Hungary's three biggest export categories for both the Soviet Union and RCMEA. DCAP differs from the Soviet Union and RCMEA because the share of machinery and equipment is relatively low in DCAP's imports of Hungarian goods, while the shares of industrial consumer goods, fuels, and food are relatively high. From a Hungarian import point of view, the Soviet Union, RCMEA, and DCAP are clearly distinct. Imports from the Soviet Union are much more heavily weighted towards fuels, ores, metals, and minerals than from any other of Hungary's trade partners, and less heavily weighted toward machinery and equipment. RCMEA (as summarised by the behaviour of GDR, Czechoslovakia, and Poland) provides Hungary with a greater proportion of manufactured goods than any other market. DCAP is a notable source of high quality machinery and equipment, chemicals, and non-food raw materials.

Finally, the sixth dimension of Hungary's trade behaviour is the potential contradiction between enterprise interests and the centre's interests (the centre being defined as the National Planning Office, Ministry of Finance, and Ministry of Foreign Trade) during CMEA trade negotiations.[15] Because CMEA trade is bilateral barter within designated pairs of contingency lists, the centre's interest may diverge from an enterprise's interest. The former wants to ensure that Hungary receives valuable goods in exchange for its exports, and is therefore concerned with the terms of trade inherent in the barter, and the quantities involved. However, an enterprise is more profit-oriented, and hence it is concerned with the prices it receives times the quantities involved. Consequently, the centre often adjusts the bilaterally negotiated *ftps* for either exports or imports via enterprise-specific per-unit subsidies or taxes in order to establish some consistency between its interests and an enterprise's interests. Thus the centre has a perfectly justifiable institutional reason to ignore negotiated prices and to intervene bureaucratically into an enterprise's affairs.

A CRITICAL ASSESSMENT OF THE BENEFITS AND COSTS ASSOCIATED WITH HUNGARY'S MULTIPLE TRADE ATTACHMENTS

Let us begin by considering how Hungary could have used its multiple trade attachments to improve its foreign trade performance, and then examine why such an ideal situation did not emerge. Hungary's benefits from trade with the Soviet Union are numerous: a secure supply of imported fuels and raw materials at *ftps* below corresponding *wmps*; a stable market for Hungarian exports, especially exports of manufactured goods (Table 3.5); subsidised loans in the form of bilateral TR-trade deficits with the Soviet Union while simultaneously enjoying $-trade surpluses due to Hungarian $-exports of wheat and meat to the Soviet Union at *wmps*; and low marketing and market-penetration costs for Hungarian exporters into the huge and largely unexploited Soviet market.

Ideally, Hungary could have capitalised on these advantages to develop large-scale manufacturing capacity based on relatively inexpensive fuel and raw material inputs. Then Hungary could have exploited the economies of scale inherent in its Soviet-oriented large-scale manufacturing sector to export: (*a*) its better quality machinery and equipment and industrial consumer goods to DCAP and RCMEA (along with its agricultural exports) for raw materials, otherwise unavailable parts and components, advanced machinery and equipment, and licenses that embody new technology; and (*b*) its more traditional quality manufactured goods to RCMEA and perhaps DEV for industrial consumer goods and other items that could serve as substitutes for imports from DCAP. In turn, Hungary could have utilised its imported Western technology to modernise its export structure and thus ensure continued high demand for its exports in the Soviet Union, RCMEA, and eventually DCAP.

The evidence presented in section three strongly suggests that this ideal picture is far from reality. In this section the results of a survey of twenty large Hungarian manufacturing enterprises and nine Hungarian foreign trading organisations (FTOs) conducted by the Institute for World Economics of the Hungarian Academy of Sciences during 1982–84 and focusing on enterprise and FTO perceptions concerning the evolution of their relations with CMEA from 1970 to 1981–83 are summarised. The survey provides excellent insight into why Hungary has been unable to capitalise on the advantages of bilateral trade with the Soviet Union.[16]

A study of the survey results for five engineering enterprises and two FTOs reveals the following.[17] The five engineering manufacturers accounted for over 25 per cent of Hungary's TR-exports of engineering products (by 1981 between 58.6 and 90.0 per cent of their TR-exports were directed to the Soviet Union). The two FTOs handled over 60 per cent of the TR-exports of these enterprises and the enterprises themselves arranged for the export of the remainder. Also, the TR-exports of these enterprises represented a substantial but declining share of total sales over time (between 13.3 and 46.5 per cent of total sales in 1971 versus between 9.6 and 38.6 per cent of total sales in 1981). Finally, the survey showed that TR-exports of these enterprises contained a very low proportion of $-imports.

The failure of these enterprises to implement the hypothetical ideal scenario was due to the following reasons:

1. The quotas embodied in the contingency list system frequently did not allow these firms to export enough to exploit economies of scale. This is partly due to the inter-governmental nature of CMEA trade agreements and partly due to the Soviet's fear of being dependent on any foreign market.

2. The prevailing system of intra-CMEA pricing did not reward Hungarian products that embodied greater levels of technological sophistication.

> In the setting of TR prices, the enterprises have only the right to make proposals to the FTOs, be it concerning their entire range of exports or concerning a novel product. Such proposals, however, tend not to have any palpable influence on the prices thrashed out, as proven by the fact that, so far, rising costs of production have not been followed by any rise in sales prices. One result of this has been a distortion of price patterns.
>
> In setting the prices of certain new products, the Hungarian and Soviet specialist FTOs have, without consulting the manufacturers, agreed upon the application of a pricing proportional to physical weight, based on the Soviet pricing approach which does not remunerate any quality parameter whatsoever. In this case, then, the Bucharest pricing principle has ceased to operate even as a principle. It has been replaced by a practice that keeps Hungarian export prices permanently low and thereby hamstrings technological progress.[18]

3. Often the Soviet partner preferred traditional products over new products because a new product would have caused at least a temporary disruption of Soviet production.

4. 'In regard of the intra-CMEA relations of the Hungarian engineering enterprises, it is inappropriate to speak of market strategies in the usual sense. Strategies of sorts do exist, but they have the

common feature of obeying more or less compelling product patterns rather than the enterprises' sovereign long-term decisions. The product patterns in question are in their majority the results of high-level pre-1968 decisions.'[19]

These pessimistic observations are not the only viewpoints expressed in the survey. A more positive evaluation follows from studying the experience of six Hungarian enterprises that produce electronics-intensive products.[20] To begin, it is crucial to note that the complaints of enterprises in this group that have incorporated electronics of average hardness into their products (thus these enterprises are constrained by contingency lists in which manufactured goods are bartered for manufactured goods) are essentially the same as those of the five engineering enterprises.[21] We will call all such enterprises traditional TR-exporters. However, for enterprises that participate in multilateral CMEA specialisation programmes and incorporate vanguard technology into their products, the Soviet market offers excellent prices and is completely open and anxious to receive new technology. Therefore, let us focus only on the latter type of electronics-intensive enterprise, namely on several enterprises participating in the data processing programme and another enterprise that specialises in nuclear instruments for medicine and geophysics. We will call these latter enterprises high-tech TR-exporters and note that their marketing strategy is simple: buy Western licenses and perhaps components to produce a product that is on the frontier of CMEA technology. Thus Hungarian high-tech enterprises utilise $-imports to generate TR-exports (in fact, their $-exports are negligible).

High-tech TR-exporters have an essentially positive attitude towards the Soviet market – their primary market – because (*a*) as participants in a CMEA specialisation programme they enjoy priority access within Hungary to investment funds, $-imports, and Western licenses; and (*b*) they obtain excellent prices for their TR-exports to the Soviet Union and RCMEA. The contingency lists corresponding to these high-tech products provide Hungary with hard goods such as oil. Since oil has a clearly documentable *wmp*, it is in the interest of the Hungarian Ministry of Foreign Trade and FTOs to bargain strenuously for high *ftps* because in these instances prices play a role in the terms of the exchange. Often the resulting *ftps* of high-tech TR-exporters are too high from a 'domestic distribution of income' perspective, thus the Hungarian government levies export taxes on these high-tech commodities. This is in sharp contrast to the export subsidies the Hungarian government pays many traditional TR-exporters in order to ensure fulfilment of CMEA obligations that otherwise would be unattractive from an enterprise point of view.

Thus far two types of TR-exporters have been examined – traditional and high-tech. Now let us turn our attention to four light manufacturing enterprises – three textile producers and one footwear manufacturer – whose main function has been to supply the domestic market, yet nonetheless has developed almost exclusively according to CMEA standards and priorities.[22]

Given that light manufacturing's primary task has been to supply the Hungarian market, why have the Soviet Union and RCMEA had such a decisive influence on the long-term development of light manufacturing? In the 1950s Hungary recognised the need to import cotton, leather and other materials, for its light manufacturing industry and to import fuels, minerals and other raw materials for its rapidly developing heavy industry. TR-exports of light manufacturers were selected as a means of paying for these imported industrial inputs. CMEA rather than ROW was chosen as the source of these industrial inputs because of East–West tension and Hungary's $-shortage. In the 1960s Hungary's light manufacturing industry enjoyed its dual role as the main supplier to the domestic market and an important TR-exporter because 'it offered unprecedented expansion, replacing as it did the production series of a few thousand acceptable to the world market with its high quality demand . . . by series in the hundreds of thousands to be absorbed by the Soviet market with its comparatively low quality demand. All this promised apparently unlimited growth and the concomitant prosperity, organisational growth and positional advantages.'[23]

Unfortunately, the economies of scale inherent in Hungary's light manufacturing did not prove to be advantageous with respect to $-exports because the quality of most Hungarian light manufactures was well below DCAP standards. This substandard output was due to poor-quality raw material inputs, inferior capital equipment, and inadequate incentives. Moreover Hungary, which had a high wage structure relative to that of DEV, was not able to compete on DEV markets.

Let us now concentrate on Hungary's inability to compete on DCAP markets. Central to this problem is the fact that Hungary's TR-exports of light manufactures are soft goods. Hence, they suffer from the same pricing problems that face Hungary's exports of engineering products. In other words, the *ftps* for Hungarian light manufactures did not increase as a consequence of quality improvements or adaptability to consumer preferences, but rather tended to move in line with the prices of the Soviet soft goods embodied in the contingency lists. In fact, a large portion of these Soviet soft goods have been low-quality industrial raw materials and machinery destined for Hungarian light manufacturing. To complicate the picture even more, twenty to 60 per cent of the value of the TR-exports of the four light manufacturing firms has been composed of Hungarian $-imports (because of Hungary's lack of raw material inputs).[24] The Hungarian central authorities would not have accepted such a vicious circle – using $-imports and enterprise subsidies to export low quality consumer goods to the Soviet Union at unsatisfactory prices in order to obtain low quality inputs for the consumer goods industry – were it not for the overall presence of implicit Soviet trade subsidies.

Thus the survey of the traditional engineering, electronics-intensive, and light manufacturing enterprises indicates that:
• TR-export capacity for Hungarian manufactured goods does nothing to generate Hungarian $-exports;
• TR-exports of Hungarian manufactured goods require $-imports as inputs, therefore are characterised by dollar-to-TR conversion and have significantly contributed to Hungary's $-debt; and
• all but high-tech TR-exports of Hungarian manufactured goods are relics of a bygone development strategy and their persistent presence in Hungarian–Soviet trade is a distressing sign of the stagnating influence of outdated contingency lists and all of the other characteristics of CMEA trade mentioned in section two.

The survey of both chemical enterprises and metallurgical enterprises reveals the more advantageous aspects of Hungary's trade with the Soviet Union. The primary task of these enterprises is to process fuels and raw materials, the majority of which is imported from the Soviet Union, then to use the processed products to satisfy domestic needs and to earn convertible currency. Alongside Hungary's indispensable need for its $-exports of fuel products, metals, and chemicals, Hungary has been experiencing growing problems since the mid-1970s with respect to imports of fuels and raw materials from the Soviet Union. Therefore let us analyse the survey results for these raw material processing enterprises more closely.

Two metallurgical enterprises – one in ferrous metallurgy and the other in aluminum – were surveyed.[25] Both have increased their production capacities since the mid-1970s, which has made them more dependent on Soviet imports of raw materials, equipment, and technology while allowing them to increase their $-exports to ROW.

Integrated ferrous metallurgy in Hungary was constructed according to Soviet design and technological specifications, and the ferrous metallurgy enterprise under consideration here received most of its equipment from the Soviet Union. Moreover, this enterprise was completely satisfied with the Soviet equipment's actual performance and simplicity of handling. Much more problematic for this Hungarian enterprise was the poor quality of Soviet iron ore, containing just 45–50 per cent Fe as opposed to 60–70 per cent Fe for prime grade. Hungary's opportunities to export ferrous metal products to DCAP were severely restricted by the low quality Soviet iron ore. In fact, until 1984 the enterprise had not been able to diversify its sources of iron ore partly because of the fear of damaging the overall exchange embedded in this bilateral contingency.[26] In 1984, a six-year research effort (the length of time dictated by the difficulties involved in altering established bilateral traditions with the Soviet Union) by Hungarian officials from the National Planning Office and Ministry of Foreign Trade was concluded. This research demonstrated the advantages available to Hungary if better iron ore could be obtained. Therefore, for 1986–1990, Hungary decided to import higher quality iron ore from Brazil rather than to increase dependence on lower quality Soviet iron ore.[27]

The fortunes of the aluminum enterprise stem directly from the Hungarian–Soviet Alumina-Aluminum Agreement signed in the early 1960s. Hungary agreed to ship alumina to the Soviet partner so that it could be processed in the Soviet Union, then shipped back to Hungary as slabs of aluminum for processing into semi-finished and finished aluminum products. In this manner, Hungary has been able to utilise excess Soviet smelter capacity. Initially, Hungary's alumina exports paid for 38 per cent of the value of the aluminum it received from the Soviet Union, with other Hungarian goods being used to offset the remaining 62 per cent. Since the agreement was signed, the quantities involved have remained the same, but now Hungary's alumina exports pay for only 24 per cent of the value of aluminum it receives and the $-content of Hungarian goods used to offset the remaining 76 per cent has increased. Overall, both sides seem willing to continue this arrangement since the agreement has been prolonged beyond 1990. Thus, Hungary has decided not to invest in its own smelter capacity, but rather to continue its dependence on Soviet capacity.[28]

Three chemical enterprises were interviewed: one is responsible for Hungarian fuel imports, another transforms basic materials such as natural and synthetic rubber into more processed basic materials, and the third is a producer of basic chemical products. Each obtains its inputs predominately from the Soviet Union. Their first priority has been the domestic market, second $-exports, and third TR-exports to fulfil long-term CMEA obligations.[29]

The three enterprises' share in overall Hungarian exports rose from 3.6 per cent in 1978 to 6.1 per cent in 1983 and in Hungarian exports to the Soviet Union from 2.1 per cent to 2.9 per cent. Their share in overall Hungarian imports rose from 11.8 per cent in 1978 to 14.5 per cent in 1983 and in Hungarian imports from the Soviet Union from 24.0 per cent to 40.1 per cent. These shifts were due primarily to changes in relative prices rather than to changes in the relative quantities exchanged.[30]

The development of these enterprises provides another view of the pluses and minuses of bilateral co-operation with the Soviet Union. On the plus side, since Hungary participated in CMEA specialisation programmes with respect to fuel products, chemicals, and metal products, it was able to construct facilities that embody significant economies of scale. Also, Hungary received relatively secure supplies of fuels and raw materials at favourable prices. On the negative side, the quality of some of the imported raw materials was so poor that it mitigated against exporting the processed products to DCAP. Delivery deadlines were broken more often by Soviet suppliers than by alternative ROW suppliers. Moreover, the production facilities at these enterprises are not energy efficient or internationally competitive mostly because of the complex and ever-changing regulatory (rather than market) environment which surrounds these enterprises.

ECONOMIC REFORM ⇔ FOREIGN TRADE POLICIES

For an economy as open as Hungary's, economic reform and foreign trade policies are closely interwoven. If central authorities would have implemented a reform characterised by relatively uniform regulators across all enterprises (namely, imposed hard budget constraints and not engaged in bargaining over firm-specific regulators), then enterprises that had performed well (poorly) would have received more (less) than they actually did. Presumably, enterprise accountability would have forced enterprise managers to be more sensitive to fluctuations on the world market. Moreover, in a reformed environment in which central authorities would have accepted the decisions dictated by market-determined prices, it seems reasonable to expect that investment decisions would have better reflected long-run efficiency considerations including those of the world market and CMEA and, hence, the deterioration in Hungary's terms of trade would not have been so severe.

However, such a scenario would not have addressed the issue of Hungarian trade transacted in TRs, which has represented between 45 and 50 per cent of Hungarian trade turnover. Within CMEA, Hungarian enterprises have not actively engaged in most trade decisions and bilateral barter constrained by contingency lists has not been an effective way for Hungary to adjust to a rapidly changing world environment or to encourage specialisation. The cumulative impact of these CMEA obstacles to flexible, decentralised decision-making can be understood from the lessons of section five:

- TR-export capacity for Hungarian manufactured goods has done nothing to generate Hungarian $-exports;
- TR-exports of Hungarian manufactured goods have required $-imports as inputs, therefore have contributed significantly to Hungary's $-debt; and
- all but high-tech TR-exports of Hungarian manufactured goods have been relics of a bygone development strategy and their persistent presence has been a distressing sign of the stagnating influence of CMEA institutional characteristics.

In effect, Hungary has built two foreign trade strategies, one for $-trade and one for TR-trade. Thus even if Hungary would have implemented a more comprehensive and uniform reform, Hungarian central authorities still would have bureaucratically interfered in enterprise decisions in order to guarantee that CMEA obligations would be met.

In order to discuss the impact that improved foreign trade policies might have had on the Hungarian reform process, it should be understood that investment mistakes have been the fundamental cause of Hungarian foreign trade failure.[31] Investment in industries that export to the Soviet Union has met Hungary's short-run need to acquire fuels and raw materials at prices lower than corresponding *wmps*. However such investment has had debilitating long-run consequences. The policy tools used to stimulate $-exports and restrict $-imports have been just as short-sighted because they have been designed to generate only minor changes in Hungary's production structure; they have focused almost entirely on *short-term* $-export targets while neglecting long-term efficiency considerations; and they have been based on enterprise promises – a notoriously unreliable indicator of future enterprise performance – rather than on market criteria.

Thus discussing improved foreign trade policies is a complex matter that requires different recommendations with respect to Hungary's trade with the Soviet Union, RCMEA, and ROW. In order to improve its foreign trade policies with the Soviet Union, Hungary would have had to risk losing some of the implicit subsidies connected with such trade by changing its bargaining apparatus. On the Hungarian side, enterprise representatives could have bargained directly with Soviet negotiators. Under this scenario, enterprises would not have received TRs for their exports or imports, but rather the Soviet goods offered in exchange. Then the Hungarian enterprise would have had the option of either retaining the goods received from the Soviet side or selling these goods to Hungarian distributors. Such a policy may well have forced a much greater proportion of relative Hungarian–Soviet *ftps* to approach corresponding relative *wmps*. In this manner, Hungarian enterprises would have negotiated with Soviet officials and not with Hungarian central authorities.

In order to improve its foreign trade policies with RCMEA, Hungary would have had to risk loss of market share by striving to transform TR-trade into $-trade. (This also could have been an option with Hungarian–Soviet trade.) Once again, Hungarian enterprise representatives could have negotiated directly with representatives from the partner country, and Hungary, over time, could have pressed for a greater and greater portion of Hungarian–RCMEA trade being transacted via convertible currencies, perhaps subject to some sort of temporary bilateral balance constraint. However, unemployment in Hungary might have developed due to cutbacks in trade with those trade partners unwilling to participate in the switch from TR-trade to $-trade.

These suggestions designed to improve Hungary's trade with the Soviet Union and RCMEA fall under the category of the 'Finlandisation' of Hungarian intra-CMEA trade.[32] Finnish–Soviet trade is influenced by short-, medium-, and long-term governmental agreements; yet Finnish enterprise representatives negotiate directly with Soviet officials and transactions are based on current *wmps*, not on past bilateral price trends or a moving average of *wmps* for the previous five years.

In order to improve its foreign trade policies with ROW, Hungarian domestic prices should have moved closer to relative *wmps* at a more rapid pace and Hungarian export subsidies and import quotas should have been eliminated. Under these conditions, central authorities could have manipulated the exchange rate in order to control the $-trade balance.

Presumably healthier foreign trade performance would have freed Hungarian policy makers from preoccupation with short-run emergencies such as repayment of loans from Western banks. This, in turn, may well have lead to the introduction of a more comprehensive and internally consistent economic reform. However, for a country like Hungary, economic reform and foreign trade reform should have been implemented simultaneously in order to reinforce one another, rather than in a piecemeal, sequential manner.

Notes

My special gratitude goes to my many Hungarian colleagues, especially to János Kozma and Margit Rácz, who assisted me during my 1986–87 research stay in Hungary as an IREX scholar. IREX funds are provided by the National Endowment for the Humanities and the United States Information Agency. I also am very grateful to Josef van Brabant, George Dalton, Raimund Dietz, András Köves, Marie Lavigne, Gábor Oblath, Ádam Török, and the participants of the conference, 'The Challenge of Simultaneous Economic Relations with East and West', for their helpful suggestions on an earlier version of this paper. Finally, I wish to thank Scott Johnson, Thomas Maycock, and Lauren Wittenberg for their outstanding research assistance, and Paula Nielsen for her excellent word processing. All remaining errors are my full responsibility.

1. Kornai (1986, pp. 1694–1710). For statistical evidence, see Kornai and Matits (1984, 1987).
2. Kornai (1986, pp. 1729–1730).
3. See Kornai (1980) for an exhaustive discussion of soft budget constraints, which is another way of discussing firm-specific treatment of enterprises.
4. Kornai (1980; 1986).
5. Marrese (1986b; 1989).
6. See Kornai (1988) for a comprehensive list of references. Also Marrese (1980; 1981a; 1981b; 1982; 1983; 1986a).
7. Hewett (1985, pp. 20–35) discusses ways by which the Hungarian Central Statistical Office may be introducing upward bias in its GDP calculations. However, on the whole, Hewett *guesses* that the Hungarian official GDP index found in Table 3.1 is closer to the 'true' index than the Alton index (discussed below).

8. Alton *et al.* (1987, p. 23).
9. For a more detailed account of the separability of Hungarian foreign trade, see Marrese (1989).
10. The remarks that follow are not unique to Hungarian–Soviet bilateral trade; rather they apply to bilateral trade between most East European CMEA-members and the USSR. The post-1973 period differs from earlier years due to the first oil-price shock which contributed to terms of trade improvement for the USSR and deterioration for Hungary.
11. The rationale behind the Soviet goal for independence has been strongly influenced by Soviet decisions to adhere to taut central planning; act as a superpower; and value Eastern Europe highly as a component of Soviet defence. See Marrese (1986b) for details.
12. The differential between the *ftp* of Soviet oil paid in TRs by Hungary and the *wmp* of oil has decreased steadily since the beginning of 1985. Yet the only way known to this author of evaluating whether the price paid by Hungary for Soviet oil is less than the corresponding *wmp* is to employ the implicit subsidy methodology, which yields an estimate for a realistic TR/$ exchange rate. However, implicit subsidy calculations are available only through 1984. See Marrese (1986b) or Marrese and Vanous (1988).
13. Ausch (1972, pp. 85–86); Marrese and Vanous (1983, pp. 58, 59).
14. An exponential time trend was chosen over a linear time trend and a trend based on time and time-squared because of goodness-of-fit considerations.
15. The centre, as argued in section two, is not homogeneous and its interests are many. Therefore, this divergence of interests is much more difficult to solve than is implied in the discussion above.
16. A comprehensive summary of the survey is contained in the seven articles found in Inotai (1986a).
17. The discussion concerning engineering enterprises and FTOs comes from Rácz (1986a), Török (1986), and interview material I gathered from the Institute of World Economics.
18. Rácz (1986a, p. 26).
19. Török (1986, pp. 67–68).
20. The discussion concerning electronics-intensive enterprises comes from Rácz (1986a, 1986b) and interview material I gathered from the Institute of World Economics.
21. Rácz (1986b, p. 76).
22. The discussion concerning light manufacturers comes from Rácz (1986a), Pártos (1986), and interview material I gathered from the Institute of World Economics.
23. Pártos (1986, p. 80).
24. Pártos (1986, p. 81).
25. The discussion concerning metallurgical enterprises comes from Rácz (1986a), Réti (1986), and interview material I gathered from the Institute of World Economics.
26. Réti (1986, pp. 44–45).
27. Interview material.
28. Réti (1986, pp. 47–53).

29. The discussion concerning metallurgical enterprises comes from Rácz (1986a), Inotai (1986b), and interview material I gathered from the Institute of World Economics.
30. Inotai (1986b, p. 55).
31. Discussed in more depth in Gács (1987) and Marrese (1989).
32. Oblath and Pete (1983); Oblath (1990).

Bibliography

T. P. ALTON, K. BADACH, E. M. BASS, G. LAZARCIK, and G. J. STALLER, 'Economic Growth in Eastern Europe, 1970 and 1975–1986', Occasional Paper No. 95 of the Research Project on National Income in East Central Europe (New York: L. W. International Financial Research, 1987).

S. AUSCH, *Theory and Practice of CMEA Cooperation* (Budapest: Akadémiai Kiadó, 1972).

J. GÁCS, 'Import Substitution and Investments in Hungary in the Period of Restrictions (1979–1986)', revised version of a paper presented at the 10th US–Hungarian Economics Roundtable (Budapest, 1987).

E. A. HEWETT, 'The Gross National Product of Hungary: Important Issues for Comparative Research', World Bank Staff Working Paper No. 775 (Washington, D.C.: The World Bank, 1985).

A. INOTAI, (ed.), *The Hungarian Enterprise in the Context of Intra-CMEA Relations* (Budapest: Hungarian Scientific Council for World Economy, 1986a).

A. INOTAI, 'Intra-CMEA Relations of Some Hungarian Chemical Enterprises', in Inotai (ed.), 1986a (1986b) pp. 55–60.

J. KORNAI, *Economics of Shortage*, (Amsterdam: North-Holland, 1980).

J. KORNAI, 'The Hungarian Reform Process: Visions, Hopes, and Reality', *Journal of Economic Literature*, XXIV (December 1986) 1687–1737.

J. KORNAI, and Á. MATITS, 'Softness of the Budget Constraint – An Analysis Relying on Data of Firms', *Acta Oeconomica*, 36, No. 3–4 (1984) pp. 223–249.

J. KORNAI, and Á. MATITS, *Vállalotok Nyereségének Bürokratikus újraelosztása* (The bureaucratic redistribution of enterprise profit) (Budapest: Közgazdasági és Jogi Könyvkiadó, 1987).

KSE (annual volumes) *Kúlkereskedelmi Statisztikai Évkönyv* (Hungarian Foreign Trade Statistical Yearbook) (Budapest: Kózponti Statisztikai Hivatal).

M. MARRESE, 'The Hungarian Economy: Prospects for the 1980s', in Economics Directorate NATO (eds.), *Economic Reforms in Eastern Europe and Prospects for the 1980s* (Oxford: Pergamon Press, 1980) pp. 183–201.

M. MARRESE, 'Is Unemployment the Only Answer to Labour Shortage in

Hungary?', in Jan Adam (ed.) *Employment Policies in the USSR and in East European Europe* (London: Macmillan, 1982) pp. 96–119.

M. MARRESE, 'Agricultural Policy and Performance in Hungary', *Journal of Comparative Economics*, 7, No. 3 (1983) pp. 329–345.

M. MARRESE, 'Hungarian Agriculture: Moving in the Right Direction', in *East European Economies: Slow Growth in the 1980s*, Vol. 3 of the Joint Economic Committee of the US Congress (Washington, DC: US Government Printing Office, March 1986a) pp. 322–340.

M. MARRESE, 'CMEA: Effective But Cumbersome Political Economy', *International Organization*, 40, No. 2 (1986b) pp. 287–327.

M. MARRESE, 'The Separability of Hungarian Foreign Trade with Respect to the Soviet Union, the Rest of CMEA, and the West', *Comparative Economic Studies*, XXXI, No. 2 (1989) pp. 1–41.

M. MARRESE and J. VANOUS, *Soviet Subsidization of Trade with Eastern Europe: A Soviet Perspective* (Berkeley: Institute of International Studies, University of California, 1983).

M. MARRESE and J. VANOUS, 'The Content and Controversy of Soviet Trade Relations with Eastern Europe, 1970–84', in Josef C. Brada, Ed A. Hewett, and Thomas A. Wolf (eds.), *Economic Adjustment and Reform in Eastern Europe and the Soviet Union: Essays in Honor of Franklyn D. Holzman* (Durham: Duke University Press, 1988) pp. 185–220.

MINISTRY OF FINANCE, 'Foreign Exchange and Customs Regulations', Booklet No. 16 of Public Finance in Hungary. Budapest: Ministry of Finance (1984).

G. OBLATH, and P. PETE, 'The Development, Mechanism, and Institutional System of Fino-Soviet Economic Relations', manuscript (1983).

G. OBLATH, 'Internal Regulation of Foreign Trade with Respect to Socialist Trading Partners: A Comparison of the Finnish and the Hungarian Systems', in Michael Marrese and Sándor Richter (eds.) *The Challenge of Simultaneous Economic Relations with East and West* (London: Macmillan, 1990).

G. PÁRTOS, 'The Hungarian Light Manufacturers' Link with the CMEA Region', in Inotai (ed.), 1986a (1986) pp. 79–86.

M. RÁCZ, 'A Summary Analysis', in Inotai (ed.), 1986a (1986) pp. 9–41.

M. RÁCZ, 'On the Intra-CMEA Relations of Some Hungarian Manufacturers of Electronics-Intensive Products', in Inotai (ed.), 1986a (1986b) pp. 69–78.

T. RÉTI, 'Metallurgical Enterprises in a Constrained Room for Manoeuvre', in Inotai (ed.), 1986a (1986) pp. 43–54.

SE (annual volumes) *Statisztikai Évkonyv* (Hungarian Statistical Yearbook) (Budapest: Központi Statisztikai Hivatal).

Ä. TÖRÖK, 'Intra-CMEA Relations of the Hungarian Engineering Enterprises', in Inotai (ed.), 1986a (1986) pp. 61–8.

J. VANOUS, 'A Review of Developments in Soviet and East European Hard Currency Trade, Balance of Payments, Debt, and Assets, 1980–86', PlanEcon Report Nos. 36–37–38 (1987).

4 *Perestroika* in the Soviet Union: The Domestic and International Dimensions
Nikolay Shmelev

Perestroika in the Soviet Union has beyond a doubt international as well as domestic ramifications. Modern economic progress in large and small countries alike is impossible without fully utilising the international division of labour. But in order to take advantage of the international division of labour, it is imperative that beneficial impulses from the world economy reach the domestic economy unimpeded so that short- and long-term economic decision-making proceeds with full awareness of both domestic and international options.

In the early 1980s the Soviet rate of economic growth slowed down significantly. The economy entered a precrisis state. The pace of economic advance slowed while the productivity of capital investments fell, and social problems worsened, which in turn caused the international economic position of the Soviet Union to deteriorate. One notices three principal defects of the Soviet economic system which have been developing since the late 1920s: first, the primacy, or the monopoly of the producer in all spheres of the economy; second, the lack of incentives for workers to improve productivity; and third, the enterprises' anti-innovation bias.

The principal growth factors that the Soviet Union relied on since the first five-year plans – a growing labour force, cheap natural resources, and an increasing share of investment in national income – were exhausted. The era of extensive growth in the Soviet economy came to an end. At the same time, the era of 'administrative socialism', of running the economy by decree, came to a logical conclusion having fulfilled its historic role.

At the time of writing the Soviet Union faces the complicated challenge of accelerating the rate of economic progress, by using the existing economic potential more efficiently, while simultaneously creating a new economic mechanism based on economic rather than administrative incentives. This process was started at the 27th Congress of the Soviet Communist Party. As the 1990s begin the Soviet economy is searching for an optimum balance: between centralisation and decentralisation; among the interests of the state and those of enterprises and individuals; and between the plan and the market place.

The programme of reforms the Soviet government has in mind is long-term and consists of several stages. It is anticipated that these new economic mechanisms will come into full force in the late 1990s.

During the current five-year plan period (1986–1990) realistic progress can be expected in several sectors of the economy. First, the Soviets have the potential to exploit its most obvious reserves which are organisational rather than economic in nature. For example, through poor or negligent management alone, up to 25 per cent of working time in industry is lost. On the other hand, in agriculture up to twenty per cent of total produce is lost but a statistic of 50 per cent for vegetables and fruit alone is not beyond reality. Second, the Soviets expect to accelerate the progress of their machine-tool industry and to improve the quality of manufactured products, primarily that of machinery. Third, an economy-wide transition to new conditions of work based on the Enterprise Act is planned involving the independence of enterprises and self-financing. Fourth, a far-reaching change in the mentality of economic managers and work collectives is expected to be accomplished. People in all walks of life should realise that obligatory methods of economic management, such as orders, pressure, and directives are gone for good, to be replaced by the inexorable advent both in ideology and in practice of the purely economic incentives of the 'universal and consistent cost accounting'.

The strategy for the 1990s envisages far-reaching changes in the whole economic environment as well as the entire system of the country. The essence of these changes are as follows: first, a new structural investment policy, and, second, a new macroeconomic framework which will determine all spheres of life of enterprises and their work forces.

The new structural investment policy will emphasise high technology industries, modernisation in existing plant and equipment, increases in production of consumer goods, and finally, improvements in the services and the social infrastructure. At the same time, it will give lower priority to investment in energy industries which at present is too high – approaching 60 per cent of the country's total investment expenditure.

The new macroeconomic environment, which is being created as I write and will, hopefully, determine economic activity in the 1990s, involves a combination of directive and indicative planning and a free market. This system will have the following main characteristics.

1. The overall long-term planning of the State Planning Committee will be strengthened, while its role in the day-to-day activities of the economy will diminish. Its functions will cover the direct planning of 250–300 of the most important types of products (out of the 24 million currently being produced) and the distribution of the all-union investment fund among the national priority projects. At the level of individual industries, planning will be performed by ministries, whose number will apparently be drastically reduced.

Competitive government procurement through tenders will become the principal instrument of direct planning. By the mid-1990s direct procurement is expected to take up on average around 30 per cent of total output. The rest will be determined by the market by means of direct contracts between enterprises and through wholesale trade, namely, through market mechanisms.

2. The role of indicative planning, that is, of centrally setting the overall 'rules of the game' will be enhanced. These controls include centrally established tax rates, depreciation allowances, interest rates and rents for the services of land, and water and natural resources. The prices of several hundred of the most important products will also be centrally planned. Simultaneously, target ranges will be established for the 'floating' prices of several thousand types of goods, the production and sale of which the government considers to merit control. The rest will be determined by the market.

3. Enterprises will switch to complete cost accounting, current expenditures and bonus funds will be financed out of their revenues. New investments will be financed out of profits and bank credit. It is also possible (although the problem is not completely resolved) that enterprises will sell shares and bonds in order to drive personal savings and involve the idle capital of other enterprises.

In principle, loss-making enterprises will in principle go bankrupt. However, the government will take steps to rescue them on a case-by-case basis.

4. Agricultural production will be organised in a more flexible manner. Innovative forms of production will be employed both within and outside of the framework of collective and state farms, including agribusinesses, agrocombines, work team and family contracting, and family long-term rent of land. Meanwhile, all kinds of

agricultural co-operatives will be developed, including those in the fields of sales, supplies, and credit.

Good prospects for individual, family, and co-operative enterprise exist in the cities (especially in small-scale manufacturing, technological innovation and services). However, given Soviet social traditions, the revival of even small businesses using hired labour is unlikely, or unfavourable.

5. The Soviet Union hopes to complete a radical price and finance reform. This is probably the most difficult and sensitive component of the Soviet economic programme of reform.

They will be aimed primarily not at the redistribution of income but at the creation of a framework of guidelines which will put an end to arbitrary decision-making and allow and even encourage decisions based on sound economic information. As the 1980s close it is still very difficult. Since the 1930s the Soviet Union has experienced energy and raw materials prices that are artificially low in comparison to the world market level, while the prices of machinery are artificially high; at the same time, in the consumer sector the prices of food and utilities are artificially high. In the future massive price subsidies, which now take up to a quarter of government expenditures, will be phased out.

In accordance with the decisions of the July 1987 plenary meeting of the CPSU Central Committee, the price reform will proceed in a way that will not harm the interests of the population. The possible rises in consumer prices will be compensated by a rise in wages and pensions and lower prices of manufactured goods.

The goal of financial reform is to eliminate inflationary methods of financing from our economic system and to encourage sound and normal credit. *Perestroika* needs financing and one of the possible sources will be credit in all its forms.

Currency reform is an indispensable and integral part of financial and price reform. There are two interrelated goals that the Soviet Union would like to achieve in the near future: the establishment of a realistic and unified rouble exchange rate, and second, a transition to partial rouble convertibility (that is, convertibility at the central bank level) as a first step towards full convertibility. The Soviet Union hopes that by the early 1990s we will achieve full rouble convertibility within CMEA.

6. The Soviet Union hopes that economic reforms will accelerate the transition towards an 'open economy' and more active integration into the international economic activities. Some progress can already

be discerned, especially in connection with the rights to access world markets that many enterprises have received.

The reforms will allow the establishment of a direct link between domestic and international prices, the introduction of cost accounting into foreign trade activities and the creation of improved incentives for manufacturing and agricultural enterprises to participate in export activities, industrial co-operation and other types of activities as well as the opening of the Soviet market to their CMEA partners and to other countries and the establishment of multilateral patterns of co-operation. The convertibility of the rouble will permit debt conversion (shifting between different types of debt instruments). The Soviet government also hopes that the reforms will give a fresh impetus to the creation of joint ventures in the country.

The activities of international organisations such as GATT, IMF and the World Bank are of a growing interest to the Soviet Union. In the light of the positive international developments that are taking place in the late 1980s, these organisations should assume a truly universal character and take into account the interests of all members of the world community.

Whether the existence of regional preferential trading regimes is warranted is a separate issue. However, regional integration is a natural process; it has not started by accident. Some degree of preferentiality for the members of integration groups is probably natural also. The Soviets can dislike the agricultural policies of the EEC that discriminate against outsiders, but the Soviet Union understands why they emerged. Therefore, the preferential treatment for members of the CMEA is undoubtedly natural too. Now it is enforced through planning decisions; tomorrow, tariffs can become its most important instrument, but this is of secondary importance.

The real issue is whether the free cross-border movement of goods and factors of production between countries with different social systems can be achieved even in the distant future. Economic developments point in this direction, but do political developments point in that direction too? It would be premature to answer 'yes' to that question. No one is going to argue that far-reaching reforms in the Soviet Union are going smoothly. It is a revolution and revolutions, as can be seen by history, are not easy. The Soviet Union needs to conquer the incredible inertia entrenched in its economic system, as well as conquer the resistance of interest groups which are threatened by the transition from administrative management to economic self-regulating systems. Finally, the scepticism of parts of the population towards some of the aims of the reform must be taken into account, in particular towards the price reform and the possible closure of many unprofitable enterprises. The Soviet Union faces challenges aplenty. But they are not insurmountable given the necessary perseverance from all sectors of society.

Contrary to what some people in the West think, the radical economic reforms in the Soviet Union are not a gradual return to capitalism. In fact, the reforms are a return to Leninism, to Lenin's notions of building an efficient, highly competitive socialist economic model. These ideas were successfully realised under Lenin's direction, but because of the well-known historic developments Lenin's socialist economic model was phased out. Today's task is to revive Lenin's ideas in a way that will fit new historical realities and new economic challenges.

5 A new situation in Hungarian–Soviet trade: what is to be done?
András Köves

During 1975–1988 Hungary's relations within the CMEA have been marked by the following difficulties: the narrowing of purchasing opportunities (the stagnation or fall in the quantity of imports that Hungary wished to purchase); the faltering of the earlier stability of purchase and sale; and the considerable deterioration in Hungarian terms of trade and in non-price conditions of trade.

DETERIORATION IN THE CONDITIONS OF CMEA CO-OPERATION: CAUSES AND CIRCUMSTANCES

To a large extent these difficulties can be attributed to unfavourable developments in the Soviet economy. The Soviet economy has suffered from a slowdown in economic growth that also affected those raw material extracting sectors which play a decisive role in exports. Other Soviet problems have included the structural rigidity of the economy, the increasing technological gap, the deteriorating efficiency, and the worsening agricultural situation in spite of gigantic investments. All these factors – aggravated by the compelling Soviet need to increase convertible currency earnings – hindered Soviet exports to Hungary. Thus Hungarian trade with the Soviet Union has ceased to play the same role of stimulating economic growth that it had played previously. Consequently, this trade could not offer an adequate basis for solving the most serious problem of the Hungarian economy, namely managing the convertible currency debt, either by increasing convertible currency exports or by substituting for convertible currency imports.

All of these problems have affected not only Hungary but all of the Soviet Union's CMEA partners. In particular, these problems were very largely responsible for the unfavourable events Hungary experienced within the CMEA. The CMEA region, which until the second half of the 1970s grew faster than most other regions of the world and was characterised by technological catch-up and a rising standard of living, has since increasingly shown a standstill in growth and a deterioration in its position within the world economy.

It may be a subject of separate examination whether or not Hungarian economic policy recognised this change and reacted to it adequately. In this chapter we can only refer to the fact that the recognition was at least belated[1] and that belated recognition was not followed by an adequate reaction because *the practice of economic policy systematically overestimated the potential of developing relations with the socialist countries.* Even after long years of stagnation Hungary reckoned that the volume of imports from the CMEA would grow and be used as a substitute for convertible currency imports. Hungarian economic policy was formulated as if Hungary had been caught by a surprise which could not have been foreseen. For instance, Hungarian economic policy did not anticipate the failure of its CMEA partners to fulfil long- and short-term intergovernmental agreements, especially with respect to consequent shortfalls of imported oil.

One important element of the deterioration in conditions was obvious from the beginning, namely that Soviet external economic policy changed since the mid-1970s. The change in attitude consisted of two elements: first, the increased emphasis on the *quantitative* limits of Soviet deliveries, and second, the tightening of the *conditions* of delivery (prices, counterdeliveries, contribution to investment projects, and so forth). The Hungarian leadership – like that of the other CMEA countries – appeared willing to accept the stricter conditions in the hope that the quantitative limits of Soviet deliveries could be softened. This reaction – which I have elsewhere termed import-maximisation[2] – is connected to many circumstances. It is mostly explained by the change in relative prices after 1973 on both the world and CMEA markets. Consequently, it was a rational endeavour to purchase the largest possible quantity of hard goods – primary energy and raw materials – at intra-CMEA foreign trade prices and for roubles. It should be immediately added that the freedom of action of economic policy was very limited: the Hungarian leadership would not have been able to react in any other way. I attribute a bigger role to the notion that even in the midst of the considerable changes which have occurred in Hungarian economic policy during the 1980s, the traditional Hungarian strategy of economic development remained dominant. This strategy determined both the nature of Hungary's endeavours within the CMEA and the sectoral priorities of economic policy. Hence, the survival of the import-maximising attitude primarily indicates that Hungarian economic policy-makers did not or were not able to perceive that the *change in Soviet economic policy* was not merely the result of 'subjective' factors, that could be influenced, but was mostly the *consequence of the deterioration and increasing tensions in the Soviet internal economic situation.*

NEW DEVELOPMENTS IN HUNGARIAN–SOVIET TRADE

Since 1980, Hungarian rouble terms of trade have deteriorated continuously and heavily. As is well known, this can be explained by the increase of oil and other raw material prices within the CMEA. During the same period, the *increase in the volume of rouble-accounted Hungarian imports first slowed down and then in essence stopped.* More concretely, in the first half of 1970s, rouble-accounted imports rose by an average 9.5 per cent annually, in the next five-year period (1976–1980) by only 3.2 per cent annually, and between 1981 and 1986 by 0.6 per cent annually. The trends of the volume of Hungarian rouble-accounted exports took a different turn. Export growth did not later reach the high dynamics of the years 1971–1975 (10.8 per cent annual average), but its annual rate in the 1980s was about five per cent. Consequently *Hungarian trade has continued to pay for essentially stagnating rouble-accounted imports with a permanently growing volume of exports.*[3]

While the declared endeavour of Hungarian policy has been the improvement of the convertible currency balance of trade through reducing imports from the non-socialist countries and increasing exports to them, in fact the growth of the Hungarian economy became increasingly dependent on convertible currency imports, and began to rely less and less on imports from socialist countries. Between 1971 and 1975, the growth of the GDP by one per cent was still matched by an increase of 1.51 per cent in rouble-accounted imports. In the 1980s this ratio has been as little as 0.35 per cent. In volume terms, between 1971 and 1975 rouble-accounted imports still grew twice as fast as non-rouble-accounted imports, and between 1981 and 1986 it was already non-rouble-accounted imports that exceed rouble-accounted imports threefold.

Obviously, even without dwelling on these figures any longer these trends of rouble-accounted imports and rouble-accounted exports in combination are sources of serious tensions in the Hungarian economy and render the improvement of the equilibrium in Hungary's convertible currency trade very difficult. It is also well known (although no published statistics are available in this respect) that the different volume processes of imports and exports in rouble-accounted trade are caused by the diverging changes in imports from and exports to the *Soviet Union*, while the trade volume processes with the other CMEA countries are more or less balanced.

After these preliminaries I wish to raise but one question in this chapter: this question is linked to the latest developments in Hungary's rouble-accounted trade, namely that the terms of trade with the Soviet Union improved in 1987 and will presumably improve for some years.[4] Due to the improvement in the terms of trade – which however is not accompanied by any noteworthy growth in the opportunities to import – a situation may arise where Hungary can accumulate a considerable surplus in its trade with the Soviet Union in the coming years. What are the alternative choices for Hungarian economic policy in such a situation concerning the *volume processes* of trade with the Soviet Union? Depending upon whether we consider it necessary to avoid such a forthcoming surplus and upon our view concerning the possibilities of increasing imports from the Soviet Union, we may select one of the alternatives outlined in the next section.[5]

THE ALTERNATIVES

Describing them schematically, policy-makers have the choice of at least three alternatives.

1. *A further rapid growth of the volume of exports – regardless of the growth of imports.* This would eventually mean a large Hungarian surplus in trade with the Soviet Union.

This alternative primarily corresponds to the endeavours of the Hungarian companies and authorities mainly interested in exports to the Soviet Union. They assert that maintenance of the growth in the volume of exports and the associated high level of capacity utilisation represent a value in and of themselves, and even the performance of the Hungarian economy on other markets is dependent upon this. Consequently, growth in the volume of exports to the Soviet Union must remain an important objective of Hungarian economic policy, without regard to whatever other consequences may arise.

2. *Growth of exports should be conditional on growth of imports* in

order to prevent the emergence of a significant Hungarian surplus. Hungarian–Soviet *trade should be more or less balanced*.

This alternative corresponds primarily to the aspirations of the central functional organs which are sensitive to the macroeconomic interests of the country. Their positions can be summed up in the wish that the above mentioned endeavours to increase exports should be given ground only to the extent that they make additional imports possible. It is obvious that in this alternative *the necessity of increasing imports has a distinguished place*. According to the advocates of this view, the increase of imports from the socialist countries is one of the most important objectives of economic policy.

It is important to note that this alternative, as opposed to the first one, aims at taking partial advantage of the improvement in the terms of trade. Under the circumstances of improving Hungarian terms of trade, balanced trade (at current prices) means that the growth rate of Hungarian exports in volume terms should exceed that of imports, in the future as well.

3. The third alternative would make it possible to change this situation. This sets out from the assumption that in bilateral clearing trade within the CMEA a country can actually exploit the potential benefits derived from the improvement in the terms of trade if the increase of the volume of its exports lags behind that of its imports. In the present situation of the Hungarian economy, it is improper that economic policy does not try to realise the potential benefit to be derived from the improvement in the terms of trade. Imports from the socialist countries cannot be increased substantially. In this situation *the slowing down of the increase of rouble-accounted exports, and presumably even some reduction of its volume cannot be avoided*. Of course, this should not mean a policy which would reduce exports to these countries universally, but rather the implementation of policies designed to stimulate or restrict the volume of exports on the basis of efficiency considerations.

ARGUMENTS AND COUNTERARGUMENTS

The main argument for the *first-mentioned* alternative is that the existing export capacities of Hungarian industry must be exploited. The basis for this argument is that the overwhelming part of the commodities manufactured for the Soviet Union cannot be sold to Western or developing countries, or can be sold to them only at big losses. The manufacturing capacities cannot be switched over to production for other markets, or only at the expense of great efforts and costs, and even then only to a small extent.[6]

The Soviet market must not be lost. It is a huge market, and is certainly the most important market for Hungarian products – and will remain so. Reduction of Hungarian exports, if any, would cause uncertainty among Soviet buyers, and they would look for other partners – within or outside the CMEA. This problem is more serious since Hungarian–Soviet trade is characterised by an asymmetry of interests: the Soviet Union has much less need for the products supplied by Hungary, than Hungary for the goods supplied by the Soviets (particularly for fuels and raw materials). Moreover, oil prices will certainly not always be as low as in the second half of the 1980s, and with rising oil prices the problems of equilibria can also take a different turn within the CMEA. It is necessary to prepare for the changing conditions through the continuous increase of exports.

Another element to the first alternative is that it should certainly be possible to increase rouble-accounted imports. Ignoring the fact that all CMEA countries have the same experience as Hungary as far as imports from the Soviet Union are concerned, supporters of the first alternative assert that the present stagnation of imports is mainly due to the lack of interest on the part of the Hungarian companies. Those companies favour convertible currency imports even when competitive imports from the socialist countries would in fact be available.

Finally, political considerations also support the necessity of the permanent expansion of relations.

In opposing the above arguments, the advocates of *the second alternative* relative to those of the first alternative consider the exogenous constraints of imports from socialist countries to be more serious, and the problems of Hungary's macroequilibrium to be greater. They regard any further rapid increase in exports which have a high convertible currency import content yet are destined to go to socialist countries as impermissible. They see the balancing of export increments to the socialist countries by imports as being necessary. In fact if imports from socialist countries are available, they have no objections to the further increase of exports to the socialist countries. On the contrary, they believe – with special regard to the acute problems of balancing convertible currency trade – that this is the desirable trend.

THE CASE FOR RESTRUCTURING

In this section the most important arguments in favour of the third alternative are presented.

1. The cardinal point is that no positive change can be expected during the early 1990s in the existing trends of Hungary's trade relations with CMEA countries. This applies first of all to Hungary's import potential. *In the next couple of years there is no way in which the volume of imports from the Soviet Union could be substantially increased.* Statements made by the Soviet economic policy decision-makers and planners in this respect must be taken very seriously. It would be an illusion to believe that any kind of Hungarian endeavour in the next few years should be able to change this situation. Moreover, it would be a grave error to build the plans for the restoration of the foreign economic equilibrium and consolidation policy generally on this illusion.

The stagnation of Soviet deliveries can be explained fundamentally by the situation within the Soviet economy. Soviet endeavours to restructure the Soviet economy cannot lead rapidly to lasting results which would change its ability to export within the next few years. Moreover, the change in the trend of world market prices (the fall of oil prices from December 1985) has already led to a rapid growth of Soviet debt to the West, which means that the Soviet Union should make maximum efforts to keep up (and possibly even increase) the volume of its traditional fuel and raw material exports to the West. These endeavours, along with the well known production problems of the Soviet raw material sector and the slowness of domestic energy rationalisation and raw material saving measures, can even lead to the reduction of Soviet energy – and other raw material exports to CMEA countries. These considerations certainly indicate that it is unrealistic to believe that Soviet fuel and raw-material deliveries can be increased.

Additionally, I see no opportunity for the substantial increase in the quantity of non-traditional (manufactured goods) Hungarian imports from the Soviet Union. The Soviet intention that co-operation within the CMEA should rely on the mutual delivery of industrial products and that the Soviet Union should not have to play primarily the role of a raw material exporter in this co-operation, already has a history of several decades. But during all of this time the constraints which impede these endeavours have not been reduced. As long as there is no substantial change in the actual economic conditions of the Soviet enterprises and their domestic market situation, there is no foundation for believing that substantial additional import opportunities could be opened up – even by creating new forms of co-operation such as direct inter-enterprise links or joint enterprises.

In view of the vast size of the Soviet economy, the assumption is undoubtedly justified that in this huge economy there are always additional goods (even if it is not always easy to find them) which Hungary needs. In fact, the justification of this claim is incontestable. But first, the question is whether these additional goods discovered by many method *can be mobilised* for delivery to Hungary – and if yes, on what terms – and second, whether the inclusion of new goods discovered in this way in Hungarian–Soviet trade are sufficient to counteract those economic processes which have led to the stagnation of Soviet exports. (In other words: can enough new goods be included in trade which replace the possible loss of the old ones?)

On the other hand, the danger exists that even if it were possible to avoid the stagnation of the total volume of deliveries, Hungarian endeavours at increasing imports – just as the policy of import-maximisation followed thus far – can lead to huge losses and additional costs. By undertaking the obligation of Hungarian deliveries, the increase in imports of some raw materials from the Soviet Union can be imagined. The experience with the Yamburg investment project indicates that this would be an even much more costly policy than before. The possibility also exists that the superfluous part of imports can also increase, the part which figures already in the bilateral agreements, but which is unusable or can be used only at low efficiency, and which consequently should be eliminated from the trade.

2. It may seem that the potential Hungarian surplus in trade with the Soviet Union is an entirely normal and logical consequence of the development of relations thus far. If from the mid-1970s to the mid-1980s the Soviet Union extended a credit for part of the deterioration of Hungary's terms of trade, Hungary cannot refuse to extend a credit for financing part of the Soviet price loss due to the reversed price trends. However, Hungary became indebted while the volume of its exports to the Soviet Union rose by five or six per cent annually at least, and covered the bigger part of the price loss by the much faster increase of the volume of exports than that of imports. In other words, the deterioration in Hungary's terms of trade was accompanied by a huge outflow of resources. There is no sign of the

reversal of *this process*. On the contrary, its continuation seems to unfold.

The dynamic growth of Hungarian exports to the Soviet Union had the consequence that despite the stagnation of the quantity of imports, the Soviet Union's share in total Hungarian exports reached a record level. This obviously and greatly narrowed the investment-, manpower- and import-resources available for exports to other countries. If this trend of an increase in the volume of exports remains essentially unchanged, this would inevitably place a further burden on Hungary's balance of convertible currency trade.

The present situation of the Soviet economy and the policy of accelerated Soviet growth for the 1990s imply the quantitative and qualitative growth of Soviet import requirements. The fact that the demand was becoming more selective could already be sensed at the long-term trade negotiations for the 1986–1990 period. The Soviet endeavour became more determined that the structure of the Hungarian deliveries should change in accordance with the priorities of Soviet economic policy, and that Hungary (similar to the other CMEA countries) should participate more intensively in Soviet development projects, whether in the development of the energy base or in a programme of technical–scientific progress. It is a serious problem that the structure of Hungarian exports to the Soviet Union should change in a manner that is exactly opposite to the direction than would be demanded by efficient adjustment to the world market. The Soviet demands concerning quality and structure have intensified concerning Hungarian deliveries while these demands do not make it easier for Hungary to sell those goods which are produced for the Soviet market on Western markets for convertible currency.

The general experience (especially that of the years 1985–1986) indicates that the Soviet market is more uncertain with respect to sales potential than is claimed in textbooks and newspaper articles. Even if this is understandable, this uncertainty is more unfavourable since it involves a market to which one-third of Hungarian exports is directed.

3. The seemingly strongest argument in favour of maintaining the existing trend concerning Hungarian exports to socialist countries is indeed that the productive capacities intended for the Soviet Union cannot be switched over to production for other markets. Consequently, their possible closing would exacerbate the trends of stagnation or regression in the Hungarian economy. Arguments of this

kind could undoubtedly be correct in themselves, even though, in my opinion, some reserves for reorientation exist (namely reorientation towards exporting to the developing countries or to China). However, I believe these arguments are put forward because it is easier to export to the Soviet Union, from the point of view of sectoral ministries, investors, producers, and traders, than to reorient. The last comment does not diminish the actual gravity of the problem. However, what in the first approach seems to support the necessity of the continuation of the present practice, proves to be in fact – in the course of a more thorough analysis – the most weighty argument for the revision of this practice.

The recent interruption of the growth of the Hungarian economy and the lagging of the Hungarian ability to generate convertible currency exports selective to Hungary's increasing requirements of convertible currency imports have been caused exactly by the Hungarian way of thinking about economic policy and by Hungary's development strategy since 1950. These have attributed a decisive role to the importance of Hungarian adjustment to Soviet requirements and to Soviet export capacities in the determination of Hungary's macro and micro structure. What is involved is not only that this direction of economic development was allotted the decisive part of Hungary's resources, on account of which everything else was inevitably pushed into the background, but also the well known consequence that if development and production policy adjusts to a market the requirements of which differ dramatically from those of the world market, this necessarily leads to a reduction of the ability of standing one's ground in the world market. In circumstances when the maintenance of Hungary's convertible currency solvency and credit standing is the key question of economic progress, when the elements of instability have appeared in CMEA relations, when it is much less possible than earlier to rely on CMEA countries in the satisfaction of the qualitative and *quantitative* demands of the Hungarian economy, then the further economic progress of the country can depend to no small extent on the revision of this development strategy.

The revision of development policy undoubtedly meets tremendous difficulties: the economic policy – as is often stressed – has to face constraints, and a restricted freedom of movement. But it also must be recognised that today's barriers are so high precisely because of the economic policy of yesterday and of the day before yesterday. The revision – which has been due for a long time – was again and again postponed. If today it is again delayed, tomorrow the limitations for action will be even greater, and any attempt aimed at a successful change will be even riskier and perhaps even more hopeless.

4. It can be argued that in the case of a possible fall in the volume of Hungarian exports, the reduction of imports would also become inevitable. Such a reduction would primarily affect those imports Hungary considers most important, such as raw materials. This has to be acknowledged, and undoubtedly would greatly affect the Hungarian economy, even if the terms of the purchase of raw materials from the Soviet Union differ less conspicuously than earlier from conditions on the world market due to the combined consequence of the fall of world market prices and the deterioration of the terms of importing within the CMEA. But the decline in the quantity of delivered hard goods from the Soviet Union could occur without a decline in the volume of Hungarian exports. In fact, the greater the extent to which the Hungarian economy adjusts to Soviet demands, the more adversely it would be affected by a reduction of Soviet deliveries of hard goods.

This question has a more general aspect, which I now address. It is a widespread view, especially in the West, that the Soviet Union is not interested *economically* in trade with the smaller European CMEA countries (including Hungary). The Soviet Union has disadvantages only from this trade, which it accepts exclusively out of political considerations, and which it wants to reduce. This view, which has been explained within economic literature most conspicuously and supported by a great deal of material in the book by Marrese and Vanous,[7] takes its arguments mainly from the well known fact that in rouble-accounted trade between the Soviet Union and the other CMEA countries, the balance of delivery of hard goods is positive for the Soviet Union. In other words, a considerable part of its exports consists of goods which can also be sold in the West – against convertible currencies, and for which the other CMEA countries pay in soft, bad quality, obsolete products, which cannot be sold on the world market – or can be sold there only at considerable price rebates. *Economically* the Soviet Union would benefit, as a result, if it sold these products in the West, and if it does not do so, this only has political motivations. I have already commented in detail on this theory of 'implicit subsidies'.[8] Here I will only touch upon some aspects of the problem.

It is obvious that for the Soviet economy the diversion of the exports of hard goods from the CMEA to convertible currency countries – to the extent that it is possible – could offer considerable benefits. For instance, it would be possible to increase the quantity of total Soviet imports (or to minimise its decrease) and to change the import structure of the Soviet Union in a manner that would improve Soviet conditions for modernisation, restructuring, and acceleration of growth.

However, some qualifications are appropriate here. In the years of rapidly growing world market oil prices, intra-CMEA prices followed them gradually. It was related to this circumstance, as Marrese and Vanous found, that exporting oil and other hard goods to the CMEA countries, instead of to the world market, imposed growing opportunity costs on the Soviet Union. As I write the situation has changed. As it could have been supposed as early as 1983[9] the fact that CMEA prices have been following the fall in world oil prices with a lag is a stabilising factor for the Soviet economy. Slower deterioration of Soviet terms of trade within the CMEA enhances the relative economic significance of its relations with European CMEA countries. In other words, the economic benefit to be derived from a reorientation of Soviet commodity funds from CMEA countries to the world market are shrinking and the costs of such a regrouping are increasing. This is an especially important conclusion in the light of the global decline of Soviet imports (first of all, imports from the West).

With respect to costs, it can be asked whether it would be possible for the Soviet Union to substitute imports from convertible currency markets for those imports that no longer will come from CMEA markets. In the Soviet Union, *the principles of allocation of convertible currencies for imports are much different from those determining the pattern of imports from the CMEA countries*. Imports from the West mainly consist of up-to-date machinery used in basic production processes, steel pipes, other raw materials and essential foodstuffs. Imports of machinery and equipment for non-industrial production uses and industrial consumer goods are at the low end of the Soviet import priority list – however important they are for Soviet end-users. Since Soviet foreign exchange difficulties imply that the Soviet Union has to export more oil to the West in order to limit the cutback of traditional imports from the CMEA-countries, there is little hope of reduced CMEA imports being offset by deliveries from hard currency sources. This can lead to aggravating shortages in many fields of the Soviet economy.

5. As mentioned above, the high and growing convertible currency

import content of Hungarian exports to the Soviet Union is a major concern for everyone analysing Hungarian–Soviet trade from the point of view of the Hungarian convertible currency balance of payments. The significant convertible currency import content of exports to the Soviet Union is not a recent phenomenon. There are, however, two new elements in this respect related to the changes in the conditions of Hungarian–Soviet trade. On the one hand, the possibilities and conditions for converting rouble imports into convertible currency exports have deteriorated – partly because of stagnation of imports from the Soviet Union, and partly because Hungary has lost its earlier cost benefits related to import prices in the CMEA being lower than world market ones. On the other hand, because of the deteriorating Soviet balance of payments situation, the Hungarian surplus in convertible currency trade with the Soviet Union has been reduced.[10]

6. Finally, I wish to emphasise again that every claim which argues that the quantitative growth of trade within the CMEA is of great value in and of itself, must be rejected as irrelevant. Such views are not only irrelevant merely because of the contention that the *one-sided* increase of useless trade is useful. It is no less important that we evaluate the growth of trade from the point of view of quality and economic efficiency. Everybody who is dissatisfied with CMEA co-operation in its present form is justified. This cannot be changed while maintaining the former policy. Only if we radically break with the policy of the maximisation of trade can we realistically reach the goal that the structure of CMEA relations should be transformed in accordance with efficiency considerations.

This recommendation is more topical than ever before. In the world economy of the 1980s, the depreciation of primary energies and raw materials has been a lasting process. Although the possibility cannot be excluded that the world market oil prices should, for a longer or shorter time, increase compared to today's price, such a development has strong limitations. The basic problem of economic policy in the oil importing countries is no longer how to provide for and pay for their energy and raw material imports, but rather that the markets of the energy and raw material exporters have become narrower, and consequently it is more difficult to export to them. The only exception to this is perhaps the CMEA region, where it continues to be accepted as axiomatic truth that the countries of the region must satisfy their energy and raw material requirements basically from internal sources, and that the economy of the importing countries must develop in such a way that they should be able to pay for fuels and raw materials imported from within the region. It is, of course, very difficult to break with this policy, but until this is done, export orientation – the indispensable condition for standing one's ground in the world market – is a pious wish.

CLOSING REMARKS

Up to this point, we have discussed Hungarian–Soviet trade as a bilateral problem. It is logical to ask whether this problem, and the solution recommended by the author, is a more general one relevant for the other smaller Eastern European countries. Basically, we have to answer this question in a positive way. The difficulties related to importing from the Soviet Union in Eastern Europe are as general as is their dependence on exports to the Soviet Union. As in the case of Hungary, this is the consequence of 40 years of economic policy. Moreover, the economic situation in every East European country is very difficult, with debt burdens growing and the problem of managing debt service becoming intractable. That is why all of them are *compelled* to revise the traditional policy of quantitative increase of exports.

Of course there are considerable differences as to how this necessity is implemented. In some countries (Poland for example), the economy has been disrupted, with a tremendous shortage in production inputs (imported inputs included). This has impeded the export activities of *firms*. Firms simply do not have enough imports to be able to export more. In others, such as in the GDR, the motivation has a *macroeconomic* character. It means that East German economic policy makers, wishing to stop imbalances from growing, are compelled to decrease exports to the Soviet Union. Otherwise, indebtedness would grow even more rapidly, domestic expenditure would be cut in a more radical way, and inflationary pressures would increase.

These observations suggest that a decline of intra-CMEA trade in the next years may occur. Since the quantitative increase of CMEA trade does not have a value in itself, and its decrease is not necessarily disastrous. The consequences depend upon the policy reactions in the member-countries. This is precisely why changes in the trends of the trade are exceptionally important. Namely, they indicate turning points, and should alert Hungarian policy makers to the limits of CMEA co-operation.

Various problems of CMEA co-operation are well known. In

Hungary, at least since Sándor Ausch's essential book[11] was published, it has been common knowledge that this co-operation is not efficient, that it hardly contributes to covering the qualitative and high-technology needs of CMEA member economies, and impedes adjustment to the international economy. Despite all of these factors, the volume of intra-CMEA trade increased dynamically – until the mid-1970s essentially in a balanced way. Notwithstanding growing signs and experiences to the contrary, the idea has survived that there is a possibility to further increase the volume of inter-CMEA trade. The belief has persisted that via 'appropriate' policies related to the strategy of import maximisation, quantitative constraints *can be* and *should be* eased because quantitative growth of trade with the socialist countries is the key to domestic stability, economic growth, and the maintenance of living standards. In other words, the belief in quantitative growth has served as the main argument and excuse for the essentially unchanged character of economic policy. I think the time has come for that illusion to vanish.

Of course, I do not think that there are no possibilities for a reasonable future quantitative growth of intra-CMEA trade. But this is a function of overcoming the critical (using Gorbachev's words: pre-crisis[12]) situation now characterising CMEA economies by means of radical economic reform and by revision of economic policy – a less emphasised but inseparable concomitant to radical reform. However, the closed nature of CMEA economies, together with the system of intra-CMEA co-operation based on inward-looking policies are among the most important factors and structural causes of the crisis that haunts both Eastern Europe and the Soviet Union.

Notes

1. It is already a commonplace statement as I write that in the 1970s Hungarian economic policy did not adjust adequately to fundamental changes in the world economic environment. It is mentioned less frequently that this misadjustment was mostly linked to the idea that the country's relations within the CMEA would grow dynamically, in a balanced way, and under conditions that would be advantageous to Hungary even in the changed world economic situation; thus no changes were needed in economic policy.
2. See, for example, A. Köves 'The Import Restriction Squeeze and Import

Maximising Ambitions', *Acta Oeconomica*, 34, 1–2 (1985), pp. 99–112; A. Köves 'Some Questions of the Energy Policy of the East European Countries', in R. Dietz and K. Mack, *Energie, Umwelt und Zusammenarbeit in Europa* (Energy, Environment and Cooperation in Europe) (Springer Verlag, Wien–New York, 1987), pp. 57–67.

3. Thus, between 1980 and 1986, the average annual growth rate of the volume of Hungarian exports exceeded *more than eightfold* that of rouble-accounted imports.
4. I can do so, because of an excellent analysis covering a broad range of questions concerning Hungarian–Soviet trade. See: Margit Rácz and Sándor Richter, 'A magyar-szovjet gazdasági kapcsolatok néhány kérdése' (Some Questions of Hungarian–Soviet Economic Relations), *Közgazdasági Szemle* (November 1987), pp. 1302–1324.
5. There is a question whether it is worthwhile to use the potential surplus to pay off existing Hungarian debts or to extending credits to the Soviet Union.
6. Similar arguments are advanced, *mutatis mutandis*, in favour of increasing agricultural exports.
7. M. Marrese and J. Vanous: *Soviet Subsidization of Trade with Eastern Europe: Soviet Perspective* (Berkeley, 1983).
8. A. Köves, '"Implicit Subsidies" and Some Issues of Economic Relations Within the CMEA', *Acta Oeconomica*, 31, Nos. 1–2 (1983), pp. 125–136.
9. Cf. A. Köves, '"Implicit Subsidies"' . . . p. 132 (footnote).
10. There are no published data on Hungarian–Soviet trade accounted for in convertible currencies. We have, however, data about Hungarian convertible currency trade with the whole CMEA. If we assume that Hungarian convertible currency trade with CMEA countries other than the Soviet Union is insignificant, those data may roughly reflect the trend of Hungarian convertible currency trade with the Soviet Union. According to the data, from 1982 to 1986, the Hungarian surplus in convertible currency trade with the CMEA countries has been reduced from 800 million dollars to about 140 million dollars. In 1987, the cutback continued.
11. S. Ausch, *Theory and Practice of CMEA Cooperation* (Budapest: Akadémiai Kiadó, 1972).
12. Cf. M. Gorbachev's speech on the 1987 June meeting of the Central Committee of the KPSV, *Pravda* (26 June 1987).

6 Economic Policy and Foreign Trade in Austria: Relations with West and East
Jan Stankovsky

INTRODUCTION

The first part of this chapter contains a short description of the main institutions, targets, and instruments of Austria's economic policy. This background section helps the reader to understand Austria's foreign economic (trade) policy.[1] Then the importance, development, and regulation of Austria's trade with the East and West are discussed and compared. The term 'East' refers to the seven European CMEA countries (Eastern Europe, excluding the Soviet Union) while 'West' refers to Western Europe (the EC and EFTA).

MACROECONOMIC POLICY IN AUSTRIA

Austria's macroeconomic policy of the 1970s and of the first half of the 1980s may be characterised as a mix of an expansive fiscal policy, tight money policy, and an incomes policy based on social partnership (Breuss, 1987, p. 205). The social partnership – certainly a noteworthy feature of Austria's economy – can be described as a system which attempts to avoid and overcome the class struggle by co-operation between labour, business and agriculture. It has its roots in the unhappy times of the 1930s with mass unemployment and civil war. It was born in the Nazi concentration camps by the former enemies on the Right and the Left and developed after the Second World War when the Soviets occupied large parts of Austria.

This combination of an expansive fiscal policy, a tight money policy, and an incomes policy is often described as 'Austro–Keynesianism'. (It is sometimes said that Austro–Keynesianism has as much in common with Keynes as Austro–Marxism with Marx, namely nothing.)[2] The mechanism of Austro–Keynesianism relies on a rather unorthodox combination of instruments and targets: the exchange rate policy (for years a *de facto* fixing of the exchange rate of Schilling on the DM) is used as an instrument for price stabilisation, fiscal policy as an instrument for influencing aggregate demand and the current account balance, and incomes policy helps to coordinate wage and price movements.[3] In view of the experience during the inter-war period, full employment has always been at the top of the hierarchy of economic targets. It was easy to achieve this aim in the 1960s, but it became more and more difficult in the 1970s and 1980s.

Austro–Keynesianism helped to overcome the consequences of the first oil-shock (1973–74), but the second oil shock (1979–80) demonstrated its limitations. The economic report of the government in 1985 stated: 'For a long lasting stagnation, however, such as that at the beginning of the 1980s, this system was not designed'.[4] Austro–Keynesianism 'faded out'.[5] Other important elements of Austria's macroeconomic policy, namely the social partnership and the tight money policy, however, are still alive.

Since the beginning of the 1980s the economic difficulties in Austria have increased. They culminated in an open crisis in large parts of nationalised and semi-nationalised industry. The core of the problem has been that the process of structural change in Austria has been too slow. In order to prevent unemployment, subsidies were granted to poorly performing enterprises in an attempt to avoid or postpone the necessary restructuring. Austria's economic policy concentrated too much on solving current problems; it failed to develop a programme of structural change. In a recent German study, the 'Austrian model' was described as 'economic policy without a plan for structural policy'.[6]

FOREIGN ECONOMIC POLICY IN AUSTRIA

In Austria, a high ethical value has traditionally been attributed to exporting. This probably has something to do with the idea of mercantilism. Moreover, since 1918 foreign economic relations have been a weak point of Austria's economy: Austria has always had a deficit in foreign trade, which in the postwar period has been balanced mostly by a surplus in services, especially tourism.[7] To overcome this structural deficit, Austria after the First World War relied mainly on import restrictions (a relic of this period is Austria's high customs tariff); then after the Second World War it relied more on export promotion. Austria now has an excellent system of export promotion which provides insurance, financing and trade information. Financial promotion is handled by the Austrian Kontrollbank, while trade information is provided by the Federal Chamber of Commerce.

In Austria's system of macroeconomic policy, foreign trade has always played a multifaceted – and sometimes delicate – role:

- The maintenance of a tight money stance – a pivotal element of the whole policy mix – required a balance in the current account. Since a 'high' schilling makes importing more attractive and exporting more difficult, a policy of export promotion was considered to be necessary.
- In the 1970s exports became more and more important as a direct instrument to maintain full employment.

Austria never had any explicitly elaborated conception of an overall foreign trade policy.[8] Important factors influencing Austria's trade policy were domestic economic goals such as the dampening of inflation and *ad hoc* reactions to new developments and problems abroad.

In relation to the *West*, Austria's two main foreign trade goals were:

- to ease market and/or to avoid discrimination in order to maintain and improve the competitive position of Austria's exporters. In this respect the trade liberalisation within the OECD and GATT, and, to an even greater extent, the West European integration (EFTA, EC) were important.
- to increase competition on the internal market by liberalising trade and capital movements. Here the total abolition of tariffs and quotas for industrial products – at first *vis-à-vis* EFTA countries (1960–1968), then *vis-à-vis* the EC (1972–1977) – has to be mentioned. By opening Austria to the world market, the process of structural adjustment was to be accelerated. A consensus developed – a *conditio sine qua non* in Austria's social partnership – for import liberalisation which depended upon the fear that failure to liberalise would provoke trade discrimination against Austria (this was the so-called 'export stick'); and the desire to penetrate new markets (the so-called 'export carrot').

The motives behind the trade policy *vis-à-vis* the *East* were in principle similar. The main instrument was export promotion, by traditional and new methods. It could be said that in this respect Austria was rich in ideas, creative and flexible.

So far as import liberalisation is concerned, East and West European countries were treated differently for two reasons:
- The countries of the East were considered to be 'State Trading' countries which were not acting according to market principles.
- The East 'carrot' has never been large and sure[9] enough to be worth the risks of 'real' import liberalisation. However, some important steps in this direction have been made. For instance, industrial countries such as the USA and Japan have been treated in the same way as the East.

TRADE RELATIONS

Regional and Commodity Structure of Austria's Foreign Trade

The structure of Austria's foreign trade by regions and main trading partners is given in Table 6.1. Austria's foreign trade is highly concentrated on Europe, especially on Western Europe (the EC and EFTA). The high share of Austrian exports to Europe, especially to Austria's neighbouring countries, could be explained by the geographical location of Austria (no sea ports), by the absence of large Austrian 'general export' houses, and by the unfavourable commodity structure of exports Austrian (the share of transport cost-sensitive goods is high). The development and the main determinants of Austria's foreign trade with East and West are discussed in more detail in the following sections.

Table 6.2 presents an overview of the commodity structure of Austria's foreign trade in 1987, for total trade, and for trade with the EC and the East. About 90 per cent of Austria's exports are industrial products (SITC 5 to 8).

The structure of Austria's *exports* to the East and the West is similar, with some exceptions. The share of machinery and consumer goods (for short, sophisticated products) in Austria's exports to the East lies below the average of total trade, the share of manufactured goods (mainly steel) and chemicals (for short, basic inputs for the industry) far above the average. Similar relations can be found in the export structure of Germany; the export structure of Switzerland shows some differences (Table 6.3).

The share of sophisticated products in Austria's exports to the

Table 6.1a Austria's foreign trade by regions: exports (share in percentages)

Year	Industrial West (OECD)						CMEA			Yugoslavia	Developing Countries	Total	Billion Austrian Schillings
	Total	Western Europe Total	EC-12 Total	FRG	EFTA-6	Total	USSR	Eastern Europe Total					
1953	71.2	65.7	–	–	–	–	–	–	–	–	–	100.0	13.2
1954	72.1	66.7	–	–	–	–	–	–	–	–	–	100.0	15.9
1955	73.2	66.3	–	–	–	–	–	–	–	–	–	100.0	18.2
1956	72.0	65.1	–	–	–	–	–	–	–	–	–	100.0	22.1
1957	69.4	63.9	–	–	–	–	–	–	–	–	–	100.0	25.4
1958	70.3	63.9	–	–	–	–	–	–	–	–	–	100.0	23.9
1959	71.9	64.0	–	26.1	8.2	–	–	–	–	–	–	100.0	25.2
1960	72.4	66.0	–	26.8	9.1	–	–	–	–	–	–	100.0	29.1
1961	72.9	67.2	–	27.5	10.4	–	–	–	–	–	–	100.0	31.3
1962	74.2	68.6	–	27.9	11.4	–	–	–	–	–	–	100.0	32.9
1963	74.6	69.1	–	26.4	10.9	–	–	–	–	–	–	100.0	34.5
1964	74.6	69.0	–	27.9	12.6	–	–	–	–	–	–	100.0	37.6
1965	73.6	67.8	–	28.6	12.4	15.3	3.6	11.7	2.4	–	100.0	41.6
1966	74.0	67.6	–	26.7	13.6	15.4	3.5	11.9	2.3	–	100.0	43.8
1967	72.0	65.7	–	22.2	14.4	16.2	3.3	12.9	3.2	7.8	100.0	47.0

1968	73.3	66.5	—	23.4	14.7	14.8	3.4	11.4	3.8	7.2	100.0	51.7
1969	75.4	68.3	—	24.2	15.9	13.5	2.8	10.7	3.7	6.6	100.0	62.7
1970	74.9	68.3	—	23.4	17.4	12.9	2.9	10.1	4.6	6.8	100.0	74.3
1971	75.4	69.0	50.8	22.9	17.8	12.2	2.2	10.0	4.2	7.3	100.0	79.0
1972	76.9	70.1	51.4	22.4	18.2	11.8	2.4	9.4	3.2	7.3	100.0	89.7
1973	76.4	69.8	52.0	21.8	17.3	11.9	1.7	10.1	3.9	7.0	100.0	102.0
1974	70.2	64.5	47.1	19.7	16.5	15.1	2.6	12.4	5.1	8.7	100.0	133.4
1975	66.1	61.8	46.4	21.9	14.8	17.1	2.9	14.2	4.6	11.4	100.0	130.9
1976	67.8	63.5	48.8	23.4	13.9	15.1	2.8	12.4	3.6	12.7	100.0	152.1
1977	69.9	65.2	51.6	26.6	13.0	14.5	2.8	11.6	3.7	11.3	100.0	161.8
1978	72.4	67.4	54.3	29.1	12.4	13.7	3.1	10.7	3.5	10.3	100.0	176.1
1979	72.4	68.2	55.4	30.3	11.9	12.9	3.3	9.6	4.0	10.2	100.0	206.3
1980	72.6	68.8	56.2	30.8	12.1	12.1	2.7	9.4	3.3	11.5	100.0	226.2
1981	70.4	66.1	53.9	29.1	11.7	11.5	3.1	8.4	3.0	14.4	100.0	251.8
1982	70.9	66.2	54.3	29.3	11.3	11.1	3.5	7.6	2.9	14.4	100.0	266.9
1983	71.7	66.7	55.6	30.8	10.5	12.1	3.9	8.2	2.6	13.1	100.0	277.1
1984	72.8	66.4	55.1	29.6	10.6	12.2	4.5	7.7	2.4	12.0	100.0	314.5
1985	74.3	67.3	56.1	30.1	10.5	11.1	3.8	7.3	2.3	11.9	100.0	354.0
1986	78.8	72.4	60.1	32.7	11.8	9.6	3.1	6.6	2.2	8.9	100.0	342.5
1987	81.2	75.2	63.4	34.8	11.1	9.0	2.5	6.5	2.0	7.5	100.0	342.4
1988	81.3	75.3	63.8	35.0	10.7	9.1	2.9	6.3	2.0	7.1	100.0	383.2

Table 6.1b Austria's foreign trade by regions: imports (share in percentages)

Year	Industrial West (OECD)					CMEA			Yugoslavia	Developing Countries	Total	Billion Austrian Schillings
	Total	Western Europe Total	EC-12 Total	FRG	EFTA-6	Total	USSR	Eastern Europe Total				
1953	75.9	61.0	–	–	–	–	–	–	–	–	100.0	13.3
1954	78.7	67.7	–	–	–	–	–	–	–	–	100.0	17.0
1955	79.6	66.7	–	–	–	–	–	–	–	–	100.0	23.1
1956	79.8	64.8	–	–	–	–	–	–	–	–	100.0	25.3
1957	80.3	65.4	–	–	–	–	–	–	–	–	100.0	29.3
1958	79.5	67.4	–	–	–	–	–	–	–	–	100.0	27.9
1959	79.5	70.3	–	40.2	6.1	–	–	–	–	–	100.0	29.8
1960	79.3	70.2	–	40.0	6.4	–	–	–	–	–	100.0	36.8
1961	81.5	73.9	–	42.9	6.9	–	–	–	–	–	100.0	38.6
1962	81.2	74.0	–	42.3	7.0	–	–	–	–	–	100.0	40.3
1963	79.8	73.5	–	41.4	7.4	–	–	–	–	–	100.0	43.6
1964	81.3	74.6	–	41.7	8.0	–	–	–	–	–	100.0	48.4
1965	81.3	75.3	–	41.8	7.9	10.8	2.5	8.3	1.3	–	100.0	54.6
1966	81.9	75.8	–	42.4	8.6	9.6	2.1	7.5	1.9	–	100.0	60.5
1967	82.9	78.0	–	41.7	10.4	9.1	2.1	6.9	2.0	5.6	100.0	60.0

Year										
1968	81.8	77.1	—	41.4	10.3	9.8	2.3	7.4	1.8	6.1	100.0	64.9
1969	81.6	77.1	—	41.3	10.8	9.7	2.3	7.3	1.6	6.6	100.0	73.5
1970	82.1	77.0	—	41.2	11.0	9.4	2.2	7.1	1.4	6.5	100.0	92.3
1971	82.4	76.7	64.9	41.0	11.3	9.1	2.6	6.6	1.1	6.9	100.0	104.5
1972	83.5	77.8	66.4	41.9	11.0	8.5	2.2	6.3	1.0	6.4	100.0	120.6
1973	83.3	77.8	65.8	41.7	11.6	8.4	1.9	6.5	1.0	6.7	100.0	137.9
1974	78.5	73.6	62.7	40.1	11.0	9.7	2.6	7.1	1.0	10.2	100.0	168.3
1975	79.2	74.1	63.4	40.0	10.5	10.2	3.4	6.8	.9	9.2	100.0	163.4
1976	79.4	74.1	64.3	41.1	10.3	9.5	3.7	5.9	.8	9.7	100.0	206.1
1977	81.3	75.6	66.2	42.2	9.5	8.8	3.6	5.2	.8	8.6	100.0	234.8
1978	81.0	75.5	66.3	43.3	9.0	8.8	3.8	5.0	.7	8.9	100.0	231.9
1979	79.8	74.1	65.6	42.3	8.8	8.8	3.8	5.0	.8	10.2	100.0	269.9
1980	77.4	71.0	63.1	40.8	8.1	9.7	4.2	5.5	.8	11.6	100.0	315.8
1981	74.8	67.2	59.6	38.9	7.6	11.9	6.2	5.7	.8	12.2	100.0	334.5
1982	76.8	69.5	61.9	40.6	7.3	11.2	5.1	6.1	.9	10.8	100.0	332.6
1983	78.7	71.3	63.6	41.5	7.4	10.5	4.3	6.2	1.0	9.5	100.0	348.3
1984	76.7	69.3	61.4	39.9	7.5	11.7	5.0	6.7	1.1	10.2	100.0	392.1
1985	77.6	70.0	62.1	40.9	7.6	10.7	4.4	6.2	1.1	10.2	100.0	431.0
1986	83.0	74.9	66.9	44.0	7.7	8.3	3.1	5.3	1.0	7.3	100.0	408.0
1987	84.5	76.2	68.0	44.2	7.8	6.8	2.1	4.7	1.0	7.4	100.0	411.9
1988	85.0	75.9	68.1	44.5	7.4	6.4	1.9	4.5	1.0	7.3	100.0	451.4

Table 6.2 Commodity structure of Austrian foreign trade with the East, the EC-12 and total in 1987

	Food	Raw materials and fuels				Manufactured goods						
							Semi-finished products					
	Total	Total	Raw materials	Fuels	Total	Chemicals	Total	Iron, steel	Other	Machinery	Consumer goods	Total
Exports to:												
CMEA	5.4	8.7	2.2	6.5	85.8	14.5	33.5	15.0	18.5	30.8	7.0	100.0
USSR	5.2	.2	.0	.2	94.6	11.6	50.0	41.1	9.0	25.4	7.6	100.0
Eastern Europe	5.5	12.0	3.1	8.9	82.5	15.6	27.2	5.1	22.1	32.9	6.7	100.0
EC-12	3.0	8.2	6.4	1.8	88.7	7.8	32.3	6.8	25.5	34.9	13.7	100.0
Germany	1.8	6.1	3.0	3.1	92.0	7.1	30.6	6.1	24.5	38.3	16.1	100.0
Total	3.4	7.1	5.3	1.8	89.4	9.0	33.0	7.4	25.5	33.4	14.0	100.0
Imports of:												
CMEA	8.9	65.7	18.7	47.1	25.3	7.6	9.6	3.3	6.3	4.9	3.3	100.0
USSR	.8	90.9	19.7	71.2	8.3	2.0	3.5	1.1	2.4	2.4	.4	100.0
Eastern Europe	12.5	54.8	18.3	36.5	32.7	10.0	12.2	4.2	8.0	6.0	4.5	100.0
EC-12	4.6	4.9	3.1	1.8	90.5	11.7	21.6	3.0	18.6	37.6	19.6	100.0
Germany	3.0	4.5	2.7	1.8	92.4	11.4	21.3	2.6	18.7	41.5	18.2	100.0
Total	6.0	12.4	5.2	7.2	81.5	10.3	19.2	2.7	16.5	34.7	17.3	100.0

Table 6.3 Commodity structure of foreign trade with the East and total of Austria, Germany and Switzerland in 1987

| | Food | Raw materials and fuels | | | | Manufactured goods | | | | | | |
| | | | | | Chemicals | Semi-finished products | | | Machinery | Consumer goods | Total |
	Total	Total	Raw materials	Fuels	Total		Total	Iron, steel	Other			
Exports:												
Austria CMEA	5.4	8.7	2.2	6.5	85.8	14.5	33.5	15.0	18.5	30.8	7.0	100.0
Total	3.4	7.1	5.3	1.8	89.4	9.0	33.0	7.4	25.5	33.4	14.0	100.0
Germany CMEA	5.1	2.4	1.9	.4	90.6	18.5	28.1	15.0	13.1	36.5	7.5	100.0
Total	4.8	3.1	1.8	1.3	89.9	13.0	17.7	4.0	13.7	48.4	10.8	100.0
Switzerland CMEA	1.8	1.4	1.3	.1	96.8	33.8	6.5	.2	6.2	49.0	7.5	100.0
Total	3.1	1.3	1.2	.1	95.2	21.9	19.2	1.4	17.8	33.1	21.0	100.0
Imports:												
Austria CMEA	8.9	65.7	18.7	47.1	25.3	7.6	9.6	3.3	6.3	4.9	3.3	100.0
Total	6.0	12.4	5.2	7.2	81.5	10.3	19.2	2.7	16.5	34.7	17.3	100.0
Germany CMEA	8.3	45.6	7.6	38.0	42.7	6.2	17.2	3.6	13.6	4.7	14.5	100.0
Total	11.2	15.8	6.1	9.6	69.9	9.4	17.5	3.3	14.2	28.0	15.0	100.0
Switzerland CMEA	14.3	28.3	4.1	24.2	57.3	14.0	28.9	4.3	24.6	4.7	9.7	100.0
Total	7.2	7.4	2.9	4.5	85.2	11.3	21.7	2.9	18.8	31.6	20.6	100.0

West is higher (and thus more future oriented) than that to the East.

The commodity structure of Austria's *imports* from the East differs considerably from the composition of total imports and also from the structure of exports to the East. Only 25 per cent of Austria's imports from the East (eight per cent from the Soviet Union, 33 per cent from Eastern Europe) are industrial products. This share is considerably lower than in Germany and in Switzerland. The relatively low share of industrial products (and especially of consumer goods and manufactures) in Austria's imports from the East is probably due partly to the high level of customs protection in Austria. The very high share of energy and raw materials – which can, at least partly, be explained by geographical factors – also contributes (statistically) to the low importance of industrial products in Austria's imports from the East.

Austria's Trade Relations with the East

The East is an important trading partner for Austria. Until 1985 about eleven per cent to fifteen per cent of Austria's exports went to the East, with a peak in 1975 (seventeen per cent). The share of imports has always been a bit lower. Since 1985, the East's share of Austrian trade has been on the decline. In 1987, a historical low was reached – nine per cent of Austrian exports and seven per cent of Austrian imports.

The importance of Eastern trade in Austria is two to three times higher than in Western Europe (1987 average, 3.2 per cent, including inter-German trade). Among Western countries, only Finland has had a higher share of Eastern trade than Austria. In Germany during 1987, the share of exports to the East was 3.4 per cent (including inter-German trade, 4.7 per cent), while in 1975 it was 7.2 per cent (including inter-German trade, 8.8 per cent).

Austria's trade with the East is more oriented towards the smaller East European countries, mainly Hungary and Czechoslovakia but also Poland and the GDR, than to the Soviet Union. However, between 1974 and 1984, the share of Austrian exports to the Soviet Union increased, while the share of Austrian exports to Eastern Europe declined considerably. Austria has a share of between five and six per cent of all exports of OECD countries to the East. Inside this region Austria holds a strong position in Eastern Europe (between eight and ten per cent of all OECD exports). This can be compared with Austria's market share in total OECD exports, which is only about 1.5 per cent. In Hungary and Czechoslovakia, Austria has usually been the second largest western supplier after West Germany.

A detailed survey of Austria's trade with the East and of Austria's trade regime is contained in a survey by Levcik and Stankovsky (1984). The main conclusion of that survey and other studies can be summarised as follows:

- Austria's *trade regime* has formally been the same *vis-à-vis* the East and West. However, there have been some *de facto* differences both in exports and imports.
- Austria's *export* financing scheme has served mainly for the promotion of exports to the East and to the developing countries.
- Austria has engaged heavily in the financing of trade with the East: with ten to fourteen per cent the share of Austria in total credits of Western banks to the East is considerably higher than Austria's export market share in the East (six per cent).
- Austria's exports to the East have been supported by numerous co-operation promotion agreements, industrial co-operation at the enterprise level, a relatively high number of joint ventures, and flexible and experienced use of countertrade.
- With few exceptions, those have been mainly with Hungary, 'real' co-operation between Austrian enterprises and East European enterprises did not develop. Industrial co-operation agreements have served primarily as instruments for export promotion.
- In the first half of the 1980s, heavy export financing produced some success. However, in 1986 and 1987 Austria's exports to the East shrunk considerably.
- In 1985 and 1988 Austria introduced new legal measures for supervising high technology exports. These legal provisions have been formulated in a non-discriminatory manner. For instance, any country that exports high technology products to Austria can request Austria to forbid the re-export of these products. However, it is clear that these provisions were introduced mainly to prevent illegal exports of Western high technology to the East. They have not been applied to exports of genuine Austrian products. Any negative impact on legal Austrian exports towards the East cannot be expected.
- *Imports* of industrial products from the East have been fully liberalised, namely, have become free of quantitative import restrictions. Only for some imports from the East (and also from Japan), a countersigning procedure (*Vidierungsverfahren*) is applied. This system is not designed for, but sometimes is used as, a means of restricting imports.

- For imports from all Eastern countries – also from non-members of GATT – the lower most-favoured-nations (MFN) tariffs are applied. In spite of this, industrial products from the East have been discriminated against relative to products from EFTA and EC countries which can be imported duty free. In general, Austrian tariff protection is rather high, especially for some labour-intensive products (textiles, clothing, shoes).
- Bulgaria, Romania and Hungary (in 1988) were granted the General System of Preferences (GSP) for developing countries. As a rule, the GSP tariffs in Austria are 50 per cent of the MFN-tariffs.
- Due to the high share of energy in Austria's imports from the East the collapse of oil prices caused a steep decline in the value of Austria's imports from the East in 1986 and 1987.

Austria's Trade Relations with Western Europe

About two-thirds of Austria's foreign trade has been directed towards Western Europe. In 1987, this share was as high as 75 per cent.

Austria's trade with Western Europe was – in a rather complicated manner – influenced by the various stages of West European economic integration. In the beginning of the 1960s, two integration groups – the EC and the EFTA – were formed. Within each group tariffs were abolished, but they were maintained against the other group. Austria became a member of the EFTA. In the 1960s, trade with the EFTA countries expanded greatly whereas there were serious difficulties – due to mutual discrimination – in trade with the EC.

In 1972 two former EFTA members (Great Britain and Denmark) became members of the EC, while other EFTA countries – including Austria – concluded free-trade agreements for industrial products with the EC.

This free-trade agreement proved to be favourable for Austria, in spite of some problems (agricultural trade, proof of origin). The share of EC-12 in Austria's export increased from 55 per cent in the first years of the 1980s to 60 per cent in 1986 and 63 per cent in 1987. Austria gained substantial market shares in the EC. On the other hand, the share of EC in Austria's import also increased (to 68 per cent).

In 1985, the EC published a plan (White Paper) for the completion of the EC internal market by 1992. The White Paper envisages the abolition of all material, technical and fiscal barriers for the free movement of goods, services, labour and capital within the European Community. At the same time a programme for research promotion was introduced.

The deepening of integration within the European Community will cause discrimination against outsiders. This discrimination is not intentional, but it is inevitable. As mentioned, Austria was already discriminated against by the EC in the 1960s. In addition to this 'new discrimination', an increase of the ECs 'old protection' is also possible. Up to now, individual EC countries have passed some instruments for implementing national trade barriers. After completion of the ECs internal market, trade protection will be applied only at the community level.

The consequences of discrimination against Austria's exports on such an important market as the EC are self-evident. The Austrian government therefore set as a policy target the 'full participation' in the internal EC market, at first without EC membership. In the meantime it became more and more clear that full access to the EC internal market will be possible only with EC membership. Thus, in December 1987, Austria's government declared EC membership – with a neutrality clause – to be an Austrian 'option'.

Austria's EC membership would certainly influence its economic relations with the East,[10] including the loss of Austria's treaty-making power. As an EC member, Austria would have to accept the common trade policy. Not all possibilities for an individual trade policy would be eliminated. Individual EC countries are able to conclude co-operation agreements with other countries. Export promotion schemes among EC countries would be harmonised, not unified.

An EC membership would by no means lead to a decrease of Austria's trade with the East. On the contrary, positive impulses could be expected. As an EC member, Austria would have to apply the Common Customs Tariff, which is in general lower than the present Austrian tariff. This would ease access for the East European suppliers to the Austrian market. With EC membership some obstacles for export-oriented industrial co-operation with the East would be eliminated (for instance, no need for proof of origin for Austrian exports to the EC). However, some problems could be caused by the lower level of import liberalisation in the EC.

As an EC member Austria could certainly play an important role in the formation of the EC's future 'East European Policy'. The great competence of Austria in this area is fully acknowledged by all

European countries. Finally, in a somewhat visionary vein, one could imagine – probably not for the 1990s, but for the next millennium – the emergence of a free trade area between the EC and Eastern Europe.

Appendix Austria's East–West Trade: A Descriptive Background Survey[11]
Friedrich Levcik and Jan Stankovsky

DEVELOPMENT OF AUSTRIA'S TRADE WITH THE EAST

The Historical Basis of Austria's East–West Trade

The intensive trade links between Austria and Eastern Europe are based on elements of geography and history. Austrian exporters have comparative advantages over competitors, based on short distances and lower transportation costs (Danube), to East European markets. Likewise East European suppliers often find the Austrian market more easily accessible for their products than other markets.

After 70 years of independent statehood and 40 years of separate social and political development there are hardly any remnants of former economic relations between the successor states of the Austro–Hungarian empire. However, previous common history aids mutual understanding, and some knowledge of each others' languages often plays a decisive role in the commercial and economic relations between Austria and Eastern Europe.

Before the Second World War Austria conducted about a third of its foreign trade with the countries now belonging to the East (European CMEA). Of all Austrian imports, 42 per cent in 1929 and still 32 per cent in 1937 came from this region (excluding imports from what is now the GDR). In the same years, 35 per cent and 28 per cent respectively of Austrian exports went to that region. Czechoslovakia's share in these transactions was eighteen per cent of imports and almost fifteen per cent of exports in 1929; and in 1937 that country's shares were still eleven per cent of imports and seven per cent of exports. Also Hungary and Poland were important trading partners of Austria before the Second World War. On the other hand, trade with the Soviet Union was not then important at all.

Economic relations with the East were restored immediately after the war, but remained below the level of the pre-war period. Nevertheless, about one-fifth of total Austrian foreign trade went to or came from this region – and about half of these transactions were concluded with Czechoslovakia.

The political and social changes in the East European countries after the war diminished their involvement in foreign trade. At the same time a geographical reorientation of their exports and imports occurred. Austrian trade with the East suffered from this development and its importance for the Austrian economy shrank considerably. In the mid-1950s the share of the East in total Austrian foreign trade diminished to roughly nine per cent, with Poland, the traditional supplier of coal, becoming the most important trading partner. Most of foreign trade with the Soviet Union in that period was statistically not recorded.

After the war the Soviet Union took possession of all enterprises formerly in German ownership in the part of Austria occupied by its forces. Among these enterprises there were several large industrial undertakings, the major part of the Austrian oil industry and the Danube Steamship Company. All foreign trade transactions of these enterprises were conducted under Soviet administration, thus remaining outside Austrian jurisdiction and unrecorded in Austrian statistics. It has been estimated that the statistically uncontrolled exports of these enterprises to the Soviet Union in 1954 amounted to AS 2.7 billion, namely, seventeen per cent of total Austrian exports in that year (Breuss, 1983). In the autumn of 1955, the enterprises under Soviet administration were handed over to Austria, who undertook, in lieu of compensation, to deliver to the Soviet Union for six years running goods to the value of AS 650 million ($25 million), as well as 10 million tons of crude oil annually, all free of charge. The total costs of these compensatory deliveries amounted to AS 6.6 billion or to .5 per cent of the cumulated GDP for the years 1955 to 1963. These compensatory deliveries are not included in Austrian foreign trade statistics.

Austria's Trade With the East Since the State Treaty in 1955

The State Treaty of 15 May 1955 restored Austria's sovereignty in international law. On this occasion Austria undertook to adhere to a state of neutrality in perpetuity.

After conclusion of the State Treaty of 1955 Austrian trade with the East expanded considerably: part of this expansion can be explained by the statistical inclusion of the foreign trade transactions of enterprises previously under Soviet administration, another part by various Soviet purchases after the end of the compensatory deliveries. Thus the growth of Austrian East–West trade pertained mainly to trade with the Soviet Union, but trade with the other East European countries also developed favourably.

On average, *exports* from Austria to the East grew by 17.5 per cent annually between 1955 and 1959 and by 10.8 per cent between 1960 and 1964. These growth rates were higher than those for total exports. The share of the East in total Austrian exports increased from 9.4 per cent in 1954 to 14.6 per cent in the first half of the 1960s. The Soviet Union took about one quarter of the value of exports to this region. The expansion of Austrian exports to the East continued in the 1960s and contributed considerably to the dynamic development of total exports. Austrian exports to Western Europe were hampered at that time by the discrimination of all external imports into the European Community (EC). The expansion of exports to other EFTA countries, promoted by the abolishment of tariffs within this group, was only an insufficient compensation for the losses incurred in trade with the EC. In the second half of the 1960s the share of the East in Austrian exports increased, especially the market of the smaller East European countries which at that time attracted a growing share of total exports.

At the beginning of the 1970s Austrian exports to the East were hampered for a time by the switchover from clearing settlements to convertible currency transactions (see below). Therefore Austria hardly participated in the overall expansion of East–West trade in the early 1970s. Only after the problems of settlements in convertible currencies were mastered, could Austria recuperate some of the losses incurred earlier. In 1974 Austrian exports to the CMEA region expanded by 66 per cent; part of this expansion was of course due to the inflation in world trade. Between 1970 and 1974 Austrian exports to the East grew at an average of almost nineteen per cent annually. Nevertheless, due to the more dynamic development of trade with other regions the share of East in total exports diminished. In the second half of the 1970s the development of exports to the East slowed down considerably. Especially trade with Eastern Europe flattened out while trade with the Soviet Union continued to grow quite well. The share in total exports increased to an average of 14.5 per cent in the second half of the 1970s.

In the first half of the 1980s exports to the East grew at an annual rate of 7.4 per cent, at constant prices by 5.4 per cent. Again, exports to the Soviet Union performed better than the exports to Eastern Europe. It is possible that the Soviet Union was ready, by increasing its purchases in Austria, to diminish its extraordinary trade surplus with this country (AS 13.1 billion in 1981). In 1986 and 1987 the exports to the East collapsed: they shrunk by 11.1 per cent annually (10.6 per cent in constant terms). The share of the East fell to a historical low of only nine per cent in 1987.

Also *imports* from the East to Austria after the State Treaty of 1955 expanded at a fast pace, especially those from the Soviet Union. In the 1960s the demand for products of the CMEA countries grew less rapidly. The share of the East in total Austrian imports was always somewhat smaller than its share in Austrian exports. The import share amounted to 10.3 per cent in the second half of the 1950s; it was 11.1 per cent in the first half of the 1960s but shrunk to under ten per cent in the second half of that decade. In the first half of the 1970s imports from the East to Austria expanded by eighteen per cent annually. In part this was due to the 'explosion' of the prices of crude oil and of other fuels. The growth of Eastern imports slowed down considerably in the second half of the decade whereby the imports from the Soviet Union continued to grow fast while at the same time imports from Eastern Europe almost stagnated. The CMEA region recorded a share of about nine per cent of total Austrian imports during the 1970s.

In the first half of the 1980s imports from the East grew at an annual rate of 8.3 per cent (2.5 per cent in constant terms). Both the Soviet Union and the smaller East European countries increased their share in Austrian market. In the second half of the 1980s the development changed considerably. Austria's imports fell from AS 46 billion in 1985 to only AS 28 billion in 1987 (−21.9 per cent annually). This was mainly due to the breakdown of prices of energy on the world market. In real terms the imports from the East increased by 2.1 per cent annually in 1986–1987.

Up to 1979 the foreign *trade balance* with the East was always in surplus. The foreign trade surplus expanded in trade with Eastern Europe (during 1970 and 1974 an average of AS 1.8 billion annually was achieved, growing to AS 6.9 billion annually between 1975 and 1979) while trade deficits mounted in trade with the Soviet Union (between 1975 and 1979 a deficit of AS 3.2 billion annually was incurred). Also in the 1980s Austria's imports from the East were considerably higher than the exports. The trade deficit peaked in

1981 with AS 11 billion, but diminished in the following years. In 1987 a surplus (AS 3 billion) was achieved.

AUSTRIA'S TRADE REGIME VIS-À-VIS THE EAST

Austria's trade regime in relation to the East can be divided into two areas: the area of traditional trade policy and the area of specific trade promotion. The realm of traditional trade policy includes rules on import- and export-licensing, plus regulations of payment settlements and of customs duties, while the second area encompasses governmental co-operation promotion agreements and export financing measures.

Import and Export Rules for Austria's East-West Trade

The legal foundation of Austria's trade regime was enacted in the Foreign Trade Law 1968 (newly notified in 1984).[12] The law postulates the principle of free trade according to which neither imports nor exports should be restrained unless otherwise prescribed by specific rules. However, the law contains a relatively large number of items (positions) where import (list B1 and B2) or export (list A1 and A2) authorisations are required (so-called customs authorised or 'controlled' goods, as against 'free' goods, for which no authorisations are required). The Federal Ministry of Economic Affairs or the Federal Ministry of Agriculture are authorised to grant the necessary permits.

Since 1962 the right to issue import licenses was gradually delegated to the customs authorities. In the so-called 'customs authorisation procedure' (*Zollämtermächtigungsverfahren*) the license is issued automatically when customs clearance takes place. Thus the customs authorisation procedures constitutes as *de facto* import-liberalisation.

Since the beginning of 1967, the authorisation procedure has been applied to almost all imports of industrial products from member countries of GATT. It has also applied, with some minor exceptions, to the exports of 'controlled' goods.

East European countries (including countries which were also GATT members) did not fall under the privilege of this procedure. It did, however, apply to the Soviet Union, to whom the trade agreement of 1955 conceded most-favoured-nation treatment.

In the 1950s and 1960s imports from the East were relatively tightly controlled. For imports of 'controlled' goods requiring a special import permission, quantitative quotas were agreed (or renewed) in annual trade agreements. Austria promised in these agreements to grant import licenses at least up to the limit of the quantitative quotas. Since 1962 the procedure of automatic licensing of imports was introduced in trade with the East, whereby requests for import permits were granted automatically and without quantitative restrictions. This, too, was a *de facto* liberalisation. The number of products for which this regime of automatic licensing was applied has been successively broadened.

Since the beginning of 1975 the regime of customs authorisation procedure has been also applied in dealings with all Eastern countries. By this regulation Austria was the first West European country after Finland to have completely liberalised imports of industrial origin from the East. However, since 1975 a new regime, the so-called countersigning procedure (*'Vidierungsverfahren'*), has been introduced for certain products from the East (but also from other overseas countries, for example Japan). This regime stipulates that at the time of customs clearance a pro-forma invoice approved by the competent Federal Ministry must be produced which tallies with the customs clearance papers. It is the purpose of this regulation to enable the Ministries to judge *ex ante* the volume of goods on offer from the East (and some other countries) to avoid possible market disruptions. The procedure should not be applied in a restrictive manner. Nevertheless, it is being criticised by the East European countries which see in it an administrative restriction not applied to imports from the West.

Imports of agricultural products are restrained by various Austrian regulations, such as customs duties and by various charges and levies.

In the beginning of the 1980s the liberal attitude of Austria's trade regime with respect to exports came under criticism from the USA in connection with alleged high technology transfers to the East. The Austrian government has repeatedly assured the USA that Austria is not a passageway for illegal high technology transfers to the East. However, the introduction of tighter export controls became necessary, in order to secure the unrestricted flow of high technology from the USA to Austria. In 1985 (see Stankovsky, 1985) and 1988 (see Stankovsky, 1988) amendments to the Foreign Trade Law enacted supervision and export authorisation for special manufactures. These new measures are formulated in a non-discriminatory manner but *de facto* they have to prevent illegal re-exports of Western (USA) technology to the East. Exports of genuine Austrian origin are not restricted. For years similar provisions have been applied by Switzerland, Sweden and Finland. In 1985 export licensing for computers, computer parts and some other articles became statutory. Moreover, the Import Certificate (IC) was introduced as a legal instrument. The IC in which the use of the product was stipulated, was issued by the Austrian Ministry upon request of the Austrian exporter. The IC had to be submitted by the foreign (American) exporter to his authorities in order to receive an export license. The Austrian authorities supervised the correct application of the IC. In 1988 a list C was amended to the Foreign Trade Law, which contains products requiring an export license. The IC is no longer in use. The export authorisation procedure was extended also for products which are on transit through Austria.

Payments Settlements

International settlements are regulated in Austria by the Currency Law 1946 (Devisengesetz 1946, BGBl 162/1946) according to which all payments for imports have to be approved by the Austrian National Bank. Settlements for imports from countries with convertible currencies were freed soon by notifications of the National Bank. Settlements with the East European countries were regulated after the Second World War by bilateral clearing arrangements. The switchover to settlements in convertible currencies *vis-à-vis* the Soviet Union took place at the end of 1970, in relation to Bulgaria, Czechoslovakia, Hungary and Poland by the end of 1971, in relation to Romania by the middle of 1973 and in relation to the GDR by the end of the same year. During the period of clearing settlements payment arrangements with the East European countries were regulated by the following rules: the imports of 'controlled' goods required, in addition to an import license according to the Foreign Trade Law, a payment permit by the Austrian National Bank. For 'free' commodities an authorisation to accept the payment obligation of the National Bank was required.

At present, no restrictions whatsoever are imposed on payments in connection with foreign trade with the East. For settlements of capital accounts there are some general constraints.

THE AUSTRIAN CUSTOMS REGIME

General Principles

Austrian customs are regulated by the Customs Law 1955[13] and the Customs Tariff Law 1988.[14] Austria has a two-scale tariff. The higher scale is the autonomous scale, the lower contains treaty rates. The Austrian tariff consists mainly of *ad valorem* duties.

The law envisages the possibility of tariff reductions for reasons of price policy if the commodity in question is not produced in Austria. Until 1970 the higher (autonomous) tariffs were applied *vis-à-vis* those East European countries which were not members of the GATT, but frequently Austria granted tariff concessions. *Vis-à-vis* the Soviet Union the lower (contractual) tariffs were applied on the basis of the trade agreement of 1955, which contained the clause of most-favoured-nation treatment. As of 1 January 1971, the lower (contractual) tariffs on the basis of the Gatt Extension Law[15] are generally applied by Austria, namely also in relation to all East European countries. Austria has granted these tariff concessions without receiving reciprocal concessions from East European countries.

The Tariff Burden on Austrian Imports

By tradition Austria is ranged among the countries with a high level of import duties. Calculations for the years 1913, 1927, 1952, and 1960 yielded an average tariff of almost twenty per cent.[16] However, the actual burden of the tariffs for imports was much lower after the Second World War, since many tariff items were temporarily cancelled or reduced by Austrian autonomous decisions. This was done mainly to combat inflation and to increase the competitiveness of Austrian exports.[17] In 1960 the ratio of actual customs collections to the value of imports (measuring the actual average tax burden on imports) amounted to not more than 7.6 per cent.

Since the 1960s the level of Austrian import duties have been considerably reduced in three different ways:
- All members of GATT (including Austria) have reduced their contractual tariffs in three rounds of tariff reductions (Dillon, Kennedy and Tokyo Round). Austria reduced the tariffs for industrial produces during the Kennedy Round by eighteen per cent, during the Tokyo Round by 31 per cent to an average of eight per cent. These reductions also applied to the East European countries.

- On the basis of Free Trade Agreements customs for imports of manufactures were abolished during 1960 to 1967 in relation to the EFTA-countries, and during 1972 to 1977 in relation to the European Community. In addition to Customs Unions, Free Trade Areas are exempt by the GATT treaty from the principle of most-favoured-nation treatment.
- In 1972 Austria enacted the Law on Tariff Preferences (*Präferenzzollgesetz*), on the basis of which tariffs on imports from developing countries were lowered by about 50 per cent. Since 1982 a second Law on Tariff Preferences has been passed. Among the countries favoured by this law are Bulgaria, Rumania and Hungary (in addition to Yugoslavia).

By these measures, the average tariff burden on Austrian imports has been considerably reduced. By the end of the 1980s it amounted to only one per cent. For industrial imports, customs are collected only from industrial overseas countries (such as the United States and Japan) and Eastern countries; the reduced preferential tariffs are also collected on imports from developing countries.

Computations made by the GATT secretariat indicate that, in 1976, Austria had an average customs level for industrial products of approximately ten per cent. These tariffs were considerably higher than in other Western industrial countries.[18] Average tariffs for raw materials (weighted average 0.9 per cent) and semi-finished products (5.8 per cent) in Austria were approximately on the level of other Western industrial countries. However, the tariff averages for finished products (weighted average 18.5 per cent, simple average 13.4 per cent) were very high. The average tariff[19] for industrial products in 1984 in Austria was 4.9 per cent, compared with 4.2 per cent in the EC. The actual tariff average[20] for imports from the East in Austria in 1985 for all commodities was 3.2 per cent, for industrial products 5.5 per cent. According to these statistics, Austria still has high tariffs for imports of clothing, footwear, tools and electrical equipment.[21]

Governmental Co-operation Promotion Agreements

Inter-governmental agreements have always played an important role in economic relations between East and West. The content and purpose of these agreements have changed over the course of time: originally the agreements regulated the traditional sectors of trade policy, such as payment regulations, import quotas, and so forth. Subsequently, measures for the promotion of bilateral economic relations gained in importance. In this connection a changeover to long-term agreements for five, later for ten years can be observed.

During the 1970s the trade agreements previously concluded were complemented by agreements on economic, industrial, technical and scientific-technical co-operation. The first long-term trade agreements between East and West were concluded at the end of the 1950s, the first co-operation promotion agreements at the beginning of the 1960s.[22] In 1960 there were 23 long-term trade agreements, increasing to 55 in 1965 and in addition seventeen co-operation promotion agreements. In 1974 the number of both types of long-term agreements rose to 175, in 1980 to 284 and in 1983 to 313. Sometimes economic relations between two countries are regulated by several long-term agreements with different content and scope (trade agreement, industrial co-operation agreement, agreement on scientific-technical co-operation, and so forth).

Austria was one of the first Western industrial countries to conclude long-term agreements with the East. In 1960 Austria had four trade agreements. In 1976 there were fourteen long-term trade and co-operation agreements between Austria and Eastern countries in operation, which amounted to eight per cent of all agreements; in 1987 the number rose to 22 agreements, but the share dropped to 6.2 per cent.

Of the 22 agreements which Austria had concluded by 1987, fourteen covered the scope of economic co-operation. Eight of these agreements could be classified as long-term trade agreements.

Financing Austria's East–West Trade

An important element in Austrian trade promotion is the system of export guarantees and of export financing. The two systems are complementary. They are based on public guarantees and operate in principle on cost accounting.

Since 1950 the Austrian Control Bank has been acting as the sole agent for the Republic of Austria in the field of *export guarantees*. The guarantee may be related to individual deliveries and services exported by Austrian firms. In practice an Austrian value added of 70 to 80 per cent is required. Another group of guarantees serves as warranty of financial transactions in direct connection with Austrian exports (namely for tied financial credits, forfeiting, and so forth). Also activities serving Austrian exports only indirectly, such as direct investments abroad, can be insured. The liability limit which can be used by the Austrian Control Bank for issuing guarantees stands at present at AS 290 billion. Insurance covers both commercial and political risks.

The promotion of *export financing* is necessary in cases where traditional financing by Austrian or foreign credit institutions is not available or is too expensive. This may be the case in medium- and long-term financing of capital goods, mainly to less developed countries and Eastern countries, or in extending finance at low cost to small- and medium-sized enterprises. These are mostly short- or medium-term credits for exports of consumer goods or intermediate products to industrial countries. Various export financing schemes developed in the course of time are taking care of the two fields mentioned.

Export guarantees and export financing expanded vigorously from 1973 until the beginning of the 1980s: they then stagnated or decreased. This was mainly due to the stagnating and later shrinking exports to the East and to the developing countries: the gross turnover of both forms of export promotion grew tenfold until 1982 (guarantee issued from AS 8 billion to AS 88 billion, and financing utilisation from AS 5 billion to AS 53 billion). The value of total exports increased less than three times in the same period. Until 1986 the guarantee turnover fell to only AS 42 billion, the financing turnover to AS 21 billion. The guarantee amounts and the disbursements outstanding under the export financing scheme increased ten times between 1973 and 1982 but stagnated in the following years. The insured sums reached AS 297 billion in 1986, the disbursements outstanding under the various financing schemes AS 155 billion. In 1970 about fifteen per cent of total Austrian exports were covered by guarantees. Since 1976 the share of exports covered by guarantees amounted, with minor fluctuations, to 35 per cent. It fell to 23 per cent in 1986.

As to gross turnover of supported export financing procedures (Control Bank, National Bank), the share in total exports reached some eight per cent in the first half of the 1970s. In the early 1980s more than 30 per cent of total exports were financed in this way, but only six per cent in 1986.

Estimates on the regional distribution of the various forms of export promotion show the large involvement of exports to the East. Of the total guarantee amounts, some 30 to 40 per cent are earmarked for the Eastern countries, 40 per cent for less developed countries. Practically all exports to the East and to the less developed countries are insured. It is more difficult to determine the share of export financing according to regions. Of all export claims financed under the Control Bank scheme, some 40 to 50 per cent are financing of exports to the East, some 40 per cent for exports to the less developed countries. The huge share of the East and of the less developed countries in the total promoted financing can be explained not only by the higher share of disbursements outstanding but also by the longer-term character of export financing requirements of the regions mentioned.

Austria participates to a considerable extent in Western *credits* extended to the Eastern countries. First data of the Eastern debt in Austria are available for 1974, at which time the gross liabilities of the Eastern countries *vis-à-vis* Austria amounted to AS 19 billion. In 1984 the debt has grown to AS 190 billion, but fell to AS 167 billion in 1986.

Austria participates more than proportionally in the financing of the East. This is partly due to the involvement of Austrian banks in the untied free financing of the region by Western banks. Of the total gross debt of the East with banks in the West, Austria held about six per cent in the mid-1970s. Austria's share increased step-by-step to nine per cent in 1980 and fourteen per cent in 1983; it fell to 10.5 per cent in 1986. In the mid-1970s Austria's share in the total credit volume corresponded to the Austrian market share in the region, but in the early 1980s it was more than double of this share. It must not be forgotten also that the market share in the CMEA region and especially in Eastern Europe increased in the 1980s. Among other reasons, the fact that Austria has not followed the policy of credit restrictions *vis-à-vis* the East, together with the various forms of export promotion, may also account for the positive development in Austria's trade with the East up to 1985.

Notes

1. For a much more complete description of Austria's economic policy toward the East and toward the West, see the appendix to this chapter written by F. Levcik and J. Stankovsky.
2. Austria's economic policies and social partnership are described and analysed in numerous articles by H. Seidel, former director of the Austrian Institute of Economic Research (WIFO) and Vice Minister of Finance. On this subject see also Butschek (1985), Breuss (1987), and Tichy (1982).

3. Breuss, 1987, p. 205.
4. Seidel, 1987, p. 272.
5. Seidel, 1987, p. 271.
6. Härtel, 1986, p. 88.
7. See Butschek, 1985, p. 84ff.
8. For details, see Richter (1985, p. 352) concerning the non-existence of an Austrian trade policy *vis-à-vis* the East.
9. 'According to another view no formal reciprocity may be asked for from countries with centrally planned economy . . . Therefore the maximum that can be achieved is that by giving trade concessions Austria might gain the goodwill of the USSR and East European countries, expressed in greater willingness to buy from Austria' (Richter, 1985, p. 352ff).
10. This problem is discussed in detail in Breuss–Stankovsky (1988) and Stankovsky (1988).
11. Abbreviated and updated version of Levcik and Stankovsky (1984).
12. Außenhandelsgesetz 1968 (BGBl 314/1968); wiederverlautbart laut Kundmachung vom 27.April 1984 (BGBl 1984/84). All laws in Austria are published in the Federal Law Gazette (Bundesgesetzblatt, BGBl).
13. Zollgesetz (1955, BGBl, 129/1955).
14. Zolltarifgesetz, 1988, BGBl 155/1987).
15. GATT-Ausdehnungsgesetz, BGBl 419/1980.
16. Breuss (1983).
17. In this connection the active drawback is to be mentioned, whereby import duties are waived if the imports are to be used exclusively for exports. The application of the drawback procedure is limited in trade with EC and EFTA.
18. The computations take into account the so-called base rates only, which exclude some autonomous tariff reductions. The actual tariff averages are therefore lower.
19. Computation of the EFTA. Most-favoured-nations tariffs (four-digit level), weighted with imports, excluding imports from EC and EFTA.
20. Own calculations based on statistics of the Ministry of Finance.
21. See Breuss and Stankovsky (1988) for more details.
22. Levcik and Stankovsky (1979).

Bibliography

F. BREUSS, '"Austro–Keynesianismus"--eine wirtschafts-politische Innovation mit Folgen' (Austro–Keynesianism: an economic–policy innovation with consequences), in Hans Seidel-Festschrift (ed.), *Aufklärung und Wirtschaftsforschung* (Vienna: WIFO, 1987).

F. BREUSS, *Österreichs Außenwirtschaft 1945–1982* (Austria's external economy 1945–1982), Vienna: Signum, 1983).

F. BREUSS and J. STANKOVSKY, *Österreich und der EG-Binnenmarkt* (Austria and EC's internal market) (Vienna: Signum, 1988).

F. BUTSCHEK, *Die Österreichische Wirtschaft im 20 Jahrhundert*, (The Austrian economy in the 20th century) (Stuttgart: Fischer, 1985).

H. H. HÄRTEL, (u.a.), *Neue Industriepolitik oder Stärkung der Marktkräfte? Strukturpolitische Konzeptionen im Internationalen Vergleich* (New industrial policy or strengthening of market power? A structurally political concept in an international comparison) (Hamburg: Weltarchiv, 1986).

F. LEVCIK and J. STANKOVSKY, *Industrial Cooperation between East and West* (London: The Macmillan Press, 1979).

F. LEVCIK and J. STANKOVSKY, *A Profile of Austria's East–West Trade in the 1970s and 1980s* (Geneve: ECE, TRADE/R.480, 1984).

S. RICHTER, 'Some Aspects of Economic Relations between Austria and the Soviet Union', WIIW, *Forschungsberichte*, No. 101 (1984).

S. RICHTER, 'Trade with the Soviet Union: The Case of Austria', *Acta Oeconomica*, Nos. 3–4 (1985).

H. SEIDEL, 'Austro–Keynesianismus', *Wirtschaftspolitische Blätter*, No. 3 (1982).

H. SEIDEL, 'The Austrian Economy: An Overview', in S. W. Arndt (ed.), *The Political Economy of Austria* (Washington: American Enterprise Institute for Public Policy Research, 1982).

H. SEIDEL, 'Austria's Macro-Economic Policies in the Last Decade', in Ch. Saunders (ed.), *Management of the Economy and of Enterprises in East and West* (London: Macmillan, 1987).

J. STANKOVSKY, 'Österreichischer Osthandel 1984: Markanteilsgewinne durch Exportfinanzierung', (Austrian trade with the East 1984: Market share gains through export financing) *WIFO-Monatsberichte*, 58, No. 33 (1985).

J. STANKOVSKY, 'Starker Rückschlag im Ost–West-Handel' (Strong deterioration in East–West Trade), *WIFO-Monatsberichte*, 60, No. 3 (1987).

J. STANKOVSKY, 'Stabilisierung nach scharfem Einbruch: Ost–West-Handel 1986–1988' (Stabilisation after a sharp inroad: East–West trade 1986–1988), WIIW-Forschungsberichte (1987) 132.

J. STANKOVSKY, 'Österreichischer Osthandel 1987, Talfahrt nicht zu Ende', (Austrian trade with the East 1987: An unfinished journey), *WIFO-Monatsberichte*, 61, No. 3 (1988).

J. STANKOVSKY, 'Folgen eines möglichen EG-Beitritts Österreichs für den Osthandel' (Joining the EC and possible consequences on Austria's trade with the East), *WIFO-Monatsberichte*, 61, No. 5 (1988).

J. STANKOVSKY, 'Austria's Foreign Trade: The Legal Regulation of Trade with East and West', *Journal of World Trade Law* (1969).

G. TICHY, 'Austro–Keynesianismus – Gibt's den?' (Austro–Keynesianism – Where is it going?), *Wirtschaftspolitische Blätter*, No. 3, 1(1982).

7 Internal Regulation of Foreign Trade with respect to Socialist Trading Partners: A Comparison of the Finnish and the Hungarian System
Gábor Oblath

INTRODUCTION

In this chapter I shall compare some aspects of Hungarian and Finnish regulation of trade with socialist countries. The idea of undertaking this comparison evolved from discussions in Hungary concerning the Hungarian system of foreign trade with socialist countries. It is useful to study the experiences of a country such as Finland which has had to face challenges similar to those of Hungary. A deeper understanding of the choices made and solutions found by Finland could potentially influence the way Hungary will perceive and solve its own problems. However, I should like to stress in advance that my aim is simply to compare. A comparison of this sort might have various implications and offer several lessons. Still, I consider my attempt as just one of the possible approaches to a deeper understanding of the problems inherent in trade with CMEA countries. Hungary faces the challenge of discovering solutions to them.

I would like to offer an explanation for choosing Finland as the basis for my comparison.[1] The share of trade with socialist countries in Finland's overall foreign trade was the highest in the OECD area. It was close to 30 per cent in the early 1980s, with the Soviet Union acting as Finland's major socialist trade partner, responsible for over one-quarter of overall Finnish trade in this period.² Thus the sheer magnitude of Finnish trade with CMEA countries in the early 1980s could make the Finnish experience relevant for Hungary. However, there is another, and, at least from our point of view, more important characteristic of Fino–Soviet trade which makes it extremely interesting, namely the external international framework of trade between Finland and the Soviet Union which shows a remarkable resemblance to that of CMEA trade. The value, structure, and balance of trade between Finland and the Soviet Union is based on – and influenced by – long-, medium- and short-term inter-governmental agreements; for both CMEA and Fino–Soviet trade the yearly protocols negotiated by the respective governmental organs contain rather detailed lists (quotas) for the exports and imports of specific commodity groups. Finally, the payments between the two trading countries are conducted via a bilateral (non-convertible) currency, namely the clearing rouble.³

Besides the similarities, there are some important differences between Fino–Soviet and CMEA trade. One of these differences concerns the so-called price principle of mutual trade. According to the present CMEA price principle, transferable rouble prices should be based on the moving average of the previous five- years' world market prices. However, the price principle of Fino–Soviet bilateral trade has always been that prices expressed in clearing roubles should correspond to current world market prices (converted from dollars at the ruling exchange rate between the Soviet rouble and the dollar).

This apparently minor difference leads us to the third reason for looking at the Finnish experience. The price principle of Fino–Soviet trade simply states that this bilateral *trade does not have* any *special* price principle. This is by no means accidental. The Finnish authorities are not in a position to enforce the adherence to a special price principle, that is, they cannot make domestic firms accept (or charge) unreasonable foreign trade prices from the firm's point of view. The only implication of the use of 'the world market price principle' is that both partners can refer to actual or potential Western competitors' prices, but this is the normal state of things in any trade negotiation. Certainly, no Finnish authority exists that would or could interfere with price negotiations between Finnish firms and Soviet foreign trade enterprises, which differs from CMEA practice.

The existence of this sort of an authority would be deeply inconsistent with the workings of the Finnish market economy. The government of Finland might fix the domestic prices of certain commodities, might enjoy the legal right of ordering a price freeze for a limited time period, but it *still could not trade* with another country. Nevertheless, the inter-governmental framework of Fino–Soviet trade does not seem to imply that, not only on the Soviet side, but also on the part of Finland, it is the government which commits itself to buy and sell certain quantities of specified products. However, the inter-governmental agreements contain only a mutual declaration that both governments will do their best to ensure that actual trade corresponds to the agreements. One of the questions I should like to examine is how the Finnish government gathers and uses the information to negotiate trade flows, and what kind of policy instruments it will use to influence trade with the Soviet Union.

Though it should have become clear by now what my basic interest in this question is, I shall try to state it explicitly. In Hungary an attempt has been made to establish a socialist economy based on the combination of central planning and the workings of the market. An important condition of the latter is the decentralisation of decision-making and the granting of autonomy to firms. It is, however, difficult to conceive how this can be done in a country where the share and importance of CMEA trade is very large. As is commonly known, this trade is conducted in a framework which has different standards, involves different mechanisms, and implies different behaviour on the part of both the authorities and firms from those that characterise the reformed Hungarian economy. Therefore, one of the basic issues to be resolved in the process of the Hungarian economic reform is interrelated with the management of trade with CMEA countries. This issue is the focus of my contribution.

First, I shall present an overview of Hungarian financial regulation of its CMEA trade, then I shall describe some features of the Finnish system, and finally, while comparing the two systems, I shall draw some conclusions and point to a few questions which need further investigation.

In the following discussion I shall concentrate on institutional issues and problems related to regulation, while also referring to the implications of balances of trade flows. I shall presume that the reader is acquainted with the institutional system, mechanisms, procedures and basic economic features of CMEA trade. For reasons of exposition I shall treat trade with socialist countries, with the 'East' and with the CMEA, as well as trade in roubles interchangeably. The reader should remember that this entails some minor inaccuracies.

HUNGARIAN FINANCIAL REGULATION OF TRADE WITH CMEA COUNTRIES

Before 1968, and the introduction of the 'New Economic Mechanism', there had been an expectation in Hungary that the domestic economic mechanisms of other CMEA countries would also be reformed. It had been expected that the mechanism and institutional system of the CMEA would have transformed as well, so that the role of the market, money, and prices would increase. It had been hoped that sooner or later the nature of CMEA trade would change to the mutual advantage of all of its member countries; a real market with effective multilateralism (and later on with a convertible currency) could be established.

These expectations seem to have affected Hungary's financial regulation of its trade with socialist countries after 1968. Basically, the same kind of financial policy tools were applied to socialist trade as to trade with the West. A commercial price coefficient was introduced between the transferable rouble and the forint, which had certain characteristics of an exchange rate. It was determined using the same procedure as that for the dollar rate. In both cases, the average domestic costs of earning a unit of foreign exchange with exports were calculated. This particular way of determining the forint/transferable rouble rate naturally necessitated the extensive use of financial tools (subsidies and taxes) in rouble exports, but the practice in the case of exports to the West was exactly the same.

During the 1970s not only was Hungarian financial regulation of trade transacted in dollars and trade transacted in roubles similar, but so was the course of exchange rate policy. The forint had been revalued with respect to both the dollar and the transferable rouble. The motives for both revaluations were the same, namely the desire to prevent imported inflation.

It is not the task of this chapter to discuss whether the revaluations of the forint were justified or not. The point I wish to make is that although policy instruments had many common features and changed in a similar fashion, which applied to both trade with the East and trade, with the West, the external factors behind the formal and the similar were by no means the same.

In trade with the West, it was the balance of payments and consequently the balance of trade targets that limited the field of manoeuvre of economic policy, while trade with the East was constrained by government agreements. Thus the actual structure of trade with the East was the limiting factor. It was considered unreasonable that the Hungarian government, after having obliged itself within the CMEA to sell and buy certain amounts of specified products, would force Hungarian enterprises to fulfill their CMEA obligations at either extremely disadvantageous or advantageous terms. This consideration implied the maintenance of various taxes and subsidies in socialist trade, and this was the actual practice until 1981.

In 1981 Hungarian financial regulation of trade with the CMEA was modified. According to the new system, the profitability of each firm's exports to socialist countries was to become more or less automatically equal to the profitability of its sales in the domestic market. The latter in turn – at least in principle, or more precisely, according to the regulations of the price system introduced in 1980 – had to correspond to the profitability of sales on Western markets.

The financial regulation of rouble exports introduced in 1981 meant the implementation of a more or less automatic 'profitability equalisation' system. It is not worth going into the details of this system here, the less so since it has often been modified since 1985. The basic feature of the scheme was the following: by means of taxes or subsidies the profitability (the ratio of profits to revenues) of each firm's exports to the rouble area was, by and large, equalised to the firm's profitability on domestic sales. Some incentives to improve export efficiency were, however, added to the system: the after-tax (subsidy) rouble export profitability of firms with relatively favourable rouble export efficiency (relatively low domestic costs of obtaining a rouble) could be somewhat higher than the profitability on domestic sales, and the opposite applied to firms with relatively unfavourable rouble export efficiency. Though this condensed presentation of the system might give the impression that it was extremely complicated, in reality it was not. The technical details of the scheme were preannounced, thus each firm could calculate the approximate amount of profits it could earn by exporting to the CMEA.

As a consequence, or rather, as a 'by-product' of this type of financial regulation, the Hungarian exchange rate of the transferable rouble (namely the forint/transferable rouble rate) completely lost its economic significance, as far as its role in exports was concerned. In imports however, the role of the forint/rouble exchange rate in influencing domestic prices was – at least partially – maintained. While domestic prices of several types of manufactured products continued to be linked to the foreign (rouble) prices by the exchange rate, the domestic producer prices of primary products (raw materials and energy) were to be based on their world market prices (namely potential or actual import prices from Western sources converted at the ruling forint/dollar exchange rate). Thus it was not the domestic price of the latter commodity groups that the exchange rate influenced, but the difference between the import price from socialist countries (expressed in forints) and the domestic producer price, and thereby the differential rent, taxed away by the fiscal authorities. Summing up, Hungarian financial regulation of socialist trade introduced in the early 1980s gave a rather limited role to the exchange rate in imports and practically eliminated the exchange rate's role in exports.

The most important expectation attached to the financial regulation introduced in 1981 was that it would be automatic and simple, and at the same time it would eliminate the need for, and thus the problems stemming from regular bargaining (between firms and domestic authorities) over taxes and subsidies. If simplicity were the only criterion for judging the efficiency of this domestic regulation, the 'profitability equalisation' system might be considered superior to its predecessor.

However, relative technical simplicity is not the only criterion, and comparison with an undoubtedly clumsy and complicated system is not the only standard for evaluating financial regulation. The basic question is: what purpose does this relatively simple financial system serve? Since this question is too general, we might come closer to more relevant considerations by first clarifying for whom and from which point of view can the new regulation be considered simple.

The new system was certainly simpler than its predecessor from the point of view of financial control. The fiscal authorities were indeed relieved of the troubles involved in bargaining with firms on taxes and subsidies – on which the preceding system was based. This, as well as the fact that the new system allowed less bargaining options for the firms over the level of subsidies received or taxes paid, indicates that considerations of the fiscal authorities had a rather heavy influence on the design of the regulation introduced in 1981.

But the very fact that fiscal and technical concerns had a dominating role, indicates that we must look beyond the technical details of the system and try to clarify its economic implications.

The new regulation can be considered to be an attempt at neutralising the financial effects of CMEA trade at the microeconomic level. To put it otherwise: by linking the profitability of sales to socialist countries to the profitability of domestic sales, the Hungarian firms became, at least partially, insulated from the financial consequences of their trade with (mainly exports to) socialist countries.

The insulation, however, was only partial and inconsistent. On the one hand, as mentioned above, depending on the firms' relative rouble export efficiency they could realise somewhat higher or lower profits on exports to the East than on domestic sales. On the other hand, the overall financial results of firms could continue to depend rather heavily on sales to socialist markets, especially in those cases when the share of the latter in total sales was relatively high. In these cases the regulation did not – and, in fact, could not – avoid the possibility that firms would manipulate the product and/or market mix of their sales to the West only in order to increase – via the profitability of domestic sales – the legally attainable profitability of sales to the East.

The inconsistencies of the regulation stem from the fact that it is not possible to have it both ways: to expect firms to be executives of governmental decisions (agreements) and at the same time require that they make autonomous decisions in order to improve both the efficiency of their exports to the East and increase their overall profitability.

Naturally, there are alternative interpretations of the above mentioned inconsistency. It is possible to declare that compromises are inevitable if you wish to adjust your system to an international economic mechanism and institutional framework whose workings and logic differs from your own. According to this interpretation the inconsistencies would result from the need to accept the compromises.

But there are grounds for another interpretation as well. The inconsistencies inherent in the Hungarian regulation of trade with socialist countries might reflect a more general problem of the Hungarian economic management system and mechanism: namely the lack of clarification of the role and authority of the state, on the one hand, and that of domestic firms, on the other. If this were the case, the regulation of socialist trade after 1981 can be viewed as an attempt at maintaining this unclarified and confused state of affairs within a relatively simple, manageable, more or less automatic financial system.

The two interpretations are, of course, not mutually exclusive. However, when considering the possibilities of a change, or reaching a better compromise, it should be useful to take a look at the Finnish organisation and regulation of Fino–Soviet trade. Therefore, I now turn to a discussion of the Finnish experience, skipping the technical modifications of the Hungarian regulation of trade with the East implemented since 1985.

ORGANISATION AND REGULATION OF FINO–SOVIET TRADE IN FINLAND

As already mentioned, the system of trade and payments between Finland and the Soviet Union is remarkably similar to that of intra-CMEA trade. However, Finland is profoundly different from CMEA member countries because it has a developed market economy with a convertible currency, and is closely integrated into the world economy. This certainly suggests some sort of incompatibility.

In what follows I shall try to outline how Finland has adjusted the framework of its trade with the East – the bilateral clearing and quota system as well as the major role of government agencies – to its domestic market economy.

While presenting the main features of the Finnish regulation of bilateral trade, I shall concentrate on two principal issues. First, with what kind of information and what sort of objectives does the Finnish government (agencies of the government) negotiate with the Soviet government (agencies) and what kind of policy tools are applied for implementing the agreements? Second, what is the role and scope of action of Finnish firms in this special type of trade?

The determination of the approximate annual magnitude of bilateral trade, namely outlining the volume of exports and imports, is the result of a certain kind of planning process in Finland. Both government agencies (Ministry of Foreign Affairs, Ministry of Trade and Industry, and so forth), and the Bank of Finland (responsible for keeping the rouble clearing accounts on the Finnish side) as well as representatives of Finnish firms (the central federation of industrial associations) participate in the planning process. Because of the attempt – often in the late 1980s an unsuccessful attempt – at balancing the credits and debits in the clearing account, there are two starting points for outlining the annual volume of mutual trade. First, the previous year's clearing balance, and second, the estimated value of imports from the Soviet Union. Since these imports are concentrated on a small number of commodity groups, the most important being fuel and some raw materials, and moreover, since the major part of imports is being conducted on the basis of longer term agreements by Neste, the Finnish state-owned oil company, the estimation can be carried out rather simply. Finnish firms willing to import other Soviet products indicate their demand via their industrial associations.

Thus the approximate scope for annual exports is outlined. It is in formulating a proposal on the pattern of exports, that is, in making a preliminary offer concerning the distribution of quotas among different commodity groups – implying a preliminary distribution of export possibilities among Finnish industries – that the industrial associations have a fundamental role. These associations and their central federation act as mediators between Finnish government agencies who negotiate with their Soviet counterparts and sign the trade agreements on the one hand, and Finnish firms, who actually trade with Soviet firms, on the other. The associations convey information from government agencies toward firms concerning Soviet demand indicated on the level of various ministries, for example intragovernmental committees, and from firms (industries) towards Finnish government agencies concerning export supply conditions. Taking into consideration the demand of the Soviet Union, they try to reconcile and represent the interests of Finnish industries. This is a rather complicated task, requiring a great deal of sophistication on the part of the industrial associations, but since the whole procedure is informal, the workings of the system and the details of the procedure are not readily accessible to an outside observer. But whatever the details, the central federation of industries presents a list concerning the proposed pattern (quota distribution) of Finnish exports to the relevant Finnish government agencies, and this is what the latter represent in their negotiations with the Soviet Union. Besides, the representatives of the major industrial associations are also represented at the trade negotiations. The inter-governmental trade agreement – which is naturally affected by Soviet requirements and interests – contains the final quotas, that is, the list of goods intended to be exported and imported.

The quotas, however, are not binding obligations, either for firms or governments. They are categories to be filled by negotiations and contracts between Finnish firms and Soviet foreign trade organisations.

Still, both because of the macroeconomic implications and the special character (bilateral nature) of Soviet trade, the Finnish state must exercise some sort of control over bilateral trade flows. The policy tools which at least in principle can be applied to regulating trade, might be of a financial or an administrative type. The financial instruments are supposed to influence trade flows indirectly by affecting prices and/or profits of firms and thus the supply and demand conditions. Administrative tools serve for controlling the value, balance or structure of trade directly.

The remarkable feature of the regulation of Soviet trade in Finland is that it does not rely on financial tools; *exclusively administrative (direct) policy tools are applied.*

The control is exercised through a Licensing Office. The condition of effecting actual transactions is obtaining a license from the office. The Licensing Office, before granting a license, observes the current status of the clearing balance and the extent to which quotas have already been fulfilled. These regulations are meant to assure that actual trade flows, by and large, correspond to bilateral government agreements.

The Licensing Office has another important function. Namely, it has to check that exporting firms observe the following rule: 'the products to be delivered have to be of basically Finnish manufacture'.[4] In practice, this means that export licences are granted only on the condition that the direct Western import content of goods to be exported to the Soviet Union does not exceed twenty per cent. Although this limit is not codified – thus in case of a Finnish surplus on the clearing account the limitation might become more strict in order to restrain Finnish export supply – the limitation itself is a fact of common knowledge and is generally observed by firms intending to export to the Soviet Union.

The existence of the licensing institution and of the rules enforced by this authority can be interpreted as an attempt by the Finnish government to restrain exports to the East and to insulate the latter from imports from the West. The need for this kind of constricting institution is explained by the fact that the clearing account is linked to the domestic monetary system, and indirectly, via the convertibility of the Finnish currency to the convertible balance of payments. The link is established by such an exchange rate policy in Finland which connects the cross rate between the dollar and the clearing rouble to the official rouble/dollar rate announced by the Soviet Union. Thus the exchange rate of the clearing rouble in Finland (namely the markka/rouble rate) is mechanically derived from the ruling markka/dollar exchange rate on the one hand, and the official Soviet rouble/dollar rate, on the other.[5]

It is to be stressed that the official (nominal) exchange rate for the clearing rouble in Finland corresponds to its effective rate, that is, *no discount* (or, if that were the case, premium) *is charged* for firms converting their clearing rouble claims to the domestic (convertible) currency. This is exactly what I meant by pointing out that financial policy tools – involving special exchange rate policies with respect to the clearing rouble – *are not* relied on in Finland for regulating bilateral trade.

To sum up, by definition, there is no exchange rate at which the clearing rouble could be converted to dollars (or any other convertible currency) by the Bank of Finland – *roubles are non-convertible* from their point of view, *but only from the point of view of the Bank of Finland*. In contrast, clearing roubles *are convertible* to dollars (via the Finnish markka) at the official Soviet dollar/rouble exchange rate *for firms exporting to the Soviet Union*.

This, in my view, is a contradiction indeed which might lead to undesired consequences. Firms do not experience through changes in prices and/or profitability the macroeconomic constraints inherent in the clearing accounting system. Thus they might strive (and, in fact, have striven) to increase even if this leads to an accumulation of non-convertible currency assets on the macroeconomic level. Surpluses on the clearing account, in turn, could spill over to the convertible balance of payments, causing deficits in the latter. Moreover, even a balance in bilateral trade could imply an imbalance in convertible currency payments if the Western import content of exports to the East were high. An important implication of these possibilities is that the rouble can become overvalued with respect to the Finnish currency in case of a large Finnish surplus in bilateral trade. In fact, this is what happened, in my view, during the 1980s.

Returning to the functions and rules enforced by the Licensing Office, it should be clear that its major role is to try to avoid the dangers and undesired effects of an undervaluation of the domestic currency with respect to the rouble.

But these dangers, as explained above, follow from the fact that *in the monetary sphere* bilateral trade is integrated into the domestic economy and – by the convertibility of the markka – closely linked to Finland's Western economic relations as well. Thus, in my interpretation, one of the basic reasons for the need to maintain the insulating and restraining function of the Licensing Office with respect to *real flows* is to be found in the fact that the Bank of Finland does not consider the clearing rouble/markka exchange rate as an instrument of economic (commercial) policy. By considering it as exogenous, and by not applying financial tools that would amount to influencing the rouble/markka effective exchange rate the bilateral exchange rate is rendered no role whatsoever in influencing bilateral trade flows. This is how the clearing accounts are totally integrated into the Finnish monetary system, and this is why the use of administrative tools is inevitable.

COMPARISON OF THE TWO SYSTEMS AND SOME TENTATIVE CONCLUSIONS

In spite of some basic differences, there are certain similarities between the Hungarian and the Finnish internal regulation of trade with respect to socialist trading partners. This similarity does *not* stem from a formal comparison of the features of regulation, but rather from the fact that neither of the two systems relies on financial instruments of economic policy to influence the volume and the balance of its trade with the East.

This statement is based on the observation that the exchange rate between the domestic and the clearing currency is not used, in either of the two systems, by the relevant authorities, to affect trade accounted in clearing currencies.

Although *the way* this exchange rate plays no role is rather different in the two countries, the two systems have established close links between their trade accounted in clearing and in convertible currencies. But here again, the same statement applies to the exchange rate: *the way* financial links between trade with the East and trade with the West have been established in the two countries is very different indeed.

As far as Finland is concerned, the authorities chose to consider the rouble/markka exchange rate as exogenous.[6] The exchange rate has a role, and, in fact, a very important role, in the Finnish economy in general and in its economic policy in particular, but because of adjusting the rouble/markka rate to the official dollar/rouble rate of the Soviet Union, Finland has *one single* exchange rate policy, irrespective of the parallel existence of its convertibe and clearing accounts. In Finland it is via this exchange rate policy that the exchange rate of the clearing rouble is given no role in influencing bilateral trade and that the financial link between trade accounted in convertible and clearing currencies is established.

In Hungary similar results to those in Finland – namely the passive role of the exchange rate of the transferable rouble as well as the financial link between trade with the East and trade with the West – are achieved by profoundly different means.

A commercial exchange rate exists between the forint and the transferable rouble, which is determined autonomously by Hungarian authorities. That is, the transferable rouble/forint rate is independent of the official Soviet dollar/rouble rate; there need not be, and in fact there is no, consistency between the dollar/rouble cross rate in Hungary and the exchange rate of the dollar announced by the Soviet Union. Thus, at least in principle, the Hungarian authorities could conduct an active exchange-rate policy with respect to the transferable rouble in order to influence trade with socialist countries.

However, the scope for relying on the exchange rate is not exploited by Hungarian economic policy; the potential effects of the level and changes of the exchange rate are, by and large, neutralised by the previously discussed internal financial regulation which has linked microeconomic profitability of sales in different markets to each other.

Thus, in Hungary financial links among sales to Western, domestic, and Eastern markets have been established on the microeconomic level artificially (by rules stipulating an accounting profit rate on exports of individual firms to the East) and by consciously neutralising the potential effects of the rouble exchange rate. In Finland, in contrast, the financial link has been established at the macroeconomic level, through the exchange rate system. Although – as we have seen – the Finnish authorities also apply special administrative tools and legal stipulations which are clearly different from those applied by the Hungarian authorities.

The last observation leads us to that particular difference between the Hungarian and the Finnish internal regulation of trade accounted in clearing currencies which can be considered as fundamental: the fact that while in the Finnish system no effort is made by the authorities to neutralise the effects of individual prices in bilateral trade, the Hungarian authorities do the opposite. Hungarian officials neutralise, through financial regulation, not only the (potential) effects of the clearing currency exchange rate, but also those of individual foreign trade (export) prices. More accurately, it is precisely by neutralising the effects of external prices on the microeconomic level that the exchange rate becomes unimportant in the Hungarian system.

It is respectively the lack of, and the existence of, the above mentioned neutralisation of external prices in the Finnish and Hungarian systems that points to the basic difference in the economic logic of the two systems.

This difference stems from a contrasting perception of the role of government agencies and of microeconomic agents (firms) in conducting trade. While the Finnish government takes it for granted that it cannot meddle with foreign trade prices (and consequently with price ratios), since only firms are in a position to decide what price to charge (or accept), and therefore the government has no basis for redistributing export revenues among exporting firms, the Hungarian government, at each and every point, takes the opposite for granted: namely, that it *is* exactly the government agencies who can correctly evaluate the consequences, economic effects of changes in individual foreign trade prices. According to this logic, it is the firms who should not meddle with the external prices of their own products (or only under the supervision of government agencies) and consequently the government has ample grounds for neutralising the potential effects of foreign trade prices, in other words for redistributing export revenues among trading firms.

Naturally if we accept the premise that only government agencies are in a position to consider the consequences of individual price changes and thus decide which price increases of exports (or, if it so happens, decreases) are beneficial for the national economy, it is not rational to make firms beneficiaries or victims of prices decided above their heads.

However, it is not necessary to accept this premise, since the above logic (including the idea that firms could become beneficiaries or victims of inter-governmental price negotiations) holds only when the government has already obliged Hungary to supply (purchase) quantities of specified products. These detailed government obligations must be carried out by Hungarian firms, who – according to the principles of the Hungarian economic reform – are supposed to be profit oriented microeconomic agents. Thus although the internal regulation of Hungary's trade with the East displays certain self contradictory features, the more fundamental problem seems to me to be that its whole logic contradicts the principles and endeavours of the economic reform.

It is time to emphasise that I am personally not convinced that the Finnish internal regulation is optimal from the point of view of economic efficiency. But that is just one of the reasons why I do not consider it a norm to be followed or to be implemented.

The more important reason is that the mechanism and economic environment of Fino–Soviet and that of CMEA trade – in spite of the similarities discussed – are rather different. This has certainly become clear while discussing the role of government agencies, those of firms and their representative organisations, the non-obligatory character of quotas, and the lack of a special 'price principle' in Fino–Soviet trade. That is, even if the Finnish internal regulation were perfect (optimal) in itself, it would make no sense to suggest copying it within very different circumstances. Moreover, as I have tried to point out, the Hungarian regulation does something similar to the Finnish one – not consciously, but still, Hungarian regulation simulates some features of the Finnish system, which, in my view, happen to be the least worth simulating. Although I do not want to suggest that there is nothing to be learned from the actual techniques and solutions of Finland, I should rather like to draw attention to a more general consideration on the basis of the foregoing presentation and comparison of the two systems.

In its trade with the Soviet Union, Finland has accepted and strictly stuck to the maintenance of an institutional system which conforms to the organisational, planning and management system of the Soviet Union. But the way this trade is conducted reveals that the Soviet Union has also accepted the facts and logic of the Finnish market economy. This explains why Fino–Soviet trade has no special price principle and why quotas are not compulsory.

The mechanisms of Fino–Soviet trade are thus based on the compromise of different economic systems and logics implied by these systems. CMEA trade, in contrast, is based on a single economic logic, namely that of the traditional, directive form of central planning. This is what determines the external conditions (mechanisms, functioning) of Hungary's trade with socialist countries.

A critical analysis of the mechanism and workings of CMEA trade is far beyond the scope and intentions of this chapter.[7] The point I wish to make is that the CMEA functions the way it does, and I consider it to be an overly optimistic and unrealistic expectation that the overall mechanism of this trade would change within reasonable time in a similar way to the Hungarian economic mechanism and management system.

However, the Hungarian economic mechanism *did* change. Important and genuine, steps were made to establish an economic system based on the combination of central planning and the workings of the market. The logic of this reformed Hungarian economic system (involving the division of labour between government agencies, on the one hand, and microeconomic agents on the other) differs at very important points both from the traditional form of central planning and from the logic and mechanisms of CMEA trade. In my view, it is time not only for facing this fact, but also for reconsidering and representing its consequences, representing them toward both CMEA countries and domestic firms.

The last tentative conclusion might be considered excessively general or perhaps even vague compared to the presentation and comparison of the details of the Finnish and Hungarian regulation of trade with the East. However, I hope to have made it clear that the seemingly technical problems of the Hungarian regulation point to certain fundamental inconsistencies, for which no adequate technical solutions are presently available. The Finnish regulation might have – and, in fact, does have – its own problems, but these can be solved by applying or modifying certain policy instruments, since the regulation of bilateral trade does not try to enforce an economic logic alien to the Finnish system as a whole.

In Hungary the primary and more fundamental task is reconsidering and clarifying what kind of internal *and* international institutional framework for conducting trade with socialist countries would correspond to and assist the continuation of the economic reform. Determining the adequate financial and administrative instruments and techniques for regulating Hungarian trade with the East is a challenging but still secondary task.

Notes

I wish to thank the participants of the Bellagio conference for comments on the original version of the paper. I am particularly grateful to Michael Marrese for his helpful criticisms and suggestions. The responsibility for any remaining errors or omissions and for all interpretations is, of course, mine.
1. While describing and discussing the Finnish regulation of Fino–Soviet trade, I shall draw heavily on Oblath–Pete (1986).
2. Though this share has gone down since 1985, the significance of Fino–Soviet trade is still outstanding for both countries.

3. In 1989, some important changes were announced in the payments system between Finland and the Soviet Union. These, among others, involve a limited use of convertible currencies in clearing bilateral balances. However, since from the point of view of comparing the Finnish and the Hungarian system, the 'historic' characteristics are the relevant ones. I shall not treat the recent changes.
4. Economic Commission for Europe, 1982.
5. On details of determining the markka/rouble rate, see Hirvensalo, 1979 and Oksanen, 1984.
6. Were the rouble convertible, this would be the only appropriate behaviour of the Finnish authorities. However, since the rouble is inconvertible, no market forces exist to maintain the consistency of cross rates. The rouble/ markka exchange rate, therefore, is not predetermined. Considering it as exogenous and not applying it as a policy instrument is just one of the possible choices.
7. On CMEA trade, see the classic book of Ausch (1972), and the more recent comprehensive work of Csaba (1984).

Bibliography

S. AUSCH, 'Theory and Practice of CMEA Cooperation', Akadémia Kiadó, Budapest (1972).

L. CSABA, 'Kelet–Európa a világgazdaságban' (Eastern Europe in the world economy), *Közgazdasági és Jogi Könyvkiadó*, Budapest (1984).

ECE, '*A Profile of the East–West Trade of Finland in the 1970s* (Economic Commission for Europe (ECE), October 1982).

I. HIRVENSALO, 'The Clearing System for Payments between Finland and the USSR, Bank of Finland' (1979).

G. OBLATH and P. PETE, 'The Development, Mechanism and Institutional System of Fino–Soviet Economic Relations', Vienna Institute for Comparative Economic Studies, *WIIW*, No. 111 (1986).

H. OKSANEN, 'The Rouble in Soviet–Finnish Trade', *Kansallis-Osake-Pankki Economic Review*, No. 2 (1984).

8 Effects of Trade with Centrally Planned Economies on Exchange Rates and Prices in Market Economies

Yrjänä Tolonen

INTRODUCTION

The purpose of this chapter is to study how trading with a centrally planned economy (CPE) that has no functioning price system and an inconvertible currency can affect the exchange rates, outputs, prices and welfare in market economies (MEs). In an earlier article, I have discussed how the macroeconomic behaviour of an ME having trade with a CPE differs from the behaviour of MEs trading only with other MEs (Tolonen 1988). The framework used was one of three countries (two MEs and one CPE) and three goods. In MEs, there were Keynesian unemployment and fixed exchange rates between MEs. As a case study, the Finnish trading experiences with the Soviet Union were discussed. One of the results was that an increase in this trade leads to an increase in Finnish production and employment. The reason is that with bilateral clearing account arrangements (or, more generally, with a zero balance of payments target in the CPE), an increase in Finnish imports from the Soviet Union leads to a rise in Finland's exports to the Soviet Union. This kind of reasoning has clearly affected the purchasing practices of the Finnish government, especially Finnish state-owned companies. A preference is often given to imports from the Soviet Union instead of ME sources. Examples such as railway equipment, nuclear plants and military hardware quickly spring to mind. The most recent discussion concerns the acquisition of a new generation of fighter planes for the Finnish air forces. The choice seems to be between the Soviet MIG-29 and the Swedish JAS. The former has been promoted by presenting the employment generating reasons mentioned above.

At the time of writing there is also another type of discussion taking place in Finland. This deals with the advantages and disadvantages of adopting a flexible exchange rate system instead of the current fixed exchange rates *vis-à-vis* other MEs. The first purpose of this chapter is to show that the flexible rate system would cause the trade of an ME like Finland with a CPE like the Soviet Union to have quite different macroeconomic consequences compared with those under fixed exchange rates. More concretely, an increase in this trade would have no employment or production generating effects under flexible rates in the long run. Instead, the Finnish markka would appreciate. In other words, a shift from Western sources to imports from the Soviet Union would mean that Finnish output would remain the same while the appreciation of the markka would increase the real income of those employed. This question is analysed in section two within a model incorporating Keynesian unemployment.

The type of model where labour and product markets could be in disequilibrium is traditionally seen as a short and middle-run phenomena, while in the long run Walrasian equilibrium prevails, that is, wages and prices clear the respective markets (van Wijnbergen 1985). We apply this kind of long-run modelling. Our second main question, the long-run consequences of CPE trade on the prices and welfare of MEs, is analysed by adding a CPE to a simple, but well-established, monetary model in section three (for the model, see Dornbusch 1980, ch. 7). In this model, wages have cleared the labour markets and full employment prevails. The main interest is in what happens to prices. Heuristically, if product prices are fully flexible in ME markets, one would expect an increase in the trade of an ME (home ME) with a CPE to improve its relative prices or terms of trade with respect to other MEs. Such an increase means a rise in the demand for the goods of the home ME and in the supply of its choice of importables. However, the real balance effects in the home ME may be so strong that this outcome is reversed. Trading with a CPE may worsen the terms of trade of the home ME; this implies a decrease in welfare for a given level of output.

In analysing these two main questions, dynamics is introduced. In section two, we assume that the adjustment in the CPE does not take place instantaneously. For long-run price and welfare effects, in section three, the adjustment in both the ME–ME trade and ME–CPE trade requires time.

EXCHANGE RATES AND OUTPUT

In the next two sections, we shall study a situation in which there are three countries: two MEs, ME1 (the home ME) and ME2; and a CPE. ME1 trades with both ME2 and the CPE while ME2 trades only with ME1. The CPE uses world market prices in its trade with ME1 and ties its exchange unit to the currency of ME2; furthermore, it sets a target for its trade balance and uses direct controls to obtain this target. We shall assume, for simplicity, that this target is equal to zero and not achieved instantaneously.

In this section there are three goods, the exportables of the three countries. ME1 is assumed small in the sense that the world market prices (*wmps*) of its two imports are exogenous to it. In addition, it charges the same price for its own exports both in ME and CPE markets. There is Keynesian unemployment in the MEs, the ME–CPE trade adjusts with a lag, and the MEs' exchange rate is flexible. For simplicity's sake, we assume that there are no capital movements between the two MEs. Accordingly, trade between MEs is balanced by the exchange rate, instantaneously as assumed. For the surpluses and deficits in ME–CPE trade we assume either some kind of clearing account arrangement, or that the CPE invests its surpluses in and borrows its deficits from the capital markets of the ME with which it trades, that is, ME1. In both cases, CPE–ME trade does not directly affect the demand or supply of the ME currencies because the balance of payments between the CPE and ME1 is zero. To avoid taxonomy, we shall assume the following: the ME1 import demand for the CPE goods, which is equal to its realised exports to the CPE due to bilateral balancing, constrains ME1–CPE trade. In this situation, over time, ME1 can export as much as it can import from the CPE. (For other alternatives of CPE behaviour see Tolonen [1988]. They do not essentially change these conclusions.)

Let us now turn to the model. Because ME1 is small, we can set the prices of its imports equal to unity by suitably choosing appropriate units. We may denote the relative price of ME1's exports in terms of its imports or, in this situation, the real exchange rate between ME currencies, by p which is equal to e/P, e standing for the nominal exchange rate and P for the domestic prices of ME1's exports.

The income-expenditure equation of ME1 can be presented as

$$Y = E(Y) + T^m + X^c - pM^c(Y, p) \tag{1}$$

where Y denotes ME1's output (or income measured in its own goods); E denotes its expenditures depending upon only Y, that is, there is no Laursen–Metzler effect; X^c denotes its exports to the CPE and M^c denotes its imports from the CPE. T^m is the ME1–ME2 trade balance:

$$T^m = X^m(Y^*, p) - pM^m(Y, p) \qquad (2)$$

where X^m is ME1's exports to ME2 and M^m its imports from ME2 depending on ME2's output, Y^*, and on ME1's output, Y, respectively, and on the relative prices.

ME2s income–expenditure relation, measured in its own products, referred to by a '*', is

$$Y^* = E^*(Y^*) - T^m/p \qquad (3)$$

With flexible exchange rates and no capital movements, the real exchange rate, p, is determined from the condition

$$T^m = 0 \qquad (4)$$

What are the consequences of either an increase in ME1–CPE trade or an entry of the CPE into ME1 markets? To avoid taxonomy we shall deal with only one case: ME1 shifts its imports from ME2 to CPE. For example, consider Finland's decision to buy Soviet rather than Swedish fighter planes.

The bilateral balance between ME1 and CPE is assumed to adjust with a lag. In the case under consideration, this means that even if Finnish consumers start to buy Soviet rather than Swedish goods, the Finnish exports to the Soviet Union do not increase instantaneously. The impact effect, which is no adjustment in the imports of the CPE, may now be obtained by inserting the shift variable, $-d\bar{M}^m$, for the autonomous decrease in ME1's imports from ME2 and the shift variable, $-d\bar{M}^c$, for the corresponding increase in ME1's imports from the CPE into equations (1)–(4). Assume that $-d\bar{M}^m = -d\bar{M}^c$. After some time, the CPE imports from ME1 start to rise. The end result may be obtained by differentiating and adding the condition for a balanced ME–CPE trade into these equations. In a differentiated form this balancing condition is $d(pM^c) = dX^c$. The results are summarised in Table 8.1.

As an impact effect, the real exchange rate appreciates when there is an increase in the imports of ME1 from the CPE. The reason is obvious. At the initial exchange rate, ME1 would have a surplus in its trade with ME2 which leads to an appreciation. In addition, the flexible exchange rate isolates ME2's output from changes in ME1, a

Table 8.1 Effects of a shift in ME1 from ME2 importables to CPE importables on ME1's output, Y, on its real exchange rate, p, and on ME2's output, Y^* when the exchange rate between MEs is flexible

	dY	dp	dY^*
impact effects	?	−	0
effects when CPE-ME1 trade is balanced	0	−	0

0 = effects, − = increase, + = decrease, ? = not unequivocal.

phenomena well known in the literature. What happens to ME1's output is less unequivocal. When written out we obtain from equations. (1)–(4)

$$\frac{dY}{d\bar{M}^c} = \frac{M^c - M^m\Omega + m_2^c}{\emptyset\, M^m\Omega} \qquad (6)$$

where $\emptyset > 0$ if $\Omega = \zeta^m + \eta^m - 1 > 0$.[1] ζ^m and η^m denote the price elasticity for ME1's imports from ME2 and for ME1's exports to ME2, respectively. The latter condition is the Marshall–Lerner condition. If this condition holds, two alternatives emerge from (6). If ME1's trade with the CPE is large relative to its trade with ME2, ME1's output rises as an impact effect. The exact condition is $M^c > M^m\Omega - m_2^c$ where $m_2^c = \delta M^c/\delta p < 0$. The reason for this is that appreciation decreases the relatively large bill of imports from the CPE which stimulates domestic demand in ME1 while real exports to the CPE remain unchanged. On the other hand, if the CPE share in ME1's overall trade is small, this stimulating effect is not important and output falls because of the consequences in trade with ME2. In the extreme situation where there is no initial trade with the CPE, the Marshall–Lerner condition is sufficient to guarantee that output falls – a result consistent with the literature for a two ME case.

With time, when the CPE has balanced its trade by increasing its imports from ME1, the results are straightforward (see Table 8.1). There are no changes in output in the two MEs but ME1's currency has appreciated. The consequences of appreciation, via ME trade, decrease ME1's output. However, this is offset exactly by the stimulating effect in CPE trade, that is, the increase in ME1's exports to the CPE. While output is unchanged, the real income of ME1 has risen, while that of ME2 has fallen. Because of the appreciation, ME1's consumers can obtain a larger bundle of goods, both domestic and imported.

It is interesting to compare these results with the ones in a situation in which the exchange rates in MEs are fixed. From equations (1)–(3) we easily obtain the effects of an import shift in ME1. They are represented in Table 8.2.

The impact effects of a shift in ME1's imports from ME2 to the imports from a CPE are now clearly negative for both MEs. ME2's output falls due to the decrease in ME1's demand for its goods, while ME1's output falls because of repercussion effects from ME2 to ME1. With time, a balanced ME1–CPE trade causes an increase in ME1's output and employment. The reason is the increased CPE demand for ME1 goods made possible by the increase in ME1's imports. Even if the ME2 demand for ME1 goods falls because of the decrease in ME2 income, the increase in the CPE demand more than offsets this. These results, in Table 8.2, clearly contrast those in a situation of flexible rates (Table 8.1). The general conclusion is that the special effects of CPE trade crucially depend upon the type of exchange rate system chosen by the ME.

Next, let us focus in more detail on the dynamics of the model. For this purpose we may write the impact effect under flexible exchange rates from (1)–(4) as

$$dp = (m_1^m \, dY - dM^c)/M^m \Omega \tag{7}$$

where $m_1^m = \delta M^m/\delta Y > 0$, is the marginal propensity to import from ME2. In a similar way we may obtain the effect with balanced ME1–CPE trade as

$$dp = -dM^c/M^m \Omega \tag{8}$$

From (7) and (8) two alternatives may be seen. If ME1's output, Y, falls initially, there is an overshooting in the appreciation of the ME1 exchange rate. The impact appreciation is larger than when balancing has taken place in the ME–CPE trade. As discussed in connection to equation (6), this happens when the initial share of the CPE in ME1's overall trade is small. When ME1's exports to the CPE start to rise, ME1's output increases along with its imports from ME2. This explains the overshooting. Accordingly, less appreciation is needed over time to balance the trade between MEs. If the initial CPE share is large, no overshooting takes place; consequently, Y increases as an impact effect. By comparing (7) and (8), we may see directly that the

Table 8.2 Effects of a shift in ME1 from ME2 importables to CPE importables when the ME exchange rate is fixed

	dY	dY^*
impact effects	–	–
effects when CPE-ME1 trade is balanced	+	–

Source: Denotations as in Table 8.1.

impact appreciation is smaller than the one with balanced ME1–CPE trade.

This is true regardless as to how we choose the dynamic process. As an illustration, we may adopt the following adjustment presentation where the CPE reacts to its flow and stock imbalances of trade, denoted by $pM^c - X^c$ and $-\bar{R}^c$, respectively:[2]

$$\dot{X}^c = -h_1 R^c - h_2(X^c - pM^c), \quad h_1, h_2 > 0 \tag{9a}$$

$$\dot{R}^c = X^c - pM^c \tag{9b}$$

When the CPE has a surplus either in its trade balance or cumulative trade balance (the clearing account in case of Finland), it increases its imports from ME1. The larger the surplus, the larger is this increase. The system is stable if θ is positive.[3] For the case in which the flow balance situation has a relatively strong influence on the CPE's trading behaviour, the time paths for a shift from ME2 exports to CPE exports can be shown to be similar to those in Figure 8.1.

PRICES AND WELFARE

We now turn to the long-run consequences of CPE trade. The main question to be studied is what happens to prices and welfare in MEs if, either an increase occurs in CPE–ME trade, or there is entry of a CPE into ME markets. The basic framework is the same, as in section two (see p. 000). The main differences are that the prices clear the ME markets and the ME outputs are exogenously determined. These assumptions are standard for long-run analysis. The exchange rate between the two MEs is assumed fixed. This does not mean that the trade between MEs would be unbalanced, an impossible situation in long-run analysis. We shall, in fact, introduce a

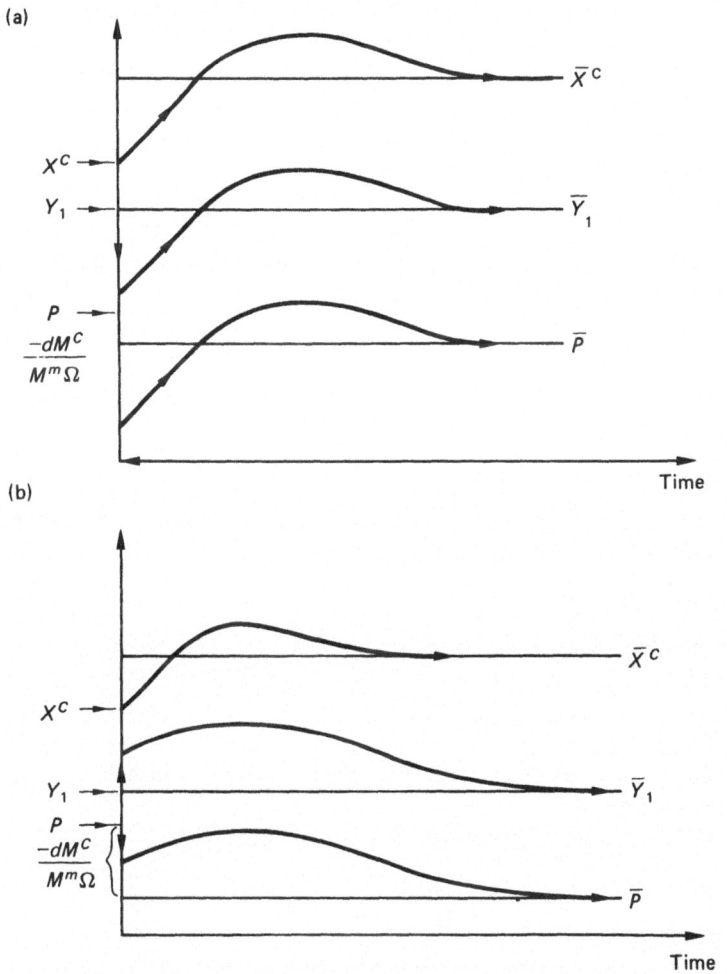

Figure 8.1 Effects of a shift from ME2 importables to CPE importables on ME1's exports to the CPE, X^c, output, Y, and exchange rate, P

Initial CPE share in ME1's overall trade (a) small, (b) large.

monetary adjustment process in MEs leading to balanced intra-ME trade. In addition, this makes the long-run results to be obtained comparable with the outcome of section two.

There are two MEs, one CPE, and two goods, the exportable of ME1, good 1, and the exportable of ME2 and the CPE, good 2. Note that because prices clear the ME markets, only two goods are needed for the analysis. Their prices are denoted by P and P^*, respectively. In choosing the units, we can set the exchange rate between the MEs equal to one.

ME1's stock demand for money, in real terms, L, is assumed to depend on its real output, Y. In linear form,

$$L = kPY \tag{10}$$

Nominal money holdings of ME1, H, are adjusted to the desired level according to the rule

$$\dot{H} = b(L - H), b > 0 \tag{11}$$

Nominal expenditure is income less hoarding. From equations (10) and (11):

$$PE = PY(1 - bk) + bH \tag{12}$$

Without essentially affecting the conclusions, a simplifying assumption $bk = 1$ can be made. Therefore

$$PE = bH \tag{13}$$

From (13), ME1's demand for good 1, D_1, can be presented as follows

$$D_1 = u(P/P^*)bH \tag{14}$$

where u denotes the expenditure share of good 1 in ME1's overall expenditures.

ME1's demand for good 2, D_2, is from (13)–(14)

$$D_2 = PE - D_1 = (1 - u)bH \tag{15}$$

For ME2, we denote the corresponding equations by adding an asterisk to the variables of (10)–(15). In what follows, we assume for simplicity's sake that $b = b^*$. [Assuming differing speeds of money market adjustment in MEs would add tedious taxonomy to the presentation.]

Using equations (14) and its unwritten counterpart for ME2, the equilibrium condition in the markets of good 1 is

$$b(uH + u^*H^*) + PX^c = PY \tag{16}$$

where buH is the nominal demand of ME1 and bu^*H^* of ME2 for good 1. The term PX^b is the nominal import demand of the CPE. PY is ME1's nominal supply of its product.

The corresponding condition for good 2 is from equation (12)

$$b((1 - u)H + (1 - u^*)H^*) = P^*Y^* + P^*M^c \tag{17}$$

where the term P^*M^c stands for the nominal export supply of the CPE and P^*Y^* for the supply of ME2 while the left-hand side is the ME's demand for good 2.

There is a connection between money markets and the trade balance in MEs. This is the well known and well established monetary adjustment mechanism (for a detailed presentation, see Frenkel and Mussa [1985]). By definition, the trade balance is output minus expenditure. On the other hand (as seen from (10), (11) and (13)), this is equal to hoarding. Accordingly, for ME1,

$$T = PY - bH = \dot{H} \tag{18}$$

where T is ME1's overall trade balance.

For the ME-CPE trade, we assume an adjustment like that presented in equation (9).

Let us now turn to the main problem of this section: what are the consequences of changes in the volume of ME1–CPE trade? In the text proper, we shall study 'true' long run effects, that is, we analyse such a situation where both the monetary adjustment and the CPE–ME trade adjustment are completed. For simplicity, we deal only with the entry situation, that is, the initial situation where there is no ME–CPE trade. The consequences of having some initial trade do not essentially affect the conclusions.

Assume that the CPE enters the ME markets because it wants to import dX^c of good 1. The effects of this when adjustments are completed may be obtained by setting $\dot{H} = \dot{H}^* = \dot{X}^c = \dot{R}^c = 0$ in equation (18) and its counterpart for ME2, and in (9). The steady state values obtained in this way are inserted into equation (16). Differentiating, this yields

$$(\hat{P}/P^*)/dX^c = \frac{P^*}{\theta (1 - u) + \Psi} (1/b \, (H + H^*)) \tag{19}$$

where $\hat{}$ denotes the relative change, θ is the share of ME1 in the ME output. Ψ is a weighted sum of elasticities of expenditure shares n and n^*: $n = (P/P^*) (u'/u)$; $n^* = (P/P^*) (u^{*'}/u^*)$; and $\Psi = - \{\theta u n + (1 - \theta)u^* n^*\}$. Obviously, much depends on the sign of Ψ. The sign of the derivative of u is negative if a rise in the relative price of good 1 reduces nominal expenditures in ME1 on good 1. This occurs when demand elasticity of good 1, in ME1, is larger than one in absolute value. The derivative is positive if this absolute value is smaller than one. The same applies to u^* and ME2. Therefore, if the demand elasticities for good 1 are larger than unity in both MEs, Ψ is clearly positive and the ME–CPE-trade leads to an increase in the terms of trade and welfare of ME1, while the welfare of ME2 falls. This result is what we heuristically expected and needs no further explanation.

If the demand elasticities for good 1 are less than unity, Ψ is negative, especially, if they are so low that $\Psi < -\theta(1-u)$. A deterioration of the terms of trade and welfare of ME1 follows. As seen from (19), this is more likely to happen if ME1 is small compared with ME2, that is, θ is small. What is the reason for this counter-intuitive outcome? When the CPE enters the ME markets, the low demand elasticities for good 1 would, *ceteris paribus*, lead to a very large increase in its price. Such an increase causes such a strong decrease in the real balances of ME1, H/P, that this real balance effect more than annuls the original effect of the CPE demand. With respect to the stability of the adjustment process, the result is that for low elasticities the system may be unstable but that the counter-intuitive results obtained above are not necessarily so.[4]

In conclusion, if a small ME faces an elastic domestic and foreign demand for its products, the trade with a CPE also improves its terms of trade and welfare in the long run. A rather similar result was obtained for middle-run disequilibrium situations where either the real income of the ME rises under flexible exchange rates, or employment improves under fixed exchange rates. However, if the demand elasticities are low, a deterioration in the terms of trade and welfare may ensue in the long run.

CONCLUDING REMARKS

The main question of this chapter was whether an increase in the trade with a CPE is beneficial to an ME. Such an increase was assumed to ensue from a shift in the import sources of this ME. As could be easily shown, the conclusions also hold for other autonomous shifts. A three period approach was applied to analyse this question so that the short and middle run disequilibrium prevail in labour and goods markets in MEs, while in the long run, prices clear the markets. In the short run, under flexible exchange rates between MEs, if the initial share of CPE trade in the overall trade of the ME under study,

ME1, is small, a shift from ME importables to CPE importables leads to a decrease in ME1's output and to an 'overly large' appreciation of its currency. If this CPE share is large, the output of ME1 increases, while the appreciation is smaller than in the middle run. In the middle run, with a completed adjustment in the CPE trade, this shift turns out to have no output effects. Because of appreciation, however, the real income of ME1 increases while that of the other ME, not trading with the CPE, falls. In the long run, this outcome was qualified. As it turned out, if the ME demand elasticities for ME1's good are low, the real balance effect can lead an increase in CPE–ME trade to cause a fall in the terms of trade and welfare of ME1.

The results obtained have additional implications. First, in the short run under flexible exchange rates, for an ME with a high relative share of CPE trade the import source change discussed above is more advantageous than for countries where this initial share is small. Finland, with its Soviet share at times more than twenty per cent, would have more reason to buy Soviet goods rather than OECD goods of the other MEs. Secondly, the exchange rate system chosen in an ME has decisive influence on the consequences of CPE trade as was shown by the comparison with the outcome under fixed exchange rates. In the latter situation, an increase in the CPE trade has tangible employment effects. In Finland, this makes trading with the Soviet Union politically more marketable than if the effects were on prices and exchange rates as in the flexible rate case or if the long run consequences were taken into account. After all, in such cases it is the firms and share owners which are likely to draw the direct benefit from an intensified trade with the Soviet Union in the form of increased profits.

Notes

1. $\emptyset = s + m_1^c + [M^c m_1^m / M^m \Omega] + [m_1^m m_2^c / M^m \Omega] > 0$ and $\Omega = \zeta^m + \eta^m - 1$ where $m_1^m = \delta M^m / \delta Y > 0$ (ME1's marginal propensity to import from ME2); $m_1^c = \delta M^c / \zeta Y > 0$ (ME1's marginal propensity to import from the CPE); $s = 1 - \delta E / \delta Y$ (ME1's marginal propensity to save, having a value between 0 and 1); $m_2^c = \delta M^c / \delta p$, the sign is not unambiguous. $\zeta^m = - (\delta M^m / \delta p)/(M^m / p) > 0$ (price elasticity for ME1's imports from ME2) and $h^m = (\delta X^m / \delta p)/(X^m / p) > 0$ (price elasticity of exports to ME2). As can be seen, $\emptyset > 0$ if the Marshall–Lerner condition for the trade between MEs holds and m_2^c is not very large in absolute value.

2. The system (9) applies both to fixed and flexible rate situations. It may be seen as a linear formulation of the way in which Portes (1979) deals with the question. Krugman (1983) has a formulation for OPEC import behaviour identical to the system if $h_1 = 0$. For our purposes such a formulation has the disadvantage that CPE surpluses (deficits) accumulate during the adjustment process which are not spent (paid for). (9) could easily be reformulated to cover such situations where the CPE adjusts its exports.
3. Solve (1) and (4) for $Y = Y(X^c, Y^*)$ and $p = p(X^c, Y^*)$. From (1) and (4), $X^c - pM^c = Y - E(Y)$. Linearise in the neighbourhood of the steady state, referred to by ss. (9) becomes

$$\begin{pmatrix} \dot{X}^c \\ \dot{R}^c \end{pmatrix} = \begin{pmatrix} -h_2 sY' & -h_1 \\ sY' & 0 \end{pmatrix} \begin{pmatrix} X^c - X^c_{ss} \\ R^c - R^c_{ss} \end{pmatrix}$$

If $Y' = \delta Y/\delta X^c > 0$, trace $= -h_2 sY' < 0$ and det $= h_1 sY' > 0$ and the system is stable. From (1) and (4) when differentiating with respect X^c, $Y' = 1/\emptyset$.

4. This can be shown, for example, by studying the special case where the adjustment in the CPE–ME trade is instantaneous. In this situation, it can be shown that the stability condition is

$$\frac{(1 - u + u^*) \theta (1 - \theta) + \Psi}{\theta(1 - \theta) + \Psi} > 0$$

If Ψ is positive, the equilibrium is always stable. If Ψ is negative, possibilities of instability emerge only if the consumption share of good 1 in ME1 is considerably larger than the share in ME2.

Bibliography

R. DORNBUSCH, *Open Economy Macroeconomics* (New York: Basic Books, 1980).

J. A. FRENKEL and M. M. MUSSA, 'Assets Markets, Exchange Rates and the Balance of Payments', in R. Jones and P. Kenen, eds., *Handbook of International Economics*, 2 (Amsterdam: North-Holland, 1985) pp. 680–747.

P. KRUGMAN, 'Oil and the Dollar', in J. Bhandari and B. Putnam, eds., *Economic Interdependence and Exchange Rates* (Cambridge, MA: MIT Press, 1983) pp. 179–190.

R. PORTES, 'Internal and External Balance in a Centrally Planned Economy', *J. Comp. Econ.*, 3, 4:325–345 (December 1979).

Y. TOLONEN, 'Some Macroeconomic Consequences of Trade with Centrally Planned Economies', *J. Comp. Econ.*, 12, 3: 345–361 (September 1988).

S. VAN WIJNBERGEN, 'Oil Price Shocks, Unemployment, Investment and the Current Account: An Intertemporal Disequilibrium Analysis', *Rev. Econ. Stud.*, 52, 4:627–645 (October 1985).

T. A. WOLF, 'Economic Stabilization in Planned Economies: Toward an Analytical Framework', *IMF Staff Papers*, 32, 2:78–131 (June 1985).

9 An Appearance of Dual Attachment in the Soviet Union's Imports: Variations in Imports from the West in relation to Imports from CMEA Countries
Urpo Kivikari

BACKGROUND FACTORS

Annual variations in Soviet imports from the West are caused partly by changes in supply. World market prices fluctuate. The activity of Western firms on the Soviet market varies with economic development in the West. The trade policy of capitalist countries offers sometimes more, sometimes less free scope for exports to the Soviet Union. The availability of Western capital and the terms of financing exports to the Soviet Union also vary.

On the other hand, Soviet demands on Western markets are variable. The impact of unique changes and turns in the Soviet economy may be responsible for deviations in the trend of Soviet imports. Repeated changes are presumably brought about by changes in Soviet production, the (unforeseen) development of CMEA trade, movements in export and import prices, fluctuation in exports to the West and variable use of operations such as countertrade.

Figure 1 illustrates the assumed influence of two crucial factors particularly characteristic of the Soviet Union. They are the discrepancy between actual production and planned production and the Soviet Union's prevailing purchasing power on Western markets.

When actual production deviates from the annual production plan, the need for imports also changes. While an imported Western

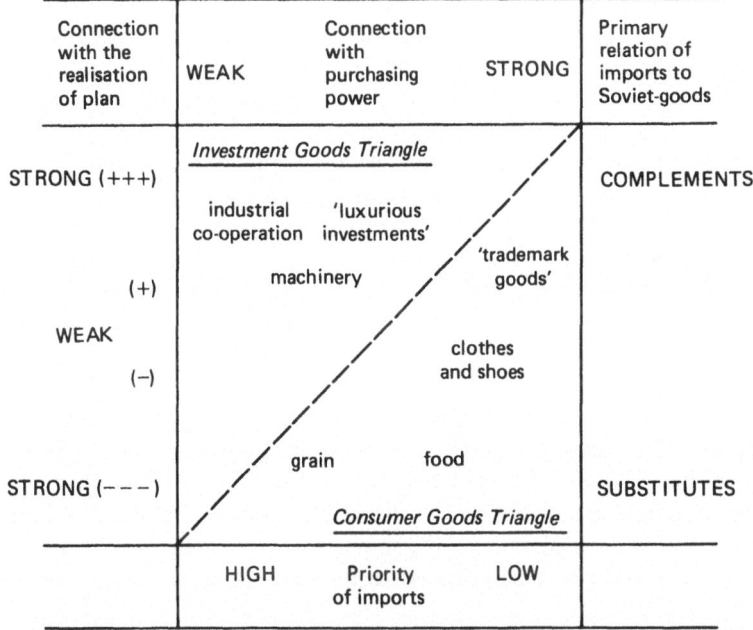

Figure 9.1 The linkage of Soviet imports from the West with the realisation of production plans and the purchasing power on western markets

commodity may be a substitute for a certain Soviet product of the same kind, it also becomes a complement to those domestic products that are used together with it. Presumably imports from the West react to fluctuations in Soviet production – parallel with respect to complements and in inversely with respect to substitutes. In some cases it is more relevant to regard the imported product as a substitute; in other cases imports are primarily complementary.

In Figure 9.1, grain imported from the West is an instance of a substitute for the Soviet Union's own production. Machinery over a one-year span acts more as a complement than as a substitute.[1] Complementary Western inputs also appear in industrial cooperation projects or as a 'finishing touch' in building projects ('luxurious investments'). Turnkey projects and imports of many consumer goods are probably not dependent on the simultaneous development of the Soviet Union's own production, thus tend to be neither complements nor substitutes.

An increase of receipts and reserves in convertible currency makes it possible to purchase more of all goods on Western markets. However in reality, a variation in Soviet purchasing unequally influences different imports. Most preferential imports, like grain, are almost independent of current purchasing power. In the case of industrial co-operation the use of special arrangements such as compensation in-kind might weaken its dependence on current Soviet purchasing power. Imports of consumer goods usually respond more strongly than other imports to changes in the availability of convertible currency.

In the simplified illustration of Figure 9.1, the role of imports from other CMEA countries is ignored. However, the purpose of this paper is to examine how annual variations in certain imports from the West relate to changes in similar imports from other European CMEA countries (the CMEA Six). Although it is quite evident that imports from these two regions are mutually co-ordinated, significant interaction between these imports has not always been found in empirical research.[2] Yet due to the stable socialist division of labour and co-ordinated planning, one might expect that imports from the CMEA would be closely linked to fluctuations in the Soviet economy.

THE DATA

This study covers the years 1965–83. During this period of stable political leadership, no radical changes occurred in the policies or the methods pursued in Soviet foreign trade.[3] In this study, parallel use of Soviet and Western statistics is employed wherever possible. However, the comparability of these two sets of statistics is problematic because the methodology and classifications are different. Moreover, Soviet imports have been collected by analysing Western exports to the Soviet Union in OECD statistics.[4] Finally, the Soviet Union has been a net importer of the commodities studied in this chapter (see below). Yet at the same time the selected subgroups represent all the main commodity groups of Soviet imports (see table at the top of the next page).

ON THE RELATION BETWEEN VARIATIONS IN TWO IMPORTS

Since in intra-CMEA trade long-term perspectives are given prominence when organising the division of labour and industrial co-

	OECD Statistics (SITC)	Soviet Statistics (CTN Categories)
Grain	041, 043, 044, 045	700 (excluding rice)
Soap, cleansing and polishing preparations	554	96503
Paper and paperboard, articles of paper	641, 642	506, 507
Textile and leather machinery, food-processing machines	724, 727	14
Footwear	851	930

operation, and since intra-CMEA prices are more stable than world-market prices, one might expect relatively small annual deviations in the trends of Soviet imports from CMEA countries. In accordance with these assumptions, the Soviet Union's total imports from European CMEA countries have varied less than total imports from the West (Table 9.1).[5] The same situation has also prevailed with respect to total Soviet exports to the CMEA Six versus those to the West. The difference between the two trade systems became especially apparent after the oil price increases of 1973 and 1979–80. The slower reactions in the value of exports to the CMEA Six is indicated by significant correlation coefficient ($r = 0.796$) with lagged changes in exports to the West. The correlation between simultaneous changes in the two imports is positive but relatively low.

Due to long-term bilateral agreements, governmental planned trade, rather stable prices, and so forth, the Soviet Union's imports and exports with other CMEA countries have varied much more uniformly ($r = 0.728$) than the trade flows with the West ($r = 0.212$). *The development of imports from the West has been more unstable, but at the same time more flexible and more independent in relation to corresponding exports.*

A few conclusions may be drawn from the figures presented in Table 9.2 about the commodity imports studied. First, in high priority imports of grain, annual fluctuations have been at their widest. Second, the crucial factor for variations of certain imports has not been the origin of the imports, but the standard deviation of changes has usually been greater for the less important import source (the one with which the Soviet Union conducts less trade). So the *less signifi-*

Table 9.1 Annual percentage changes in the Soviet Union's foreign trade in 1965–83

Year	Imports from the West (x)	Imports from the East (x')	Exports to the West (y)	Exports to the East (y')
1966	8.78	−4.54	16.44	3.61
1967	3.87	13.02	9.54	7.43
1968	16.62	9.99	8.16	10.96
1969	14.67	6.25	8.56	9.24
1970	10.99	9.85	4.67	8.42
1971	2.37	9.19	14.24	6.49
1972	27.80	18.75	−1.77	12.25
1973	28.60	7.74	42.29	9.55
1974	28.93	9.13	50.11	17.62
1975	44.96	30.91	−1.33	12.58
1979	18.73	3.24	35.89	9.20
1980	17.08	7.27	22.78	11.45
1981	14.13	9.68	9.26	15.98
1982	4.22	15.37	8.88	8.65
1983	−0.92	11.16	4.17	10.06
Mean	14.06	10.96	14.78	11.65
Standard deviation	12.73	7.42	14.99	5.64
Correlation coefficients				
$x_{t-1}, x'_t; y_t, y'_t$	0.353	0.353	−0.116	−0.116
$x_{t-1}, x'_t; y_{t-1}, y'_t$	−0.150	−0.150	0.796*	0.796*
$x_t, x'_{t-1}; y_t, y'_{t-1}$	0.093	0.093	0.101	0.101
$x_t, y_t; x'_t, y'_t$	0.212	0.728*	0.212	0.728*

Source: Soviet Foreign Trade Statistics
* Significant at the 1 per cent level.

cant part of the two imports has been more sensitive. Third, if Soviet imports from the East and from the West had compensated for each other's fluctuations, their annual changes would correlate negatively. The same would result, if the supply from these areas, when moving in a reverse direction to each other, had been the determining factor for Soviet imports. However in all the cases, annual variations correlate positively, approximately like total imports ($r = 0.353$). *This result refers to the dominant influence of Soviet demand (= imports need/purchasing power) on variations of both imports*. Of course, this conclusion is more indicative than convincing, since correlation cannot prove any causality and moreover, only one

Table 9.2 Annual percentage changes in the Soviet Union's imports from the West (X) and the CMEA six (X') in 1963–1983

Product	Imports in 1983	Annual changes		Correlation coefficient		
		Mean	Standard deviation	x_t, x'_t (n=18)	x_{t-1}, x'_t (n=17)	x_t, x'_{t-1} (n=17)
Grain						
From the West[1]	3,718	9.51	82.71	0.377	0.344	−0.214
From the East[1]	62	−0.28	117.16			
Paper and paperboard						
From the West[1]	285	11.07	25.21	0.209	0.327	−0.145
From the East[1]	46	17.98	24.37			
From the West[2]	630	6.58	14.67	0.266	0.183	−0.165
From the East[2]	64	12.15	35.63			
Machinery						
From the West[1]	218	11.07	44.48	0.308	0.155	−0.127
From the East[1]	1,299	11.10	13.73			
Footwear						
From the West[1]	151	14.79	37.70	0.567*	0.326	−0.165
From the East[1]	393	8.21	10.50			
From the West[3]	9	8.26	39.53	0.376	0.317	−0.042
From the East[3]	37	2.91	12.73			

Source: *Soviet Foreign Trade Statistics*.

* Significant at the 1 per cent level.

1 = mill. roubles; 2 = thousand tons; 3 = mill. pairs
4 = textile and leather machinery, food processing machines

correlation (footwear) is significant. In Table 9.2 the data of the whole time span, 1965–83, is included, which is not in all cases reasonable. In regression analyses, justifiable division and/or shortening of some time-series will produce different results. Fourth, the correlation usually weakens, if instead of simultaneous variations either of them is lagged.

DETERMINATION OF SOVIET IMPORTS FROM THE WEST

Regression Equations

In the following regression analyses the dependent variables are percentile annual changes in value or volume of particular Soviet imports from the West (grain; paper products; soap, and so forth; machinery for light industry; footwear). Explanatory variables are percentile annual changes of the commodity's Soviet production,[6] imports from other European CMEA countries, import price and 'free' purchasing power on the Western market.

We may for a very good reason presume that grain production and imports from the West fluctuate contrariwise. In other cases, imports from the West and *domestic production for similar types of goods* may vary annually in parallel fashion. When the purpose is to increase or decrease the total supply of a certain commodity in the Soviet Union, the desired changes may be shared between domestic production and imports.

The correlation mentioned above about simultaneous changes of imports from the West and the CMEA Six obviously needs to be studied further. But is it at all correct and well-enough established to explain variations in Western imports by simultaneous variation *in imports from the CMEA Six*? The fact is that because of different priorities and trade mechanisms most imports from the CMEA Six are actually determined earlier in the year than those imports from the West occurring in the same year. This is due to the long-range and inter-governmental characteristics of CMEA imports as well as to the Soviet Union's desire to save convertible currency.

As far as imports from the CMEA area are decided earlier than – or simultaneous with – corresponding imports from the West, there is no excuse to include this factor as an explanatory variable in the model.

The volume of imports from the CMEA countries gives unambiguous information about the role of its input in satisfying the needs of Soviet imports. The value variable in rouble terms would not be as informative as the volume, since the value in roubles indicates neither the amounts imported nor the value and expense of purchases that is in any way commensurate with the data about imports from the West. That is why the volume variable of imports from the East has been used when available. However, grain and machine imports from the CMEA Six are value variables.

The Soviet Union's *purchasing power on Western markets* could be demonstrated by many alternative variables. Here the aim has been to find an indicator of 'free' or 'natural' purchasing power, which would not reflect prevailing needs for imports from the West. *The chosen variable is the revenues of oil exports to the West minus the expense of grain imports from the West (Argentina included) in the same year.* Compared to oil income the other important sources of convertible currency, such as the sale of gold, platinum and diamonds or foreign borrowing, have been easier to change in light of the respective needs for imports. Due to its high priority imports of grain have been subtracted to reveal 'free' or 'natural' Soviet purchasing power on Western markets.

The price index of grain imports from the West has been available. In other cases, the changes in unit values have been used to approximate the price movements over time.

The following *annual percentage changes* are explanatory variables in the equations:

Q_t = Soviet production (of the commodity studied) from Soviet statistics

I_t = imports from the other European CMEA countries from Soviet statistics

W_t = purchasing power (equals oil exports to the West minus grain imports from the West) from a combination of Soviet and OECD statistics

O_t = oil exports (to the market under consideration) from OECD statistics

P_t = price index or movement in unit values from Soviet and OECD statistics

In the testing of the various models no alternative, which would all in all be better than the *model of relative first differences*, was found. Annual changes of Soviet production and purchasing power are included in equations alternatively as simultaneous variables or as variables lagged by one year compared to the corresponding change in imports. Both variants of these variables are worth testing in view of Soviet decision-making.[7]

Equations explaining fluctuations in Soviet imports of paper products and footwear have been estimated separately for imports from Finland and from the other OECD countries. This division has been implemented because of the great significance of these imports from Finland and because of the peculiarities of Finnish–Soviet trade. Finland has been a very important supplier of both commodities, namely, a 79 per cent share of Soviet imports of paper products from the West, and a 52 per cent share of Soviet imports of footwear from the West for 1983. In contrast to other imports from the West, the Soviet Union pays for its imports from Finland in *clearing roubles* used in their bilateral trade, which is based on both five-year framework agreements and annual trade protocols between the two countries. The balance of the clearing account bears no interest (when below an agreed limit of 300 million roubles).[8]

Results of Estimation

The grain imports from the CMEA Six – an insignificant factor as such (Table 9.2) – seem to be the dominating explanatory variable in the equations of grain imports from the West (Table 9.3).[9] The high correlation between these two imports ($r_{1\&2} = 0.929$, $r_{3\&4} = 0.926$, $r_{5\&6} = 0.858$) indicates that what has been decisive for variations in Soviet imports has been the need for imports rather than the supply situation in the exporting countries.

When Soviet imports from the CMEA Six are included in the equations, the coefficient of Soviet grain production is not significant. However, *lagged variation in domestic production has an assumed connection with changes of imports from the West* ($r_1 = -0.512$, $r_3 = 0.496$, $r_5 = -0.602$). When Soviet imports from the CMEA Six are excluded (lower part of Table 9.3), equation (5) has the highest R^2 and includes the volume of grain imports as the dependent variable and as an explanatory variable the lagged change in domestic production. In this equation the price elasticity is close to zero. A mutual interdependence prevails between price and Soviet imports. A high price diminishes Soviet imports, imports which on the other hand affect the world-market price.[10] As presumed, *the change in purchasing power* (= oil exports) *has no noticeable connection with the variation on grain imports from the West* ($-0.292 < r < 0.100$) and has an incorrect sign in most equations.

The value as well as the volume of Soviet imports of soaps and cleansing and polishing preparations have reacted unambiguously and strongly to changes in prices (Table 9.4). The lagged change of domestic production has a negative sign, whereas for changes in the same year the sign is a positive one. If imports from the CMEA Six are considered primary in satisfying Soviet needs, the negative sign in the equations indicates that imports from the West compensate for fluctuations in these imports. Altogether, the equations of Table 9.4 might be interpreted to mean that *the imports of soap and cleansing and polishing preparations from the West are determined primarily by changes in purchasing power and domestic production in the year preceding the imports and by the development of imports from the CMEA Six and price changes in the same year.*

Table 9.3 Regression results for annual variations (1971–1983) in the Soviet Union's imports of grain from the West* (t-values in parentheses)

	Soviet statistics (roubles)		OECD statistics ($)		OECD statistics (volume)	
	(1)	(2)	(3)	(4)	(5)	(6)
Constant	13.200	28.730	10.344	31.981	12.131	15.800
	(0.82)	(1.86)	(0.56)	(1.84)	(0.79)	(0.93)
Q_{t-1}	−0.316		−0.282		−0.519	
	(0.83)		(0.65)		(1.43)	
Q_t		0.566		0.579		0.513
		(1.12)		(1.02)		(0.93)
I_t	0.532	0.551	0.595	0.605	0.445	0.499
	(5.97)	(7.29)	(5.84)	(7.13)	(5.25)	(6.05)
O_{t-1}	−0.035		0.072		0.157	
	(0.06)		(0.11)		(0.29)	
O_t		−0.902		−0.062		−4.888
		(1.31)		(1.37)		(0.65)
P_t	−0.173	0.629	−0.254	−0.716	−0.570	−0.164
	(0.38)	(0.86)	(0.49)	(0.87)	(1.32)	(0.21)
R^2	0.940	0.948	0.935	0.946	0.936	0.026
D-W	2.43	2.42	2.02	1.79	2.13	1.94
(n)	(12)	(12)	(12)	(12)	(12)	(12)
Constant	30.575	60.024	28.803	66.368	26.671	44.172
	(0.83)	(0.98)	(0.72)	(1.48)	(0.85)	(1.16)
Q_{t-1}	−1.386		−1.481		−1.414	
	(1.78)		(1.70)		(2.12)	
Q_t		0.630		0.649		0.571
		(0.25)		(0.43)		(0.44)
Q_{t-1}	−0.399		−0.335		−0.462	
	(0.31)		(0.23)		(0.42)	
O_t		−1.879		−2.135		−1.374
		(0.63)		(1.04)		(0.80)
P_t	0.516	1.606	0.517	1.789	0.006	0.722
	(0.51)	(0.63)	(0.46)	(0.83)	(0.01)	(0.39)
R^2	0.286	0.122	0.266	0.132	0.385	0.108
D-W	2.40	2.10	2.35	2.04	2.36	2.17

* Import of grain from the OECD countries and Argentina.

Table 9.4 Regression results for annual variations (1965–78) in the Soviet Union's imports of soap and cleaning and polishing preparations from the West* (t-values in parentheses)

	OECD statistics (volume)		OECD statistics ($)	
	(1)	(2)	(3)	(4)
Constant	23.083	9.142	23.362	9.647
	(2.10)	(0.76)	(2.00)	(0.81)
Q_{t-1}	−0.933		−0.973	
	(1.61)		(1.59)	
Q_t		0.498		0.479
		(0.77)		(0.74)
I_t	−0.142	−0.129	−0.142	−0.130
	(2.02)	(1.62)	(1.92)	(1.68)
W_{t-1}	0.250		0.260	
	(2.84)		(2.79)	
W_t		−0.217		−0.250
		(2.05)		(2.37)
P_t	−1.601	−1.263	−0.693	−0.336
	(8.09)	(5.30)	(3.30)	(1.42)
R^2	0.955	0.928	0.853	0.790
D-W	2.52	1.67	2.61	1.70
(n)	(12)	(13)	(12)	(13)

* The data are available only for the years 1965–78.

In explaining Soviet *imports of machines for textile, leather and food processing industries* by far the best model both in regard to R^2 and Durbin–Watson Statistics is equation (1) in Table 9.5. *Imports from the West reinforce with a one-year lag the development of domestic production, whereas the imports from the CMEA Six have a significant negative sign.* The time span from decision-making to realisation of the imports of machinery studied may explain the independence of purchases from the degree of stringency in foreign exchange in the same and the preceding year.

The variation in Soviet imports of paper and paperboard from the CMEA Six is the best explanatory variable with a significant positive sign in all equations, when imports from Finland are excluded (Table 9.6). 'Marginal' exporters in the CMEA area and in the West have shared in the changes in Soviet imports of paper products. The

Table 9.5 Regression results for annual variations (1971–83) in the Soviet Union's imports of textile, leather and food-processing machines from the West* (t-values in parentheses)

	Soviet statistics (roubles)		OECD statistics ($)	
	(1)	(2)	(3)	(4)
Constant	36.314	32.146	−1.080	−21.234
	(2.45)	(0.84)	(0.05)	(0.49)
Q_{t-1}	3.323		2.974	
	(3.54)		(1.97)	
Q_t		−2.670		1.352
		(1.33)		(0.59)
I_t	−2.615	−0.583	−0.251	−1.911
	(2.97)	(0.35)	(0.18)	(0.99)
W_{t-1}	0.020		0.170	
	(0.18)		(0.95)	
W_t		0.010		−0.045
		(0.04)		(0.16)
R^2	0.811	0.475	0.660	0.455
D-W	2.11	1.80	1.40	1.37
(n)	(12)	(13)	(12)	(13)

* The data are available only for the years 1971–83.

variation of imports from the CMEA Six correlates much more strongly with variations in this part of imports from the West ($0.600 < r < 0.743$) than with total imports (including Finland) (see Table 9.2). The coefficients of price variable indicate that *price elasticity of Soviet demand is close to zero*. The changes in domestic production or purchasing power do not seem to have a stable effect on imports of paper products. All the equations are quite similar as regards R^2 and the negative autocorrelation demonstrated by the Durbin–Watson statistics.

Regression results concerning Soviet *imports of paper products from Finland* are quite modest, except in equation (5) (Table 9.7). *The lagged change in purchasing power has a significant positive sign.* The change in the same year has a weaker positive effect. The influence of other explanatory variables seems to be ambiguous. So the majority of Soviet imports of paper products from the West, namely, *imports from Finland, is determined within the framework of*

Table 9.6 Regression results for annual variations (1965–3) in the Soviet Union's imports of paper and paperboard from the West (excluding Finland) (t-values in parentheses)

	Soviet statistics (roubles)		Soviet statistics (volume)		OECD statistics ($)	
	(1)	(2)	(3)	(4)	(5)	(6)
Constant	−10.364	−8.035	−10.701	−8.428	1.706	−0.193
	(0.89)	(0.65)	(0.92)	(0.67)	(0.16)	(0.02)
Q_{t-1}	0.149		0.149		−1.268	
	(0.05)		(0.05)		(0.49)	
Q_t		1.092		1.185		0.620
		(0.50)		(0.54)		(0.32)
I_t	0.871	0.661	0.883	0.666	0.931	0.656
	(2.52)	(3.00)	(2.56)	(3.00)	(2.89)	(3.36)
W_{t-1}	0.036		0.038		−0.003	
	(0.23)		(0.24)		(0.02)	
W_t		0.163		0.160		0.173
		(1.12)		(1.08)		(1.35)
P_t	1.097	0.654	0.146	−0.300	0.869	0.419
	(2.04)	(1.32)	(0.27)	(0.60)	(1.74)	(0.95)
R^2	0.772	0.711	0.747	0.669	0.759	0.731
D-W	2.89	2.84	2.90	2.82	2.59	2.91
(n)	(17)	(18)	(17)	(18)	(17)	(18)

Table 9.7 Regression results for annual variations (1965–83) in the Soviet Union's imports of paper and paperboard from Finland (t-values in parentheses)

	Soviet statistics (volumes)		Soviet statistics (roubles)		OECD statistics ($)	
	(1)	(2)	(3)	(4)	(5)	(6)
Constant	5.764	7.628	1.480	7.565	1.486	8.328
	(0.67)	(0.89)	(0.14)	(1.65)	(0.18)	(0.82)
Q_{t-1}	−0.644		0.189		0.304	
	(0.36)		(0.08)		(0.18)	
Q_t		−0.743		−1.294		−0.515
		(0.54)		(0.70)		(0.32)
I_t	−0.113	−0.098	−0.095	0.098	−0.207	−0.076
	(0.55)	(0.70)	(0.37)	(0.52)	(1.06)	(0.46)
Q_{t-1}	0.246		0.596		0.643	

Table 9.7 continued

	Soviet statistics (volumes)		Soviet statistics (roubles)		OECD statistics ($)	
	(1)	(2)	(3)	(4)	(5)	(6)
	(1.29)		(2.51)		(3.51)	
Q_t		0.163		0.400		0.363
		(0.87)		(1.59)		(1.64)
R^2	0.433	0.358	0.582	0.449	0.717	0.453
D-W	3.09	2.89	2.79	2.67	2.22	2.56
(n)	(17)	(18)	(17)	(18)	(17)	(18)

five-year trade agreements and considerable deviations from its trend are caused only by the imbalance of the clearing account in Finnish–Soviet trade.

By comparing estimated equations in Tables 9.8 and 9.9, one may find *many differences in the determination of Soviet footwear imports from Finland relative to Soviet footwear imports from other OECD countries.*[11] Concerning imports from the other parts of the West the value of R^2 is higher in equations which include lagged variables, which is contrary to the results for Soviet imports from Finland. Reactions to changes in purchasing power especially differ between the two sources of footwear. Soviet imports of the consumer goods under scrutiny, when paid in convertible currency, respond to changes in Soviet reserves of foreign exchange rather with a one-year lag than during the same calendar year. In bilateral trade with Finland, it is advantageous for the Soviet Union to increase imports immediately in the case of a positive balance in the clearing account, which provides no interest. In addition to the influence of the prevailing purchasing power, footwear imports from Finland seem to react without delay to changes in Soviet domestic production evening out its fluctuation, which is not the case with imports from other Western countries. The fact is also that variations in imports from the CMEA Six have a significant positive sign only in equations explaining imports from Finland. These equations generally have quite a high R^2 and no sign of autocorrelation.

Table 9.8 Regression results for annual variations (1965–83) in the Soviet Union's imports of footwear from the West (excluding Finland) (t-values in parentheses)

	Soviet statistics (volume)		Soviet statistics (roubles)		OECD statistics ($) (1968–)	
	(1)	(2)	(3)	(4)	(5)	(6)
Constant	−9.713	−8.918	−1.568	−0.840	−0.928	3.208
	(0.82)	(0.76)	(0.14)	(0.07)	(0.08)	(0.26)
Q_{t-1}	2.292		0.890		−1.008	
	(0.61)		(0.24)		(0.27)	
Q_t		5.106		4.198		0.673
		(1.52)		(1.23)		(0.16)
I_t	0.102	0.174	0.191	0.145	−0.692	−0.796
	(0.11)	(0.21)	(0.21)	(0.18)	(0.79)	(0.87)
W_{t-1}	0.298		0.354		0.360	
	(1.56)		(1.89)		(2.03)	
W_t		0.097		0.102		−0.020
		(0.50)		(0.52)		(0.10)
R^2	0.525	0.492	0.539	0.433	0.577	0.257
D-W	1.64	1.91	2.12	2.29	3.34	3.16
(n)	(17)	(18)	(17)	(18)	(17)	(18)

CONCLUDING REMARKS

Soviet imports from the West may be seen in several senses as a continuum of imports from the CMEA Six. This is evident especially in long-range trade policy. Even in the annual variations of the two imports studied there appeared to prevail significant connections, which are indicated by estimates in regression equations. Whenever Soviet imports from the CMEA Six satisfy the overwhelming part of Soviet import needs, they have grown in a relatively stable fashion from year to year compared to imports from the West. On the other hand, the results of this investigation point to less variation in Soviet imports from the West whenever the greater part of the commodity in question is imported from the West.

In regression equations, the variable embodying the change in purchasing power produces a significant effect neither on highly preferred grain imports nor machine imports, which require a long time for implementing the investment decision. These two imports seem to have reacted with a one-year lag to changes in Soviet

Table 9.9 Regression results for annual variations (1966–83) in the Soviet Union's imports of footwear from Finland (t-values in parentheses)

	Soviet statistics (volume)		Soviet statistics (roubles)		OECD statistics ($)	
	(1)	(2)	(3)	(4)	(5)	(6)
Constant	1.425	14.136	11.183	18.826	13.607	21.499
	(0.13)	(1.86)	(0.98)	(2.49)	(1.32)	(2.64)
Q_{t-1}	0.913		−1.285		−2.247	
	(0.34)		(0.46)		(0.88)	
Q_t		−5.797		−6.200		−5.734
		(3.08)		(3.27)		(2.85)
I_t	0.445	1.231	0.797	1.293	0.872	1.223
	(0.62)	(2.65)	(1.05)	(2.80)	(1.28)	(2.46)
Q_{t-1}	0.547		0.582		0.641	
	(1.92)		(1.95)		(2.38)	
O_t		0.569		0.637		0.756
		(2.74)		(3.27)		(2.58)
R^2	0.540	0.778	0.563	0.809	0.637	0.756
D-W	1.98	2.04	1.90	1.94	1.88	1.86
(n)	(17)	(17)	(17)	(17)	(17)	(17)

production. The imports of soap and cleansing and polishing preparations from the West have also responded more clearly with a time-lag than in the same year to changes in purchasing power and the Soviet Union's own production.

In Western trade a certain dualism can also be seen. The dualism inside Soviet trade with the West has been clearly demonstrated here, when the imports of paper products and footwear have been explained. The simultaneous change in Soviet production has a negative sign in equations explaining these types of imports from Finland and a positive sign when the rest of imports from the West are to be explained. The Soviet imports seem to have reacted, as expected, more strongly – and in the purchase of footwear also more quickly – to changes in purchasing power only usable on the Finnish market.

Notes

1. Gardner, S., *Soviet Foreign Trade* (Boston: Kluwer-Nijhoff Publishing, 1983) pp. 139–140.
2. Vanous, J., 'An Econometric Model of World Trade of Member Countries of the Council for Mutual Economic Assistance', Yale University, New Haven (1985).
3. Gardner, S., op. cit., p. 5.
4. In addition to the mutual resemblance between Western and Soviet trade statistics, the relevant standpoint in defining commodity groups according to Soviet foreign trade statistics has been the similarity and availability of the production statistics needed in regression models.
5. Annual variations of all studied variables are defined as relative percentage changes calculated by the following formula: $(y_t - y_{t-1}/y_t + y_{t-1}) \cdot 200$, which indicates changes symmetrically. See Törnqvist, L.; P. Vartia; and Y. Vartia, 'How Should Relative Changes be Measured', *The American Statistician*, Vol. 39, No. 1 (1985).
6. The whole time series of the realisation of annual production plans have not been available. That is why the implementation of production plans (cf. Figure 9.1) have not been used as an explanatory variable but the variation in the actual annual production.
7. For the sake of comparability in all the equations explaining certain imports, the same explanatory variables are included. The price variable is excluded from a few models because of its low significance. Since the time series are quite short the non-lagged and lagged variables are not included in the same equations.
8. Oblath, G. and P. Pete, 'Trade with the Soviet Union: the Finnish Case', *Acta Oeconomica*, Vol. 35, No. 1–2 (1985).
9. The time series studied cover the years 1971–83, when the USSR was a net-importer of grain. Also see Brada, J., 'The Soviet–American Grain Agreement and the National Interest'. *American Journal of Agricultural Economics* (November 1983).
10. Kostecki, M. (ed.), *The Soviet Union in International Grain Markets: The Soviet Impact on Commodity Markets*, (London, Macmillan, 1984) pp. 205–211.
11. The time series begins from 1966, when Finnish–Soviet trade in footwear actually started under the auspices of a new five-year agreement.

10 Dual Systems of International Settlements: an analysis of Yugoslavia's experience and some proposals for more efficient alternative settlement systems
Ante Cicin-Sain

BASIC FACTS AND PROBLEMS ARISING OUT OF ALTERNATIVE SETTLEMENT SYSTEMS

Yugoslavia operates two or even three substantially different settlement systems for its international transactions. The overwhelming part of visible and invisible trade with the OECD and most developing countries, as well as capital transactions with these two groups of countries, are invoiced and settled in freely convertible currencies. Yugoslavia's trade with socialist countries of Eastern Europe (CMEA countries) is *mostly* settled through bilateral clearing arrangements. Official bilateral clearing arrangements still operate with five CMEA countries: Albania, Czechoslovakia, the GDR, the Soviet Union, and Mongolia. According to these arrangements, all current accounts and 'financial' transactions among partner countries should be settled through bilateral clearing.

There are, however, several notable exceptions to this general rule on bilateral clearing. Due to various factors – such as an ever-growing distinction between 'hard' and 'soft' commodities and an unplanned accrual of substantial unsettled bilateral balances – an important part of exchanges with these countries is actually settled either in freely convertible currencies or in convertible commodities, namely commodities which can be sold easily on international markets. Crude oil is the commodity which is mostly used for such purposes.

Since the early 1970s, Yugoslavia's trade with Bulgaria, Hungary, Romania, and Poland should have been, in accordance with officially concluded payments agreements, conducted in freely convertible currencies. However, settlements with these four countries over the last fifteen years show that in fact some types of informal bilateral clearing system has evolved. The essential difference with respect to official clearing arrangements is that such informal arrangements are not handled by central banks but by commercial banks. Consequently – and this is very important – there are no automatic bilateral 'swing credits' agreed to at the governmental level. Since such arrangements are not supported by the usual swing credit facility, participants are regularly forced to conclude balanced deals by providing offsetting transactions in order to 'close' each deal. It may, therefore, be said that informal clearing arrangements via commercial banks represent a step backward to simple bilateral barter. However, this is not necessarily a solution inferior to the usual official clearing arrangements.

The unavailability of automatic swing credit extensions has had ambivalent results. On the one hand, the crude and almost primitive informal arrangements have created quite a restricted settlement framework which is definitely not conducive for the desired expansion of trade among partner countries. Such a framework is certainly one of the important reasons for the relatively slow development of Yugoslavia's trade with these four countries.

On the other hand, with the informal arrangements, the trading partners have managed to avoid some of the major drawbacks and deficiencies which frequently go along with official clearing arrangements supported by large and automatically extendable swing credits.

Given the variety of alternative settlement systems which have been and still are applied in Yugoslavia's international transactions, it should be useful to see what lessons can be drawn from the country's experiences over the last fifteen or twenty years. In this context, I shall concentrate on three general areas:

1. the impact of alternative settlement arrangements on Yugoslavia's international exchanges;
2. the impact of Yugoslavia's alternative settlement arrangements on internal economic development; and
3. some proposal for improvements in alternative settlement systems.

For the first two topics I shall draw heavily on the results of a recently completed study on Yugoslavia's trade with Eastern Europe (Cicin-Sain and Mates, 1987). For the third topic, I shall draw on a set of studies which I prepared for UNCTAD.

THE IMPACT OF ALTERNATIVE SETTLEMENT SYSTEMS ON YUGOSLAVIA'S INTERNATIONAL EXCHANGES

Since it would be unrealistic to plead for the early establishment of full convertibility for the Yugoslav dinar and/or for the currencies of the East European countries, I shall concentrate on an analysis of alternative settlement systems between Yugoslavia and those countries.

The socialist countries' share in Yugoslavia's merchandise trade compared to their share in world trade is very high indeed. This is readily apparent from the figures in Table 10.1.

The share of the CMEA countries in world merchandise trade amounts to less than ten per cent, so it is evident that their share in Yugoslavia's foreign trade is extraordinarily high. Apart from the reasons of geographic proximity and a certain complementarity among their respective economies, the socialist countries' significant participation in Yugoslavia's foreign trade is no doubt related to the relative attractiveness of official clearing arrangements. Since the outbreak of Yugoslavia's balance of payments crisis, namely since 1979, when Yugoslavia was forced to restrict imports from convertible currency areas while attempting to increase its exports to those countries, the CMEA countries' share in Yugoslavia's foreign trade has increased even further. After reaching peak levels in 1982 and 1983, it started to decline but at the time of writing it remains very high. In fact, it is higher than corresponding shares for some CMEA member countries such as the GDR, Romania, and in some respects, Hungary.

If the data on the relative shares for the two groups of socialist countries are compared, the following is readily apparent:
1. There is a much larger degree of fluctuation and trade imbalance between Yugoslavia and the five genuine clearing countries than with the four 'convertible currency' CMEA countries.
2. There is a much larger degree of trade volatility or instability with the genuine clearing countries than with the 'convertible currency' CMEA countries.
3. Contrary to general predictions and numerous complaints by

Table 10.1 Socialist countries' share in Yugoslavia's merchandise trade 1976–87 (relative shares in percentage)

Year	All socialist countries		Bilateral clearing countries[a]		Convertible currency countries[b]	
	Exports	Imports[c]	Exports	Imports[c]	Exports	Imports[c]
1976	42.4	30.6	32.2	21.2	9.5	8.2
1977	40.9	29.1	29.9	20.6	9.1	7.7
1978	43.1	30.1	33.4	20.2	8.8	8.7
1979	40.4	25.4	29.8	18.9	9.8	6.0
1980	46.3	30.1	36.9	24.2	8.0	5.5
1981	53.1	33.7	45.2	28.1	7.7	5.3
1982	52.8	36.3	45.3	30.1	7.0	6.1
1983	47.8	38.0	38.9	30.6	8.5	7.2
1984	48.3	33.7	38.9	30.6	8.5	7.2
1985	50.6	32.3	39.9	24.4	9.5	7.7
1986	48.7	32.7	38.1	24.5	9.7	7.8
1987	35.1	30.3	26.3	22.5	7.9	7.2

[a] Albania, Czechoslovakia, the GDR, the Soviet Union, Mongolia.
[b] Bulgaria, Hungary, Poland, Romania.
[c] Data for imports refer to imports by origin. During the 1980s imports classified according to payments were substantially greater from the five bilateral clearing countries than indicated here.

agents involved in clearing trade, it is evident that Yugoslavia's trade with the four 'convertible currency' countries has continued to grow in absolute and relative terms since the early 1980s, whereas its trade with the five bilateral clearing countries has stagnated. It should be pointed out that an important part of the recent decline in the volume of trade between Yugoslavia and the latter group – particularly the Soviet Union – has to be attributed to the decline of crude oil prices. Nevertheless, even if this is taken into account, the overall volume of merchandise trade with these countries is stagnating.

In addition to the points noted above, two other distinctive features of trade conducted under official clearing arrangements are: the very rigid commodity structure of trade and the severe difficulties of keeping the overall volume (particularly the balance of this trade) within planned targets. The rigidity of the commodity structure is reflected in the composition of both the products traded and the trading partners involved. An analysis of Yugoslavia's trade with the Soviet Union, Czechoslovakia, and the GDR shows that the composition of imports and exports does not change much regardless of developments in these countries or on the world market.

While clearing trade on the Yugoslav side is very large in volume, it is heavily concentrated in a rather small number of branches and firms. For exports, this might be explained in terms of product specialisation. However, the most important users of imports from clearing countries are also heavily concentrated in just a few branches, and this cannot be explained in terms of specialisation. On the contrary, it might be said that official clearing arrangements, based on physical planning of the products to be exchanged and supported with automatic credit extensions, tend to create a kind of dual economy in the sense that an ever-growing division arises between sectors involved in clearing trade and other sectors of the national economy. Such a situation tends not only to generate considerable undesirable strains within a national economy, but it also impedes the development of mutually profitable trade between partners. Many products which could be traded to the benefit of both partners cannot be traded because the official bilateral trade framework is very rigid and heavily monopolised.

In their analysis of how to eliminate the unsustainably high surpluses in Yugoslavia's trade with the Soviet Union and Czechoslovakia, Cicin-Sain and Mates (1987) offer numerous possibilities for increasing Yugoslav imports of intermediary products and investment and consumer goods from these two countries. In addition to administrative problems, the absence of a keen interest to export among Soviet and Czech foreign trade organisations, and the limited knowledge that Yugoslav importers possess about available opportunities on the Soviet and Czech markets have been substantial obstacles to bilaterally balanced of trade. Although it is generally tied to comprehensive planning procedures, official bilateral clearing trade does not seem to be particularly well suited for co-ordination with other macroeconomic targets. This can be deduced from Yugoslavia's experiences, particularly for the period in which the country has been faced with a serious balance of payments crisis.

Yugoslavia runs a structural surplus with the bilateral clearing countries in the trade of services and other invisible transactions, so it is logical and necessary for it to plan at least an equally large deficit in its merchandise trade with them. Yugoslav trade planners have realised this. Consequently, they always planned that Yugoslav imports from bilateral clearing countries would exceed its exports to those countries by some $200 to $900 million annually. While the trade balances during the 1970s, namely before the outbreak of the balance of payments crisis, were realised within planned targets, after the crisis Yugoslavia started to run very large surpluses in its merchandise trade with the major bilateral clearing countries. In five of eight post-1979 years, Yugoslavia accumulated highly undesirable surpluses in its trade with these countries. The resulting accumulation of very large interest claims on bilateral accounts, particularly with the Soviet Union and Czechoslovakia, reflected a heavy drain on Yugoslavia's available resources. As a result, Yugoslav authorities were forced to undertake special actions to use up the accumulated claims, even at a considerable loss. It is important to note that Yugoslavia faced no such problems in its trade with the four 'convertible currency' countries.

This leads us to two somewhat paradoxical conclusions:
1. The official clearing trade, although institutionally closely tied to planning procedures, appears to be least suitable for efficient planning within a decentralised economic system.
2. The informal clearing arrangements, although not much different from bilateral barter trade, can provide a better framework for mutual trading than official clearing arrangements even though the latter have all the governmental support behind them.

The different dynamics of Yugoslavia's trade with East European countries are shown in Figure 10.1 and Table 10.2, which portray the development of Yugoslavia's exports and imports with bilateral clearing countries (Albania, Czechoslovakia, the GDR, the Soviet Union, and Mongolia) and with 'convertible currency' CMEA countries (Bulgaria, Hungary, Poland, and Romania) from 1976 and 1987. It is evident from Figure 10.1 that the trade balance with the 'convertible currency' CMEA countries remained remarkably stable, but there were very large and quite abrupt variations in the trade balance with the bilateral clearing countries.

Leaving aside several distinctive features and differences among alternative clearing settlement systems, the following conclusion emerges: official clearing arrangements, even when compared with very simple settlement arrangements such as informal bilateral clearing, cannot be regarded as reliable vehicles suitable for providing a necessary framework for the planned and unhindered development of trade among socialist countries. Instead of providing long-term stability in bilateral trade, official clearing arrangements turn out to be one of the most unstable and least attractive forms for participating countries to realise benefits from the international division of labour.

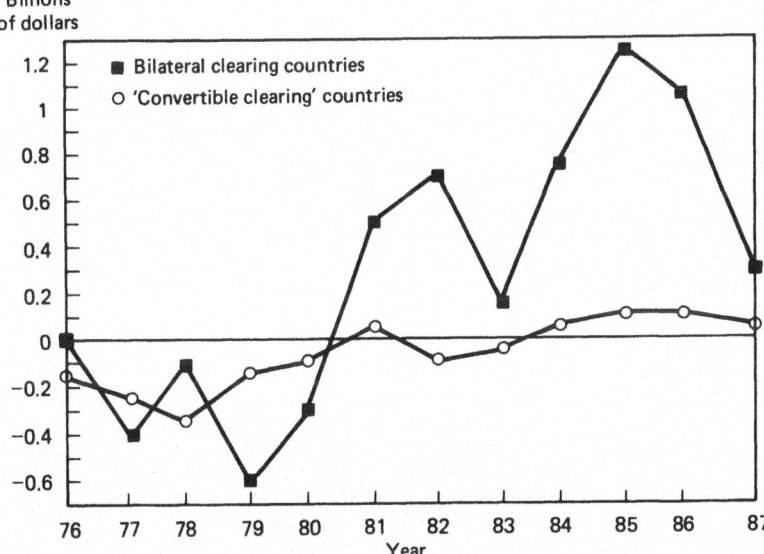

Figure 10.1 Yugoslavia's merchandise trade balance with two groups of socialist countries (in billions of US dollars)

Table 10.2 Yugoslavia's trade with socialist countries (million dollars and percentage share)

Year	Exports by destination	Imports by origin	Trade balance	Percentage share in Yugoslavia overall	
				Exports	Imports
A. Bilateral Clearing Countries Albania, Czechoslovakia, the Soviet Union, the GDR, Mongolia					
1976	1573	1560	12	32.2	21.2
1977	1574	1989	−414	29.9	20.6
1978	1895	2020	−125	33.4	20.2
1979	2022	2643	−621	29.8	18.9
1980	3317	3645	−328	36.9	24.2
1981	4615	4088	526	45.2	28.1
1982	4495	3832	663	45.3	30.1
1983	3774	3623	151	38.9	30.6
1984	3800	3047	753	38.0	26.2
1985	4245	2971	1273	39.9	24.4
1986	3928	2885	1043	38.1	24.5
1987	3429	3158	271	26.3	22.5

Table 10.2 continued

Year	Exports by destination	Imports by origin	Trade balance	Percentage share in Yugoslavia overall	
				Exports	Imports

A. Bilateral Clearing Countries
Albania, Czechoslovakia, the Soviet Union, the GDR, Mongolia

Totals					
1976–1980	10381	11857	−1476		
1981–1986	24857	20447	4410		
Averages					
1976–1980	2076	2371	−295	32.5	21.0
1981–1986	4143	3408	735	40.9	27.3

B. 'Convertible currency' countries
Bulgaria, Hungary, Poland, Rumania

1976	463	601	−138	9.5	8.2
1977	481	746	−265	9.1	7.7
1978	496	866	−369	8.8	8.7
1979	668	838	−170	9.8	6.0
1980	719	827	−108	8.0	5.5
1981	781	768	13	7.7	5.3
1982	696	780	−83	7.0	6.1
1983	825	848	−23	8.5	7.2
1984	923	857	66	9.2	7.4
1985	1009	931	78	9.5	7.7
1986	996	913	83	9.7	7.8
1987	1026	1006	20	7.9	7.2
Totals					
1976–80	2828	3877	−1050		
1981–86	5231	5097	134		
Averages					
1976–80	566	775	−210	9.0	7.2
1981–86	872	850	22	8.6	6.9

THE IMPACT OF ALTERNATIVE SETTLEMENTS ON INTERNAL ECONOMIC DEVELOPMENTS

In this section the influence of clearing trade on Yugoslavia's internal economic development will be analysed through its impact on relative prices, the behaviour and management of enterprises, and macroeconomic policies, monetary policy in particular.

The problems of price disparities arising in Yugoslavia's trade with the bilateral clearing countries have been recently analysed by Cicin-Sain and Mates (1987) on three different levels. The first level was based on surveys conducted by the Yugoslav Institute for Market Research (*Zavod za istrazivanje trzista* – ZIT). These surveys are conducted at the end of June and July of each year among a large sample of Yugoslav exporters. The data collected provide information about price ratios for exports to the convertible currency and bilateral clearing areas with respect to domestic wholesale prices and, by implication, with respect to each other. Such data have been regularly collected since 1983 for exports while data for imports were collected for the first time in December 1986.

The results indicate that throughout the 1983–1986 period Yugoslav exporters realised substantially better prices for exports to the bilateral clearing area than for domestic sales, and particularly better than for sales to the convertible currency area. However, the attractive prices to the CMEA clearing countries were rapidly disappearing by the end of the period analysed. The prices for imports from CMEA countries, without taking into account differences in quality, were only slightly higher than those for the 'same' products which were or could have been imported from the convertible currency countries.

The second level of analysis covered the regular trade in 'same products' with both currency areas for 1986 only and centred on price identifications for the same types of products. 'Same products' were defined in accordance with the nine-digit BTN (Brussels Tariff Nomenclature) classification. According to this definition, during 1986 Yugoslavia exported some 1100 'same products' and imported almost 1300 of them from both currency areas. This was at least partly due to the exchange rate policies in Yugoslavia. These products accounted for more than 90 per cent of the export value and more than 80 per cent of the import value of goods traded with the clearing currency area in regular merchandise trade.

The analysis shows that prices for Yugoslav exports were generally substantially higher in the bilateral clearing countries than in the convertible currency area. The degree of price disparities for imports was generally lower than for exports. (Detailed information about the range of price disparities for particular products or groups of products cannot yet be disclosed because these data are still considered confidential.)

The third level of investigation consisted of a comparative analysis of foreign trade prices realised in Yugoslavia's and West Germany's trade with Czechoslovakia and the Soviet Union during 1982–1984. This analysis, based on OECD five-digit SITC statistics, yielded more conclusive findings for prices of 'same products' imported by Yugoslavia and West Germany than for exported products.

It was found that Yugoslavia was paying up to 27 per cent higher prices for its imports from Czechoslovakia and the USS than was West Germany. However, the 'same products' do not amount to more than ten to fifteen per cent of Yugoslavia's imports from the Soviet Union and only about five per cent of West Germany's imports from the Soviet Union. The relative share of 'same products' in the import trade with Czechoslovakia is somewhat higher; it ranges from twenty to 25 per cent for Yugoslavia and around ten per cent for West Germany. For 'same products' exported by both Yugoslavia and West Germany to the Soviet Union and Czechoslovakia, there were only relatively small differences in realised export prices. However, the commodity structure of Yugoslav and West German exports to CMEA countries differs substantially.

Taken together, these analyses indicate that the terms of trade for Yugoslavia with the CMEA clearing countries are better than those with the convertible currency areas. This is probably one of the reasons for the relative popularity and favourable treatment given by Yugoslav economic policies to trade with the CMEA clearing countries. The finding about Yugoslavia's better terms of trade with the CMEA clearing countries fully conforms with the conclusions of Marrese and Vanous (1983) relating to the terms of trade between smaller CMEA countries and the Soviet Union.

The terms of trade with a particular currency area, however, need to be evaluated in the context of an overall balance with that area. Concerning trade with the bilateral clearing countries, the notion of terms of trade makes sense only to the extent that overall trade flows are reasonably well balanced. If that is not the case, there is hardly any justification to speak about terms of trade. With strong imbalances in bilateral trade – as has been the case in Yugoslavia's trade with the Soviet Union and Czechoslovakia for most of the time since 1980 – the outstanding balance is not being exchanged at all. Therefore, it is necessary to be prudent in making any comparisons of terms of trade with different trading areas.

The analysis of export and import prices realised in Yugoslavia's trade with the four 'convertible currency' CMEA countries indicates that price disparities are generally smaller than in its official bilateral clearing trade and that they are approximately of the same order of magnitude on the export and import side. This implies that Yugoslavia's terms of trade with this group of countries are not substantially different from those with the genuine convertible currency area. Due to the relatively strict and rigid balancing arrangements imposed by commercial banks for practically every set of export and import transactions, trade with this group of countries is reasonably well balanced. Perhaps even more important is that informal clearing arrangements, as they are practiced with the 'convertible currency' CMEA countries, do not give rise to any major distortions in domestic price and cost structures. Nevertheless, trade with these countries is not particularly popular in Yugoslavia, either with those directly involved in such trade, or with the economic policymakers.

The price and cost disparities originating from distorted export and import prices realised through official clearing trade are reflected in the majority of decision-making processes at the enterprise level. Since enterprise managers are confronted with a whole range of distorted price signals for the same or very similar products, it is understandable that individual calculations cannot be mutually consistent. Therefore, as a rule, such price and cost distortions will result in suboptimal or even perverse enterprise behaviour. *Mutatis mutandis*, the same holds, for the behaviour of consumers and savers.

When the country is systematically confronted with distorted cost and price signals at the micro level, there is no chance for successful implementation of macroeconomic policies at the national level. Distorted price and cost ratios, combined with abundant credit support for official bilateral clearing trade, can also result in some rather curious modifications of the standard tools of economic policy. Under certain circumstances, which have been present in Yugoslavia since the early and mid-1980s, such a situation may result once subsidies are granted to inefficient producers at the expense of creating additional inflationary pressure.

The interdependence between underlying conditions for economic management at the micro and macro levels can be illustrated by one of the findings of our study on Yugoslavia's trade with the bilateral clearing countries. During the period of very rapid expansion of Yugoslav exports to these countries, namely during 1980–1982 and 1985–1986, some firms engaged in this trade began granting internal subsidies for their own exports to convertible currency areas. From an enterprise point of view, such arrangements were both feasible and desirable. The funds needed to subsidise exports to Western markets were obtained from the high profits on exports to the bilateral clearing countries. At the same time, these firms were directed to provide their own sources of convertible currency in order to finance their necessary imported inputs of raw materials and intermediary products from convertible currency areas.

Since the official exchange rate was not sufficiently high to cover the production costs for exports to Western markets, several firms, particularly composite organisations of associated labour, reverted to some form of internalisation of typical macroeconomic policy measures. For the most part, such arrangements were known and tolerated by the government. They were tolerated both because of the government's reluctance to establish appropriate monetary and exchange rate policies and because of the illusion that an adequate substitute for these policies had been found. However, when it ultimately became evident that the macroeconomic costs of interest-free export financing to the clearing countries were unbearably high, such exports had to be drastically reduced – first in 1983, then again in 1986. The effects of the decline in the ratio of the exchange rate for the clearing dollar relative to the exchange rate for the US dollar were reflected not only in a reduced interest for exports to the clearing countries, which was intended, but also in the decreased competitiveness of export firms on convertible currency markets, which was highly undesired. Ultimately, the dinar had to be substantially devalued in the autumn of 1987.

As a result of the failure to co-ordinate macroeconomic policies, automatic credit extensions for official bilateral clearing transactions had significant monetary effects. The relevant relationships are illustrated in Table 10.3. These figures, limited to the years when Yugoslavia was running considerable surpluses on its trade with the CMEA clearing countries, show conclusively that the *direct net effect* of financing bilateral credit balances amounted to between fifteen and 47 per cent of an already very large creation of central bank money.

Leaving aside the question of whether net or gross effects of central bank money creation should be regarded as relevant, it is evident that automatic credit extensions for financing the official clearing trade have become one of the major destabilising factors in the Yugoslav economy. The direct and indirect effects arising out of such financing jeopardise any positive effects which might be associated with Yugoslavia's official clearing arrangements with CMEA countries. The conclusion emerges that different, better balanced, and more elastic

Table 10.3 Monetary effects of bilateral credit balances realised in Yugoslavia's trade with CMEA clearing countries

Monetary Effect	1981	1982	1985	1986
Net changes in bilateral clearing accounts (millions of clearing dollars)	1182	245	460	981
Average exchange rate (dinar/clearing dollars)	32.2	42.8	254.8	357.9
Net changes in bilateral clearing accounts (billions of dinars)	38.1	10.5	117.2	351.9
Net creation of central bank money from clearing transactions without exchange rate changes (billions of dinars)	23.6	26.0	97.5	306.8
Total creation of central bank money (billions of dinars)	94.0	55.0	664.9	992.2
Net effects of changes in bilateral clearing accounts on central bank money (4:5)	25%	47%	15%	31%
Annual inflation rate (CPI)	47%	30%	76%	88%

Source: Cicin-Sain, 1987, p. 422.

settlement arrangements have to be devised to allow for a mutually advantageous expansion of trade in goods and services among socialist countries.

AN OUTLINE FOR AN ALTERNATIVE SETTLEMENT SYSTEM: UPGRADING NATIONAL CURRENCIES AND ESTABLISHING LIMITED CONVERTIBILITY

A new settlement system needs to be devised to accommodate the growing needs and opportunities for mutually profitable trade expansion without causing significant distortions and/or imbalances at micro and macro levels of national economies. At the same time, account has to be taken of the role of planning in socialist countries' foreign trade, to the extent that it can be reconciled with postulates of economic efficiency.

The general foundation on which an alternative settlement arrangement can be structured is the gradual but systematic *upgrading of the national currencies* of the CMEA countries. These currencies should become increasingly capable of performing all the essential functions of modern money. This implies a willingness to proceed systematically towards the further monetisation of the socialist economies. In order to move in that direction it is above all necessary to *increase the free usability* of these national currencies for an ever-increasing number and volume of transactions.

Given the present nature and role of planning in the CMEA countries, it is to be assumed that the free usability of their currencies would at least initially be limited to the exchange of goods and services which cannot be reasonably well planned and directed by the usual planning and settlement methods – for example, various parts, components, intermediary products, products which have occasionally been in a very short or very abundant supply, numerous service transactions, tourism, and workers' remittances. This implies that the free usability of national currencies would initially be linked to the notion of *eligible products*. Such products would have to be somehow specified so that non-residents, holding the relevant national currencies, would be allowed to buy and dispose of these goods and services freely. To the extent that national currencies would become freely usable for an increasing number of transactions, it would also be possible to establish the *free exchangeability* of the currencies themselves.

Such regulations might be described as *limited convertibility arrangements*, where 'limited' refers both to the eligible products and the region or countries participating in the arrangements. In order to avoid the dangers which could arise from central bank presence in such arrangements – namely, their *de facto* subordination to current government policies and their unlimited capability to intervene with additional credits – *limited convertibility arrangements should be operated by the commercial banks* of the participating countries.

From a technical point of view, limited convertibility arrangements would be based on the following main pillars:
1. Full liberalisation of trade in eligible products from all licensing and exchange control restrictions among the participating countries.
2. Systematic, meaning automatic, assurance of 'foreign exchange' needed to finance the eligible trade.
3. The establishment of special limited convertibility accounts in commercial banks in the home and/or partner country.
4. The establishment of organised, official or semi-official, markets for currencies of all participating countries and the consequent application of exchange rates established on such markets to all transactions within limited convertibility arrangements.

The lists of eligible products might initially be positive, meaning that only goods and services explicitly listed would be allowed to be traded freely within the limited convertibility systems. Far less restrictive would be negative lists, which would specify the products that would be excluded from the system. Obviously, the products which would continue to be exchanged through bilateral clearing arrangements – and such arrangements could still be maintained – would not be eligible for the limited convertibility systems. In other words, all trade among the participating countries would be channelled through two independent but mutually consistent settlement systems. The trade in important 'main' products, which can be planned in physical terms and settled under long-term contracts, would continue to be settled through bilateral clearing arrangements, while all other transactions, which cannot be well planned, would be exchanged through the limited convertibility system. While the latter transactions would also be governed by rules and regulations, these would be much more liberal than present arrangements.

Limited convertibility accounts would be denominated in the home currency of the country in which such accounts were being held. Residents of both a home country and other countries – provided they were engaged in regular trade with eligible products – would be entitled to maintain such accounts. These accounts would be credited with the proceeds of eligible exports to partner countries as well as with home currency proceeds obtained by non-residents for the sale of legally imported eligible products. Moreover, they could also be credited with the proceeds of any banknote sales to authorised banks or other authorised dealers. The funds held in limited convertibility accounts would bear interest at rates comparable to those paid on internal bank accounts.

The funds in limited convertibility accounts could be used freely for any eligible transactions with participating countries or could be withdrawn in the home currency for local expenditures including the purchase of eligible goods and services for export to participating countries. Drawings on these accounts would have to be made in either the home currency or the currency of the partner country to which payment is to be made.

The following hypothetical example illustrates how the proposed limited convertibility accounts would work. An exporter from CMEA country A would be entitled to accept payments for eligible exports in the local currency of importing CMEA country B, whatever the status of that currency might be. Since this exporter would not be compelled to surrender the export proceeds to the banking system of his home country, he would deposit such proceeds into his limited convertibility account with a bank in country B in the currency of that country. The exporter could subsequently use the funds to either buy eligible export products from country B in order to export them, or make payments for eligible products to other participating countries in their currencies; he could also pay for any local expenses in country B. Clearly, the exporter himself would retain the right to decide if he was willing to enter into transactions involving payments in the currency of another participating country.

Since all these proposals are conceived with a reliance on different national currencies, some exchange rate arrangements would be required. The only appropriate method for establishing the exchange rates suitable for the efficient functioning of the proposed system would be the market mechanism with no obligatory intervention by any authority. Otherwise, there would be a great danger that transactions channelled through the system would not balance out and that excess balances would be accumulated.

Since no official interventions are envisioned, no accumulation of excess balances could be tolerated. This would particularly be the case in the early stages of the system's operation. At some later stage, when appropriate exchange rates became sufficiently confirmed by underlying market forces, it might become feasible to have some central bank involvement.

It is obvious that a great many questions are likely to be raised concerning the proposed alternative settlement system outlined here. While such questions should be discussed as they arise, it might be useful to conclude with the following remark. The proposal for the more or less free determination of exchange rates for the currencies of participating countries is less radical than it might appear. In comparison to the actual bewildering variety of exchange rate criteria in most socialist countries, this proposal would in fact greatly simplify the existing procedures and facilitate the normal development of international exchanges and internal performance of the economies involved.

Bibliography

L. ADAMOVIĆ et al., *Jugoslavija i SEV – intenzifikacija ekonomske saradnje Jugoslavije i SEV-a* (Yugoslavia and the CMEA – intensive economic co-operation between Yugoslavia and the CMEA) (Belgrad: Privredni Pregled, 1985).

J. M. VAN BRABANT, 'Exchange Rates in Eastern Europe – Types, Derivation and Application', World Bank Staff Working Papers, Nr. 778 (Washington: World Bank, 1985).

A. CICIN-SAIN and N. MATES, *Dispariteti cijena i efikasnost ekonomske razmjene Jugoslavije s klirinskim zemljama* (Disparity in prices and effective economic exchange between Yugoslavia and clearing countries) (Zagreb: Ekonomski Institut-Zagreb, 1987).

A. CICIN-SAIN, 'Dispariteti vanjskotrgovinskih cijena i efikasnost jugoslavenske ekonomske razmjene s klirinksim zemljama' (Disparity of internal trade prices and effective economic exchange between Yugoslavia and clearing countries), published in: *Problemi privrednog razvoja i privrednog sistema Jugoslavije* (Zagreb: Ekonomski Institut-Zagreb, 1987) pp. 413–428.

M. MARRESE and J. VANOUS, *Soviet Subsidization of Trade with Eastern Europe: A Soviet Perspective* (Berkeley: Institute of International Studies, University of California, 1983).

T. A. WOLF, 'Exchange Rates, Foreign Trade Accounting, and Purchasing-Power Parity for Centrally Planned Economies', World Bank Staff Working Papers, Nr. 779 (Washington: World Bank, 1985).

11 Some Specific Features of Inflation in a Heavily-indebted Socialist Country
Neven Mates

Problems of simultaneous economic relations of individual countries with the 'West' and the 'East' have until the 1980s mainly been analysed in the sphere of visible and invisible trade. In this chapter, the sphere of analysis is the financial system. With respect to Yugoslavia, it will be shown that the institutional weaknesses of the domestic financial system, which is heavily burdened with debt to Western countries and at the same time has periodically significant balance-of-trade claims on Eastern countries, constitute one of the basic causes of inflation.

SPECIFIC FEATURES OF THE SOURCES OF INFLATION IN YUGOSLAVIA

Up to the 1980s, in all countries with a high inflation rate, inflation has been accompanied by a budget deficit financed by the central bank. Attempts to curb inflation have therefore been aimed at decreasing this deficit.

The current economic crisis in Yugoslavia is unusual in that inflation grew very quickly at a time when the budget did not show any deficit. If the public sector as a whole (the central government, republics, autonomous provinces and communes) is considered, the balance of current revenues and expenditures is positive. The Federal Government occasionally takes short-term loans from the central bank, but these do not influence the overall result.[1]

Government subsidies granted to the nationalised sectors of the economy have, in countries with a high inflation rate, often been a cause of budget deficits. In Yugoslavia, the largest part of the economy is in non-private ownership, characterised by enterprises that are in principle independent economic entities and that are managed by workers employed in them.[2] In view of the fact that such enterprises are in a sort of 'half-state ownership', it could be expected that the economy receives considerable budget subsidies. These are, however, rarely paid from the budget, namely from fiscal revenue, and only receive grants for clearly specified purposes such as the promotion of exports, or the modest subsidisation of consumption of some agricultural products. The government continues (at the level of the republics, autonomous provinces, and also partly communes) by means of laws to ensure obligatory collection of funds for financing various investment projects in the fields of electricity, railways, water management and agriculture. At the federal level, funds are collected in a similar way for the development of underdeveloped republics and autonomous provinces. For all of these purposes, funds are collected by means of special taxes and their use is more or less precisely defined. Government agencies do not dispose of any significant discretionary resources for subsidising current operations of some enterprises or new investment projects.

Possibilities for subsidising inefficient enterprises from fiscal revenues or at the expense of the budget deficit are relatively small. Without considering the problems related to the inefficiency of the tax system and the overall tax load borne by the economy, it can be said that the fiscal system and this kind of use of fiscal revenues are more or less 'regular'.

In spite of this, inefficiency of enterprises and erroneous investments are the main cause of inflation because inefficient enterprises are subsidised through the banking system. Implicit subsidies are granted for current operations of enterprises through credits for working capital given at negative real interest rates; furthermore, for investment of capital in selected projects and also for the subsequent socialisation of the cost of the capital invested in erroneous projects where the enterprises involved are not able to return the capital invested. Instead of the budget, the main sources for such subsidies are bank credits obtained by enterprises under favourable terms.

INSTITUTIONAL PRESSURE FOR NEGATIVE INTEREST RATES

Enterprises are subsidised through the banking system in various ways, but basic to it is the institutional position of the banking system.

The institutional position of banks in the economic system is determined by the fact that banks are not founded as joint-stock companies. They may only be founded by organisations of associated labour, namely enterprises. Enterprises do not manage the banks they have founded proportionally to their equity since every founder has only one vote.[3] This formal right to manage banks has, however, only relatively small significance. Particularly great influence on the management of a bank is usually exercised by a small number of founders who have their representatives on the bank's managing board, and by local political circles which exercise great influence on the election of the bank's director. Since enterprises in the productive sector are highly indebted and the local political structures are primarily interested in supplying as much credit as possible to the local economy, banks are in fact managed by large debtors.

As a consequence, a bank's basic interest does not lie in maximising the profits of those who have invested capital (equity) in it. The very system of bank management acts toward exercising constant pressure on lowering as much as possible the rates of interest paid to the banks. This pressure does not only act *ex ante*, via policies favouring the stipulation of low interest rates, but also *ex post* in the sense that relatively small efforts are made to collect the stipulated interest and principal. True, banks relatively rarely write off their claims, but they frequently give up collection of interest, especially interest on arrears, while the payment of the principal is formally or informally rescheduled. Under conditions of inflation and nominally low and negative interest rates in real terms, by means of such 'rescheduling' of credits, the formal writing off of bad loans is avoided.

At the same time, competition among banks in accepting deposits is institutionally prevented. More specifically, conditions for accepting deposits are regulated by so-called self-managing (and in essence cartel-like) agreements concluded by banks. Among other things, these self-managing agreements focus on the interest rates paid on deposits. In view of the fact that bank managers are predominantly interested in the lowest possible interest rates on credits, such cartel-like agreements act toward lowering the rates of interest paid by banks. An additional factor which acts toward lowering the rates of interest paid by banks is the frequently reached upper bound on a bank's loanable funds. Since, through varied transactions by the central bank which will be discussed further below, sufficiently high liquidity of the banking system is as a rule ensured, banks are not interested in greater competition in collection of deposits, because the amount of the resources they can loan is limited.[4] Finally, the fact that banks, as a rule, operate within a limited territory also has a restrictive effect on such competition.

Monetary policy, which is shaped by the parliament and government, and which the central bank only implements, proceeds in essence from a sort of monetarist principle. More specifically, the movement of the money supply is planned on the basis of the estimated movement of nominal gross national product. From this estimate a certain percentage is deducted (which is referred to as the level of restrictiveness) and on this basis the necessary growth of money supply is assessed. If, in the course of a year, a higher than anticipated growth of national gross product (in fact of inflation) is recorded, the growth of the money supply thus set is then implemented by various instruments, among which the greatest role has, in the 1980s, been played by the limitations on bank loans. Such limitations are very important since the central bank itself pursues a very active credit policy. More specifically, economic policy has for years resorted to the distribution of selective credit (known as 'selective crediting') as an instrument for the attainment of numerous aims. Thus, selective crediting is applied to exports and preparation of production for export, production and inventories of agricultural products, and to many other purposes. For such purposes, the central bank refinances commercial banks at various percentages. This form of refinancing accounts for the entire regular credit activity of the central bank.

Credits for selective purposes are given at interest rates much lower than the so-called discount rate of the central bank. Under such conditions, pressure exercised in order to acquire the right to selective credits is considerable and the central bank can hardly withstand it. The aims regarding the growth of the money supply must therefore be additionally realised through the limitation of bank loans. The combination of, on the one hand, extensive credit activity on the part of the central bank in refinancing credits for selective purposes under very favourable interest rates, on the one hand, and of loan limitation on the other, leads to further pressure being exercised on lowering the rates of interest paid by banks. Under such conditions, when a few years ago in an agreement concluded with the International Monetary Fund, Yugoslavia undertook the obligation to pursue a policy of positive interest rates in real terms on time deposits. Since the banks did not have any interest in such arrangements,[5] this policy had to be implemented by means of obligatory prescription of such interest rates.

Finally, among the factors which have institutionally acted toward negative real interest rates, one must mention ideological attitudes according to which only income earned on the basis of labour, not of ownership, is legal and socially acceptable. The provisions of the so-called Associated Labour Act pertaining to banks specify in this sense that not only organisations which have invested resources in a bank but also those which have made use of the credits granted by this bank can participate in the distribution of the latter's income.[6]

Foreign Exchange Imbalances of Banks

The situation in the dinar domain is compounded by problems concerning the banking system in the sphere of foreign transactions. These problems are especially significant in relations with convertible currency countries, in particular with regard to external debts in foreign exchange and the foreign exchange savings of households.

The foreign exchange savings of households has developed not so much as a result of banks' interest in finding new sources of funds, but primarily due to the need of banks to obtain the foreign exchange required for foreign payments. More specifically, save for some short-lived exceptions, Yugoslavia did not and still does not have a foreign exchange market on which commercial banks are able to freely buy from each other or from the central bank foreign exchange required to make foreign payments for their clients. Payment possibilities have always in various ways been made dependent on the foreign exchange inflow of a particular bank (which the bank was never able to fully dispose of because it had to assign part of it to the central bank). And yet, possibilities for buying foreign exchange from the central bank have been limited and made dependent on special decisions of government authorities. At the same time, the right of enterprises to imports has also frequently been made dependent on the foreign exchange proceeds realised, or on the exports.

Under such conditions the primary motive of a bank for accepting foreign exchange savings is to obtain foreign exchange to finance imports of its clients rather than to collect funds for further loans. For varied reasons this foreign exchange has not been used by banks to give foreign exchange credits to their clients, but rather to sell it to them. Giving credits in foreign exchange is, as a rule, forbidden by law, and such credits are, in addition, not in the interest of bank founders who have preferred to buy foreign exchange instead of assuming foreign exchange liabilities. Commercial banks are not forbidden by law to have open foreign exchange positions, which is often forbidden to commercial banks in other banking systems in the world. Moreover, such a limitation would be unfeasible in view of this mode of using foreign exchange savings and under the condition of a non-existent foreign exchange market.

Besides household foreign exchange savings banks have frequently entered into open foreign exchange positions in their other activities. It is important to note that in this respect banks have behaved contrary to their financial interest. Under conditions of inflation and nominal interest rates which, on the credit side have, as a rule, lagged behind the inflation rate, it would have been natural for banks to be interested in trying to maintain a net positive foreign exchange position, that is, to have their foreign exchange claims exceed their foreign exchange liabilities. However, proceeding from the interests of their clients in ensuring the greatest possible volume of foreign payments, banks have entered into negative foreign exchange positions (Table 11.1). This has evolved in several ways. In accordance with law, enterprises were allowed to have foreign exchange accounts with domestic banks in which part of their foreign exchange proceeds realised by these enterprises was kept.[7] Banks have, however, used this foreign exchange to finance imports of organisations which did not earn any foreign exchange. To meet external obligations banks have frequently also used short-term foreign exchange credits, which has also resulted in the creation of negative foreign exchange positions.

Long-term credit could in principle be taken abroad by banks only on account of enterprises. In this way the external foreign exchange liabilities of banks should have in principle been balanced with their foreign exchange claims towards enterprises, so that on this basis no open foreign exchange positions needed to be created. However at the moment when payments became due, the enterprises involved were frequently not able to secure the necessary foreign exchange inflow, so they met their liabilities to their banks by paying in dinars.

Table 11.1 Balance of the central banking system

Year	Assets			Liabilities to Non-residents				
	Foreign exchange assets	Dinar assets	Other[a]	Monetary liabilities	Other dinar liabilities	Foreign exchange savings	Foreign exchange liabilities	Total
				In billion dinars				
1980	48.4	407.8	115.2	222.6	16.3	217.1	115.5	571.5
1981	77.9	539.3	177.4	289.3	30.8	305.9	168.5	794.5
1982	87.5	694.7	386.9	372.1	47.6	459.8	289.6	1169.1
1983	188.1	894.9	1064.1	434.0	75.9	915.3	721.9	2147.1
1984	334.5	1244.1	1921.5	690.5	99.4	1424.9	1285.4	3500.2
1985	582.9	1718.0	3283.6	1148.5	167.1	2295.0	1974.1	5584.7
1986	1299.0	2728.4	5940.1	2105.4	421.7	4509.4	2931.1	9967.6

	Assets			Liabilities to Non-residents			
Year	Foreign exchange assets	Dinar assets	Other[a]	Monetary liabilities	Other dinar liabilities	Foreign exchange savings	Foreign exchange liabilities
				Share of total liabilities			
1980	8.5	71.4	20.2	39.0	2.9	38.0	20.2
1981	9.8	67.9	22.3	36.4	3.9	38.5	21.2
1982	7.5	59.4	33.1	31.8	4.1	39.3	24.8
1983	8.8	41.7	49.6	20.2	3.5	42.6	33.6
1984	9.6	35.5	54.9	19.7	2.8	40.7	36.7
1985	10.4	30.8	58.8	20.6	3.0	41.1	35.3
1986	13.0	27.4	59.6	21.1	4.2	45.2	29.4

Source: International Financial Statistics, IMF.

[a] The item 'other' relates mostly to uncovered rate-of-exchange differences. This item appears in the IFS as a negative item in the liabilities. Here we have placed it as a positive item in the assets, where they should be presented.

As a result, banks again entered into open foreign exchange positions. Finally, some banks converted foreign credits directly into dinar loans.

The largest part of banks' negative foreign exchange positions was created in the 1970s. This was, however, a period when an increase in foreign debts resulted in a large deficit both in visible and invisible foreign trade. At that time the inflation rate and changes in the dinar's rate of exchange were relatively small so that losses due to rate of exchange savings were in these years occasionally taken over by the Federal Government at the moments of major changes in the dinar's rate of exchange. As a result, banks believe that they should not fear the danger of changes in the exchange rate.[8]

It should also be mentioned that in the 1970s banks were strictly forbidden to form so-called 'silent reserves'. All their income had to be distributed among the bank's founders and paid into their accounts. Only after that were the founders obliged to supplement their equity positions in their banks. Since management rights in the banks did not depend on the amount of equity invested in them, and since the income realised by the banks was not distributed exactly proportionally to the capital invested, the founders had little interest in investing in their banks' equity. As a result, banks became increasingly 'under-capitalised'.

By the beginning of the 1980s possibilities for further growth of external indebtedness had run out. This made it necessary to start to adjust the foreign exchange rate. By this fact alone the negative foreign exchange positions of banks, or the fact that they had converted part of foreign exchange liabilities into dinar loans, became a powerful generator of losses through changes in the exchange rate. A turnabout in the policy of the dinar's exchange rate came about much faster than the turnabout in the policy of interest rates. Furthermore, since part of the credits had earlier been granted at fixed and very low interest rates, a large number of banks encountered problems concerning the coverage of losses incurred through changes in the exchange rate. In an attempt to continue the policy of low interest rates in favour of their founders, banks themselves aggravated their problems even more. Under such conditions, lawmakers allowed banks as of 1980 to spread over time their losses due to changes in the exchange rate and to treat them as claims on their assets. This resulted in a gradual accumulation of uncovered exchange rate differences in the balances of banks. A steady increase in the dinar value of banks' liabilities toward foreign countries, households and other sectors having a financial surplus no longer had a counterposition in the banks' claims on the productive sector as the main net debtor (see below for more details).

The level of these uncovered losses in the banking system kept growing after 1980. Their amount can be estimated on the basis of data contained in banks' annual balance sheets and on the basis of the monetary statistics of the central banking system.

COUNTERPOSITIONS OF LOSSES IN THE BANKING SYSTEM: CAPITAL GAINS OF THE PRODUCTIVE SECTOR OF THE ECONOMY

These losses in the banking system have a counterposition in the profits of those sectors which made use of dinar loans obtained from the conversion of banks' foreign exchange liabilities. In the case of Yugoslavia this was the productive sector of the economy.

A calculation made by the author[9] has shown that for the last ten years both the average real interest rate on bank loans used by the productive sector of the economy and the average real interest rate paid on the productive sectors' deposits at banks were deeply negative. In this connection, the productive sector of the economy lost relatively more in real terms per unit of its deposits than it gained per unit of credits used. However, since the economy used many more credits than it had bank deposits, it achieved significant inflationary gains in its total transactions with banks.[10]

These gains acted differently on the balance sheets and income statements of the enterprises in the productive sector of the economy. Inflationary gains on credits for working capital directly appeared in the income statements of the enterprises using such credits. These gains either diminished the monetary costs of such enterprises,[11] or resulted in a direct increase in resources available for wages, taxes and investment.

Regarding credits for fixed assets, inflationary gains did not appear directly on the income statements of enterprises, rather showed up as an increase in the capital of enterprises because enterprise fixed assets were regularly revaluated. Obligations arising from dinar credits for fixed assets remained nominally unchanged. The effects of the revaluation of fixed assets of enterprises were therefore credited to their capital. Depreciation of fixed assets was subsequently computed on the revaluated value of fixed assets, so that inflationary gains from credits for fixed assets were on the whole eliminated from the income statements of enterprises in the productive sector.[12] However, these inflationary gains resulted over time in a steady increase in resources available for investment since depreciation allowances did not have to be used for repaying the principal.

Available data do not make it possible to assess exactly which part of the economy's inflationary gains had an influence on the income statements of enterprises and which on their capital gains. Since the rates of interest on credits for fixed assets were much more slowly adjusted to inflation than the rates of interest on credits for working capital, it can be assumed that the largest part of the inflationary effects resulted in capital gains.

Consequently, the situation was as follows: fixed assets of enterprises preserved their real value in inflation, so that their book value was correctly revaluated. Enterprises' liabilities to banks arising from dinar credits were not revaluated and nominally low and in real terms negative interest rates were paid on them. The external foreign exchange obligations of banks were at the same time automatically revaluated through the rate of exchange. Thus, there were capital gains of enterprises, on the one side, the rate of exchange losses of banks, on the other.

The effect of this inflationary redistribution was a very high degree of enterprise self-financing. Although direct investments in fixed assets were in large measure financed by bank credits, these credits kept depreciating through inflation, resulting in an increase in the level of enterprise self-financing. If we take into consideration overall real (that is, non-financial) assets of the enterprises in the productive sector, two-thirds of these on the aggregate level were financed from enterprises' own capital. In this way, a paradoxical situation was created: the country as a whole was heavily indebted abroad, the government did not have any budget deficit and the productive sector of the economy was to a great extent self-financed. The explanation of this state of affairs lies in the fact that the economy was 'freed' from its obligations to banks, and that banks remained indebted abroad and to households.

SEIGNIORAGE UNDER CONDITIONS OF CAPITAL LOSSES IN THE BANKING SYSTEM

In Yugoslavia the central bank does not monetise budget deficits. In the banking system, money is created through an increase in the net foreign exchange position of the banking system (namely, in foreign exchange reserves)[13] and by bank credits. Under conditions of high inflation for money that is created through bank credits, there is a very big difference between rates of interest collected by banks on their credits and the zero or very low rates of interest they pay on cash or deposits.[14] This difference is very large even when the rates of interest charged by banks are negative in real terms. For the purposes of this analysis we shall define the difference between the rate of inflation and low (or zero) interest rates on banks' monetary liabilities (exclusive of time deposits) created by bank credits – as seigniorage.[15] In other words, this is the income which the banking system as a whole can realise as a result of its monopoly over money creation.

The fact that for a long time banks charged, in real terms, negative interest rates on credits shows that a significant part of this seigniorage was funnelled to credit users. Since the productive sector of the economy was in absolute terms the biggest user of bank credits, the amount of which greatly exceeded the amount of money the productive sector kept in banks,[16] its monetary costs were thus diminished. While all other sectors were compelled to form their cash balances through savings, whereafter these were losing their value at the full rate of inflation, the productive sector of the economy was able to finance its money balances from credits at interest rates which were on the average much lower than the rate of inflation. Even more, through nominally low interest rates the productive sector of the economy made good not only the depreciation of its money balances, but through inflationary gains it was also able to finance part of its real assets.

The distribution of the seigniorage between the central bank and commercial banks was carried out by means of obligatory reserves, and also by means of lower interest rates paid on so-called selective credits given by the central bank. In this distribution, commercial banks always did better. It is characteristic, for example, that until 1988 for household sight deposits there was no obligation to compute obligatory reserves. On short-term resources of other depositors, obligatory reserves amounted up to 25 per cent.[17] At a time when commercial banks did not pay any or only symbolic interest rates on the sight deposits of these depositors, this rate of obligatory reserves enabled commercial banks to appropriate the bulk of the seigniorage. With rising inflation, this amount of gains stemming from differences between rates of interest charged by and those paid to the banks kept increasing. It was precisely this fact that enabled commercial banks gradually to control the problem of uncovered rate-of-exchange differences. Already in 1986 there was a decrease not only in the dollar value but also in the dinar value of uncovered rate-of-exchange differences in commercial banks. Thus, the problem of exchange rate losses is today mainly left to the central bank.

Finally, let us also consider the fate of seigniorage in the central bank system. In Yugoslavia, in addition to the National Bank of Yugoslavia, there are also eight other national banks (six republican and two provincial). In relevant legislation to date, there is *no* provision stating that the National Bank of Yugoslavia can achieve surplus income directly from interest and that such surplus income would constitute a federal revenue item. More specifically, all revenues from loans granted by the central banking system are 'owned' by the national banks of the republics and the national banks of the autonomous provinces. The National Bank of Yugoslavia must cover its costs by participating in the revenues of the republican and provincial national banks. The surplus revenues of the republican and provincial national banks, after a part is set aside for the National Bank of Yugoslavia, constitute the revenues of the republics/ autonomous provinces. These are not entered in their budgets but are directly used for financing some sectors of government expenditure. Exact data on these amounts are not available.

The largest part of revenue collected from interest on dinar credits must be used to pay interest on the foreign exchange liabilities of the National Bank of Yugoslavia. This relates both to its external obligations and to household foreign exchange savings.[18] In order to acquire enough income from interest to meet its liabilities stemming from this interest, the central banking system must achieve enough income from interest collected on dinar loans. Since dinar loans represent an ever smaller amount of the central bank's assets (and an increasing part is accounted for by uncovered rate-of-exchange differences), these interest rates on dinar loans must be nominally very high. Such high interest rates can, however, only be charged under conditions of high inflation.

If an attempt were made to curb inflation to, say, ten per cent, it would also be necessary to reduce the rates of interest on loans from the central bank, so that its revenue would rapidly drop. Anti-inflationary measures would probably lead to the remonetisation of the economy, that is, to an increase in money demand, so that credits of the central bank and then also its revenue could be raised. A radical attempt to curb inflation should, however, be accompanied by a correction of the exchange rate of the dinar, which would in turn increase liabilities arising from interest paid on foreign exchange liabilities. These two effects would in large part cancel each other.

A deficit in the revenue of the central banking system that would appear would, however, have direct effects on the creation of high-powered money. More specifically, if we were to avoid financing the payment of this interest by additional borrowing abroad, the central bank would be obliged to buy foreign exchange to pay this interest. But the central bank would not be able to buy the foreign exchange necessary for interest payments out of its interest revenues, because these revenues would drop. In view of the high level of these liabilities of the central bank, the amount of high-powered money that would be created in this way would be contrary to the aim of curbing inflation. In order to prevent such developments in the sphere of creation of high-powered money, it would be necessary to immobilise part of it through surpluses in the government budget. This shows that in order to curb inflation in Yugoslavia it is not enough to balance the budget, but a significant budget surplus must be achieved.

Considered from the aspect of seigniorage, it can be said that the central banking system is compelled to achieve large gains on the difference between the rates of interest to be collected and those to be paid in order to cover its costs stemming from the large amounts of accumulated uncovered losses incurred as a result of rate of exchange fluctuations. These losses are the consequence of the transformation of foreign exchange liabilities into dinar loans where the interest paid on them is not sufficient to cover the overall costs of these liabilities. As a result of significant subsidies to the productive sector of the economy, not only did the government in the past fail to collect seigniorage, but it also spent seigniorage in advance in the years that followed to pay interest on foreign exchange debts, which it never used to finance its budget.

EFFECTS OF THE FINANCIAL SYSTEM'S CONTACT WITH THE 'EAST'

Until now we have analysed the effects of contacts between the Yugoslav financial system and convertible currency countries. In its trade with East European countries, Yugoslavia largely applies the clearing system of payments. In trade with the countries with which this mode of payment has been stipulated, Yugoslavia has significant balance of payment surpluses. These have resulted in the creation of specific 'reserves' of the central bank. More specifically, all exports to these countries are monetised, and when there is a trade surplus the central bank has a surplus claim in its balance. No interest is charged on this surplus claim. This balance is presented in so-called accounting dollars, since world market prices in dollars are applied in trade relations with the East. In this way the central bank finds itself in a situation where, on the one hand, it has a considerable convertible currency imbalance and, on the other, a positive balance in 'accounting dollars'.

This position of the central bank causes considerable problems. True, on the one hand the position in 'accounting dollars' partly balances liabilities in covertible currencies because the rate of exchange of the accounting dollar follows domestic inflation. On the other hand, the formation of the 'accounting reserves' leads to the creation of considerable amounts of high-powered money, which is often at variance with other aims of Yugoslav monetary policy. There are, however, considerable losses in interest effects since no interest is charged on clearing account balances. Finally, in the intention of eliminating these balances, various measures are taken to stimulate imports from clearing countries, the result being a decrease in the nominal effects of the rise in the dinar countervalue of these 'accounting reserves'.

CONCLUSION

In this chapter attention has been drawn to some problems arising in contacts between the Yugoslav financial system and the West and East, and partly also in their mutual links. Until now, researchers' attention has mainly been devoted to the problems of visible trade, while here an attempt has been made to draw attention to specific problems in the financial, or more exactly, monetary–banking system. Needless to say, the main cause of these problems lies in the internal problem of the Yugoslav economic system, but some if its weaknesses come more to expression in its contacts with its environment. Although the problems in their concrete form are specific to Yugoslavia, there is a probability that they will also appear in other socialist countries which are reluctant to pay sufficient attention to the establishment of a regular monetary–banking system.

Notes

1. For more information, see data on the liabilities and claims of the federal government and other socio-political communities published in the *Bulletin of the National Bank of Yugoslavia*.
2. This independence is, however, relative. On the one hand, the election of managing bodies in enterprises is subject to the powerful influence of local political circles. Furthermore, communes can easily derogate self-managing rights in individual enterprises and introduce extraordinary measures in them. On the other hand, economic policy frequently relies on administrative measures, such as price and wage control or control of income distribution in enterprises, imposing special conditions for obtaining import licenses, determining sectors and/or purposes for which credits can be obtained under favourable terms, and so forth.
3. This was changed in the new Banking System Act of 1986. However, until now there have not been any major changes in the mode of bank management.
4. It should be noted that a securities market exists in Yugoslavia only in rudimentary form. Predominant are bills of exchange with a maturity of a maximum of 90 days, which are issued in commodity transactions between enterprises. Private individuals do not have any possibility to buy such securities, but enterprises mutually trade in them. This is, in fact, the only form of capital market that currently exists in Yugoslavia.
5. Banks have frequently found various ways avoiding acceptance of such deposits.
6. This was changed in the amendments to the Associated Labour Act passed in 1887.
7. Such a possibility has been severely restricted at various points in time.
8. In 1978 the National Bank also took over all liabilities arising from changes in exchange rates also with respect to household foreign exchange savings. Since then, foreign exchange savings has been treated as a liability of the National Bank of Yugoslavia towards commercial banks.
9. Article published in *Naše teme*, No. 4–5, 1986.
10. All other domestic sectors recorded losses in real terms in their transactions with banks. This relates to the non-profit sector (education, culture, science, and so forth), socio-political communities, and households. The

latter achieved gains in real terms on foreign exchange savings and on credits used but sustained losses on all forms of financial dinar assets, including cash. Losses sustained by households always exceeded their gains.

11. Under conditions of inflation, money (either in cash or in the form of interest free or low-interest sight deposits) loses its value. I call this loss a monetary cost.
12. In self-managing enterprises in which personal incomes (wages and salaries) and the largest part of taxes are indexed to their income, which also includes resources for wages and salaries (namely, the income of the enterprises is defined as value added minus depreciation allowances), it is of great importance whether inflationary gains appear in income statements.
13. The net foreign exchange position of the banking system has for many years now been negative, namely, its foreign exchange liabilities have exceeded its foreign exchange claims.
14. On household sight deposits, banks pay interest at a rate of 7.5 per cent; on the sight deposits of the productive sector of the economy, four per cent; and of the non-profit sector, zero per cent. The rates of interest paid on time deposits were also in the 1970s considerably lower than the rate of inflation. Only after an agreement was concluded with the International Monetary Fund was the obligation introduced for banks to pay on time deposits (but only of households and the productive sector of the economy) interest at the rates computed on the basis of the average rate of inflation recorded in the few preceding months and the rate of inflation foreseen for a few following months. The formula, according to which these interest rates were computed, was frequently changed, so that they rarely ensured the depositors a positive rate of interest.
15. Here we neglect a possible real rate of interest, that is, the part of the interest rate exceeding the rate of inflation, which should also be a source of seigniorage.
16. Enterprises are not allowed to keep any significant amount of cash.
17. The central bank pays a four per cent (symbolic) interest rate on obligatory reserves.
18. In return, commercial banks pay to the National Bank of Yugoslavia the dinar countervalue of foreign exchange savings at the moment of their deposition, actually on the dinar amounts obtained by them through the earlier conversion of household foreign exchange savings into dinar loans. Although the interest rate paid by the National Bank of Yugoslavia on foreign exchange savings is relatively low (six to seven per cent), because it corresponds to the customary interest rates paid on foreign exchange liabilities, and the interest rate on the original dinar value of savings is relatively high because it corresponds to the domestic rate of inflation, this nevertheless creates large liabilities for the National Bank of Yugoslavia. More specifically, the original dinar countervalue of foreign exchange savings amounts to only a small part of the present dinar value of these savings.

Bibliography

R. DORNBUSH and S. FISHER, *Stopping Hyperinflations Past and Present* (National Bureau of Economic Research, January 1986).

B. FISCHER and P. TRAPP, 'The Argentina Financial Sector: Performance, Problems and Policy Issues', *Kiel Working Paper No. 226* (February 1985).

B. FISCHER and P. TRAPP, 'Economic Costs of Large Public Sector Deficits and High Inflation – The Argentina Lesson', *Kiel Working Paper No. 237* (August 1985).

B. FISCHER and P. TRAPP, 'Financial Markets and Monetary Control Under High Inflation – The Case of Argentina', *Kiel Working Paper No. 232* (June 1985).

S. FISCHER, 'The Economy of Israel', *Carnegie–Rochester Conference Series on Public Policy, Monetary and Fiscal Policies and Their Application*, 20 (Spring 1984) 7–52.

R. D. MALLON, *Economic Policymaking in a Conflict Society: The Argentine Case* (Harvard University Press: Cambridge, MA, and London, England, 1975).

N. MATES, 'Gradani i naš monetarno-bankarski sistem u uvjetima inflacije – Tko gubi, a tko zaraduje' (Households and Our Credit and Monetary System Under Conditions of Inflation – Who is Losing and Who is Profiting), in *Prilog analizi tekućih privrednih kretanja i ekonomske politike u SR Hrvatskoj* (Institute of Economics, Zagreb, 1984) 49–75.

N. MATES, 'Problem nagomilanih gubitaka u financijskom sistemu SFRJ' (Problem of Accumulated Losses in the Financial System of the Socialist Federal Republic of Yugoslavia), in *Naše teme*, No. 4–5 (1986) 719–759.

N. MATES, 'Značajne promjene u poziciji bankarskog sistema u 1986.g.' (Significant Changes in the Position of the Banking System in 1986), in *Aktuelni problemi privrednih kretanja i ekonomske politike Jugoslavije* (Institute of Economics Zagreb, 1987) 49–59.

N. MATES, 'Analiza monetarnih efekata revalorizacije kredita' (An Analysis of the Monetary Effects of the Revaluation of Credits), in *Ekonomski pregled*, No. 9–10 (1987).

12 The Foreign Policy Conditions affecting Economic Relations between the Smaller European States
Peter Knirsch

The strong influence of the United States and the Soviet Union as great powers on the foreign policy of all the European states is obvious. Since the end of the Second World War, the political objectives of these two great powers have had a decisive influence on the conduct of the smaller European countries allied with them, as well as on the conduct of neutral countries. The ideologically based political antagonism between the two great powers also led to political antagonisms between the European countries – whether they desired it or not, they were part of the conflict between the great powers. However, the Europeans did not identify with the great powers in every respect. As their own power increased over time or the political dominance of the respective hegemonical power was weakened in individual cases, the desire or the necessity for European co-operation that transcended systems and alliances proved to be strong. Additionally, intersystemary relations in Europe slowly, but clearly, became more intense. This must not lead to the acceptance of the myth of Europe: the idealisation of European history as a history based on a community of interests is overstated. The concept of European unification does have some basis in reality, but it is much more limited than what the ideal aims at achieving.

What has remained of these common European interests is very difficult to put into concrete terms because, on the one hand, the East–West conflict has masked and suppressed them to some extent for the past 40 years and, on the other hand, because this common heritage is not only positive, but also includes old enmities and prejudices.

It is obvious that the improved political climate between East and

West after 1986 has thus far not had a positive influence on East–West economic relations. Such economic relations continue to stagnate for economic reasons. Political factors can considerably disrupt intersystemary economic relations, but they can promote such relations only to a limited degree, for the development of such economic relations depends to a certain extent on economic situations. At the time of writing, it seems possible to eliminate or mitigate political distortions in East–West trade, but making the necessary changes in the economic structure of some of the European countries involved, and doing so quickly enough, will probably be much more difficult.

13 Problems and Prospects of East–West Transfer of Technology
Stanislav Simanovsky

The socialist countries have become actively involved in the international exchange of technology, particularly with respect to the sale and purchase of licenses, since the mid-1960s. The last decade has witnessed the appearance of new important factors in East–West transfer of technology aiming at amelioration of legal, institutional and economic mechanisms of this process and at improving its efficiency. There is a growing trend to combine licensing with purchasing and leasing of appropriate research and technological equipment, 'turnkey' plants, and complete sets of machinery.

Meanwhile, there are factors hindering the process of mutually beneficial transfer of technology between East and West. It is an internal factor that CMEA countries are lagging behind the world level in some important areas of science and technology such as computer hardware and software, new materials, certain kinds of mechanical engineering, electronics, optics, biotechnology and others. This is combined with poor quality and low competitiveness of industrial goods manufactured on the basis of both domestic and foreign technology which considerably reduces the export potential of the machinery and equipment produced in CMEA countries. The innovative process is also delayed by a slow speed of diffusion of innovations, inadequate mechanism of stimulation of technological progress, including its economic, legal and institutional components. Among external factors, politicalisation of trade is the most important. This was especially noticeable at the end of the 1970s and in the early 1980s when some Western countries, first of all the United States, introduced strict rules regulating export to socialist countries and enforced more severe practices of export administration with the COCOM framework.

It is not the technological war, but broad international scientific and technological contacts in the interests of the co-operating countries and the whole of mankind that should enjoy priority in the development of East–West relations.

14 Towards a Comprehensive Economic Reform? A Pessi-Optimistic View
László Szamuely

The radical novelty of the present Soviet reform, initiated by the Gorbachev leadership, is the definite and openly declared intention to abandon the very backbone of the Stalinist model of the planned economy: the sacrosanct system of central 'breaking-down' of plan targets and central allocation of material resources in physical terms. One should see this as a major breakthrough in the long history of sharp, sometimes bitter debates on reforming the 'really existing' socialist economies that goes back to the mid-1950s. The history of the Hungarian reform, however, shows that departure from the directive planning system does not necessarily mean a change to a market economy, or even to a regulated one. The government does not dictate to companies directly what and how to produce but indirectly – by means of financial regulation (taxes, interest rates), pricing, and crediting – regulates the economic activities of them. The government's aim is to fulfil the centrally elaborated plans as completely and smoothly as possible by regulating the incomes of the companies. Thus, a direct control is being replaced by an indirect one.

The experiences of the Hungarian and perhaps the Polish reforms suggest that the system of indirect control possibly is an unavoidable intermediate stage or model on the way towards a full-blooded market economy. In Centrally Planned Economies (CPEs) struggling with internal and external disequilibria, with shortage economy of different degrees, the immediate abolition of the strong central control would not be possible without the danger of economic anarchy and collapse.

There are many obstacles to the reforms needed to be carried out in CPEs. The most important is the lack of attractive and convincing examples of unambiguous reform successes. Another group of obstacles is of a sociological, political and ideological nature. A less frequently mentioned but serious obstacle is the import-restricting policy that has been pursued by Eastern Europe for a decade to cure the deteriorated external economic balances. Only tough work, painful corrections, competent leadership, and the determined execution of innovations can give one hope that by the turn of the millennium Eastern Europe will be freed from its economic quagmire.

15 Reflections on Enterprise-level Currency Conversion in Foreign Trade: The Case of Hungary
Ádám Török

Currency conversion in foreign trade takes place in an economy that participates in more than one international trade and accounting system. One of these is world trade accounted in freely convertible currencies, while others include a zone of bilateral and multilateral clearing like CMEA or the bilateral clearing rouble accounting system between the Soviet Union and Finland. Currency conversion in Hungarian foreign trade as elsewhere in Eastern Europe, is a special case of which there is a very low degree of substitutability and a substantial difference of efficiency criteria between the two types of exports and imports.

Currency conversion in trade on the microeconomic level can be analysed with a 'black box model'. This means an enterprise may be analysed only on the basis of four international trade flows, that is two flows of exports and imports to and from the two separate markets – the CMEA and the West. Thus only the direct trade flows of an enterprise come into the scope of the analysis, but exactly these are the foreign trade flows that can be influenced by economic policy. Currency conversion in foreign trade takes place if the sign of the enterprise level trade balance in rouble trade is different from that in dollar trade. Conversion is 'from-rouble-to-dollar' if rouble trade has a negative balance and dollar trade a positive balance. With dollar trade showing a negative balance and rouble trade a positive balance, enterprise level currency conversion is considered to be of the 'from-dollar-to-rouble' type.

About one-third of our sample of 127 Hungarian industrial enterprises were engaged in currency conversion in 1980 and 1984. The picture is surprisingly clear.

- Out of 53 enterprises in the machinery industry, more than twenty show currency conversion, all of them dollar-to-rouble type.
- In light industry, out of 40 enterprises eleven to fourteen exhibit show currency conversion. With one exception (a spinning factory) all of them experience dollar-to-rouble currency conversion.
- Included in the sample are thirteen enterprises in the iron and steel industry, out of which nine are steel mills. This sector generally shows rouble-to-dollar type conversion – five to five enterprises in both 1980 and 1989 – stemming from the low value-added transformation of Soviet raw materials into iron and steel characterised by high energy intensity and high raw material content.
- Out of twenty enterprises in the chemical industry, nine to eleven firms show currency conversion. Dollar-to-rouble conversion is usual in light chemistry and the pharmaceutical industry (altogether five to seven enterprises), whereas two to four enterprises (above all in the petrochemical industry) show rouble-to-dollar conversion.
- Rouble-to-dollar conversion on a large scale is found in the one Hungarian enterprise that handles oil refining.

The model of 'interdependent currency conversion transactions in trade' functions in the following way. If enterprise A as a producer of machinery increases its exports with a high 'dollar content' to the Soviet Union, an increase of Hungarian 'dollar exports' becomes necessary. This is made by petrochemical exporter B, using more inputs originating from the Soviet Union. This eventual increase of 'rouble imports' is not obviously a counterpart of earlier incremental 'rouble exports' by enterprise A (because mutual deliveries of a certain sort of machinery and oil are much less than obviously linked to each other), so incremental 'rouble exports' by enterprise C would be required by the Soviet Union. If these incremental exports have a high 'dollar content', additional 'dollar exports' by enterprise D become urgent and so on.

This mediating role of Hungarian industry poses a problem, above all during 1975–1985 when conditions of both types of currency conversion in trade have significantly worsened for Hungary. Prices of imported Soviet oil decreased slower than export prices of petrochemical products on the world market, while the prices of imported Western machinery and parts have increased faster than Hungarian export prices on the Soviet market. Careful macroeconomic analysis would be necessary to show the extent to which the compensation for imports needed for rouble-dollar conversion makes further dollar-rouble conversion necessary. Based on such analysis, it is my opinion that any eventual elimination of low efficiency Hungarian productive activities would not have serious employment consequences because of given their low value-added content. However, such a reduction of productive capacity would at least temporarily diminish the structural openness of the Hungarian economy.

16 Joint Ventures between East and West
Tauno Tiusanen

In the current period of East–West economic co-operation the practice of establishing joint ventures is spreading. However, the excitement of this phenomenon should be approached with caution because there are factors which do not favour large-scale capital movements from West to East.

It seems to be unlikely that the large-scale flow of direct investment from the West to the East will occur in the extracting industries of the socialist countries in order to advance the vertical integration of Western firms. For example, the acquisition of mines in socialist countries by Western firms is prohibited; therefore, one of the still valid methods of Western direct investments in the socialist world is out of question, or at best hardly usable.

CMEA countries emphasise their relatively inexpensive and well-educated labour force as an incentive for joint ventures with Western firms. One must consider, however, that the relative importance of labour costs in production shows a decreasing tendency. In the manufacturing branches, which are always labour intensive, plentiful offers are globally available for both contract manufacturing and direct investments.

Western businessmen are not familiar with the bilateral trading system in which deliveries are purchased in transferable roubles. Therefore, many of them do not see that direct investment cannot be conducted in a CMEA country using the same methods as within the EC.

The outdated CMEA monetary system is characterised by a supply-oriented economy, a passive role of money, and the non-convertibility of national currencies. Undoubtedly, these are the main stumbling blocks of direct investments between East and West. The Western partner is normally looking for large, readily available markets in order to earn convertible currency, whereas the host country tries to avoid converting locally earned currency or transferable roubles into convertible means of payment.

A comprehensive monetary reform is an important precondition for substantial direct investments from the West to the East. Obviously, this has also been understood in the CMEA, especially in Hungary, for quite some time.

17 The Involvement of the CMEA Countries in the International Trade in Services: Can They be Competitive?
Marie Lavigne

Several reasons explain why analysis of the services sector in centrally planned economies' (CPEs) trade is difficult. In most CPEs the national accounting is based on the net material product system which excludes services. Information on the contribution of this sector to growth and national income is very limited. In CPEs the balance of payment statistics are usually not published and other public data for trade in services are very poor. At the time of writing, a quantitative study is hardly possible. Such an approach is totally excluded for countries as Bulgaria, the GDR and Rumania.

Concerning specific services, maritime transport is significant for Poland and the Soviet Union. Both countries are significant competitors for Western shipping companies and they are often accused of rate-cutting. Direct evidence is, however, difficult to provide. One should apply to this area those analyses of dumping which have been done on merchandise trade. For instance, the definition of 'normal value', the identification of subsidies, and the allocation of those subsidies are concepts that have to be defined more consistently.

In tourism, all European socialist countries have a positive balance because their citizens have limited opportunities for travel and because the export of tourist services is heavily supported through various methods. Here again, it is difficult to provide evidence of dumping. For instance, the fact that restaurant prices are very low for the tourist is due both to exchange rate subsidisation and to low food prices which also benefit the local population. In addition, there is everywhere a discrimination against tourists from socialist countries, who are hit by the special limitation of less favourable exchange rates. This leads to a 'double market' for international tourist services, the rationale of which has to be investigated.

Under the heading 'advanced services', one may include a number of services of which some categories may appear as already 'traditional' for market economies, but less so for centrally planned economies, such as insurance, banking and financial services, and construction and engineering services. The Soviet Union in particular has a long history of experience in those fields, mainly through the operation of Soviet-owned firms in the Developed West and in developing countries. The main question here is whether the Soviet Union (and East European countries) will follow the modernisation drive which characterises the evolution of such services in the international trade of developed market economies. There is a vast group of services which are only beginning to be supplied by centrally planned economies, such as sales of software or transactions in information services. Attention must be paid to a specific form of service which is offered by the Soviet Union on the international markets, namely the commercial launching of satellites. The Soviet Union already appears to be a competitor for the United States, for Europe (Arianespace) and for China, especially if account is taken of the Soviet Union's very low rates.

The need for more research in this area is acknowledged both in the West and in the East, where the lack of specialists and expertise is readily recognised.

18 Money as a Means of Communication and Reforms in Eastern Europe: Some Propositions
Raimund Dietz

1. In the capitalist Western world economic communication rests on money mediated exchange between private economic agents. In a monetarised economy the state may also act as a private economic agent.
2. When socialism stepped onto the historical stage it was widely believed that it would be able to perform economic tasks more efficiently and more humanely than capitalism. Experience revealed the contrary. The attempt to socialise from the top downward has led to *three* modes of socio–economic communication – or Marxists would say: modes of production.
3. These modes, existing side by side, are:
  - Central administration of economic activities characterised by vertical chains of order and information.
  - Quasi- or pseudo-market relations. (The combination of these two forms of communication with all its consequences is the subject of the old debate on plan and market.)
  - The intra-CMEA mechanism characterised by moneyless barter between states.
4. Each of these types is systemically inferior to money mediated exchange relations (commodity-money relations).
5. The reform politician usually takes for granted that reforms can only be successful if economies – domestically and intra-CMEA – are monetarised. The theoretician will probably sympathise, but will not be able to support this view since theoretically money is inessential (neutral or quasi-neutral). This is not a deliberate assumption, but derives logically from the models of allocative efficiency.
6. Money, however, is not neutral but extremely productive sys-

temically. Only exchange generates money, and only money renders possible worldwide economic socialisation. Exchange communication, on which Western civilisation is based, is 'up from below' socialisation, and its most important means is money. The elimination or suppression of exchange relations has immeasurable consequences.

7. Socialist economies can be interpreted as (non-profit) organisations on a national scale with semi-autonomous sub-organisations (enterprises). The economic wellbeing of the latter depends on successful bartering with the centre *and* on (horizontal) exchange communication with clients. This ambiguous role of the enterprises is reflected by unclear boundaries between them and their environment (budget constraints are soft) and by the passivity of money (quantitative rather than monetary constraints bite first.) The softness of budget constraints and the passivity of money are only two sides of the coin. Permanent shortages deprive money of its function as a means of exchange (and thus as a means of storage).

8. Intra-CMEA trade is regulated without money (exceptions notwithstanding). Plans are co-ordinated in advance, and bundles of products are bartered by state agencies who neither know costs nor real opportunities, so that world market prices have to be invoked.

9. Thus the transferable rouble is an accounting unit, applicable only in actual barter. It does not buy. Therefore it is neither transferable (if possible, credit is avoided) nor convertible.

10. Inside CPEs the use of money is supportable in spite of its softness since (unknowable) gains and losses may cancel out under the cover of State property. This is different with intra-CMEA affairs: states, whose paternalist behaviour ends at their border, avoid storing, and prevent enterprises from holding soft 'socialist' currencies: those must not be used, because they do not really buy.

11. Attempting to make the transferable rouble convertible is like putting the cart before the horse. To be real money it must be able to buy at reasonable transaction cost. Only if money is really able to buy, it may become convertible. (If not, the currency will yield only a near zero-price in terms of hard currencies.) A common CMEA currency – if it were achievable for systemic reasons after a long evolutionary process – may be not desirable for political reasons.

12. The monetarisation of socialist economies in only achievable, if the state withdraws consistently from operative interventions into the economy, that is, when economic communications will be based on exchange relations. Only then can money emerge as a means of

exchange, and shall budget constraints be hardened. This applies to domestic affairs as well as to intra-CMEA relations. Direct enterprise links are indispensable to monetarisation. However, in striving to reduce risks, rationally behaving enterprises will prefer harder (= easier buying) to softer currencies. The higher the degree of shortages in the economy, the softer the currencies – the lower is the chance for economic integration in the East. This is why the West may be economically so attractive that East–West economic relations may in the long run override East–East relations.

19 Summary Remarks
Tamás Földi

I am going to concentrate in my summary remarks on that political and institutional framework which determines the overall form and content of East–West and East–East economic relations.

In European history, deep separations between regions have been present since antiquity. I suspect, nevertheless, none of them have been of such a global nature as the separation after the Second World War. This mostly affected the countries of Central and Eastern Central Europe. The basic facts of this separation determine those problems we have focused on in our conference. But separation is not a natural state of affairs and it is even more clearly abnormal in our present world. Interdependence cannot be excluded from international relations. Huge countries with a wide variety of natural endowments and human skills and large economic potential can survive such a separation for a very long time. The history of a number of Asian countries proves this in quite a convincing manner. Another question is that a long-standing separation has its adverse consequences which are *a posteriori* very difficult to eliminate. Of course, economic separation does not mean the total abolishment of contacts, rather it means the lack of organic links such as prices, monetary system, structural adjustment, and so forth. It is a natural endeavour, especially in those small countries which, by definition, suffer the most from economic separation, that they try to find ways to overcome its consequences, as well as an optimal compromise between their attachment to a coalition and the necessity for participation in the economic and technological globalisation process. This is the case of dual attachment which is, of course, not the same for market economies (MEs), and the borderline centrally planned economies (CPEs). The mixed nature of the market economies provides the potential for these countries to cope with the conditions of trade with the CPEs in a flexible way. The Finnish case, which has been analysed and discussed, is good evidence of that: Soviet trade is largely influenced by a system of government intervention which, at the same time, tries to preserve the independence of enterprises in their decision making. MEs can assess their economic relation with CPE countries as basically successful. Less success can be observed on the part of the CPEs in their economic relations with the West. As mentioned in a number of chapters, CPEs have lost ground and are in a more and more marginal position in the external economic relations of the MEs. It is hardly possible to avoid the conclusion that just the less mixed character of the centrally planned economies is the major obstacle to their successful adjustment to the world market. Difficulties in economic relations within the CMEA area are also due to systemic causes. There exists an evident contradiction between the CPE economic system – that was originally shaped under an autarchic approach and thus lacked traditional tools of international economic relations, many of which proved to be irreplaceable – and the need for intensive external economic relations. The almost exclusive role of the government bureaucracy in shaping these relations is the major obstacle to a rational and progressive development of these contacts.

Nobody is satisfied with the present state of affairs in the CPEs, not even those who are against any substantial change either in the intra-CMEA relations or in the national economy.

At present there are three options, at least in principle, in improving the actual situation in the socialist countries:
1. To use tools of the command economy to push the economy in the direction of planned technological progress and structural change;
2. To combine central planning and economic regulation in order to do the same;
3. To abandon central planning, except for some sectors, and to replace it by full (external and internal) market orientation supplemented by state intervention to diminish adverse effects and to strengthen positive effects.

It is hardly deniable that under particular conditions the second alternative can be rather effective in the light of exhaustion of command tools. However, arguments for the third option show limitations inherent in the second option. In order to overcome problems mentioned above it is necessary to create such circumstances both within the national economies and in their external relations where efficiency and structural change are a *sine qua non* of survival and growth of enterprises. Economic reforms tend to exert such effects. The Soviet economic reform ideas clearly show such a tendency. But as it has been raised in this volume – based on the experiences of previous reforms – there exist minimum conditions of achieving the expected results of the reform policy. As pointed out, the abolition of the central breakdown of obligatory plan targets and the switchover from the so-called 'material-technical supply' to commerce in materials and means of production as well as other steps to secure the independence of enterprises are indispensable for development in this direction. While these conditions are necessary, experience has proven that they are still not satisfactory. The necessity of a parallel existence of plan and market is not self-explanatory. Those steps taken in Hungary in 1968 and envisaged in the Soviet Union for the coming years do not give an unambiguous solution to the question how central planning can be coupled with the existence of a well-functioning market. It is evident that prices, the investment system, and the system of foreign economic relations play a decisive role in this respect. Conditions for creating a real mixture of market and plan seem to be mainly political. Without a decisive political change, there is no hope for progress in this field. If such a political change can lead to changing the process of decision-making, the status of individuals and their behaviour as producers, only then can even the most widely shaped but up to now mostly empty patterns of economic organisation be filled with contents. This change cannot be introduced overnight, therefore the significance of intermediary solutions is tremendous. At the same time, we cannot forget that new intermediary solutions bear a rather great risk. They are often Janus-faced and their progressive role can be limited to a minimum because of the weight of previous conditions, routines and interests in preserving the traditional power structure. It has been pointed out many times in these pages that compromises, setbacks, and withdrawals are not excluded. If the thesis by Gorbachev that a radical reform has no alternatives proves to be an actual leading principle, there is hope that both East–West and intra-CMEA economic relations have brighter prospects.

The interrelation between politics in general and the success of economic reforms could be analysed further. What the relation is between economic reform and economic policy, or even, in a wider sense, economic strategy, is a much debated question. Hungarian experience shows that economic reform cannot by all means have a decisive impact on economic policy, but if they are not in accordance, they can mutually neutralise each other. Foreign economic policy and strategy has an outstanding role in the interrelation between policy and reform, perhaps not everywhere so much and in such a direct way as in Hungary. But even in the Soviet Union foreign economic relations should become an organic part of the economic process and foreign economic strategy has to be shaped in accordance with the principles of economic reforms. Economic isolation has deep roots in Stalinist economic policy that have to be overcome, but not as it was done in the 1970s as a *replacement* of reforms but as a supplementary source of economic development both in the real sphere and in the management system. How successfully the Soviet Union and other East European countries can cope with all these difficult tasks is the question of the future.

Index

Albania, 35
  and bilateral clearing trade with Yugoslavia, 157, 162
Ausch, Sándor, 78, 79 n4 and 11
Austria
  abolition of clearing, 9, 12–13
  Austrian Control Bank, 104–6
  Austrian National Bank, 101
  Currency Law of 1946, 101
  customs authorisation procedure (*Zollämtermächtigungsverfahren*), 99
  customs regime, 102–6
  foreign trade economic policy, 80–108
  Foreign Trade Law 1968, 99, 100, 101
  Law on Tariff Preferences (*Präferenzzollgesetz*), 103
  pre-war trade, 96
  State Treaty of 1955, 96–7, 98
  trade relations with Eastern Europe, 90–2, 95
  trade relations with Western Europe, 92–4
Austrian economic model, 81
Austro-Keynesianism, 80–1

bankruptcy, in the Soviet Union, 60
Bellagio Conference, x, 1, 124
bilateral barter, 38–40, 158
bilateral clearing, 126, 157
  compared with hard-currency settlements, 5–21
  and Fino-Soviet trade, 1
  and Yugoslav trade, 7, 157–73
bilateral contingency list, 39–40, 47
Brussels Tariff Nomenclature (BTN), and analysis of Yugoslav trade, 165
Bucharest price formation principle, 11, 15, 123
  in Hungary, 46

Bulgaria, 7, 35, 92
  and convertible currency trade with Yugoslavia, 162
central planning
  effects on trade systems, 8–10
  Hungarian National Planning Office, 44, 50
  in the Soviet Union, 58–63, 123
  parallel existence of plan and market, 209
  reform of, 60–5, 195–6
  State Planning Committee, 60
centrally planned economies (CPEs)
  effect on exchange rates and prices in market economies, 126–39
  international competitiveness of services sectors in CPEs, 202–3
  reform and obstacles to reform, 195–6
  role of money in CPEs, 204–6
China
  and Hungarian exports, 73
  and Soviet competition in trade, 203
COCOM, 194
comparative advantage, Austria, 95
Council for Mutual Economic Assistance (CMEA), 95, 97–8, 106, 109–16, 123–4, 140–56
  deterioration of cooperation, 64–6
  exports to USSR, 140–56
  institutional characteristics, 31, 38–40, 44
  monetary system, 200–1
  reform of, 10, 20–1
  specialisation, 47, 51
  trade in, 1–4, 5–21, 207–10
  trade with USSR, 74–8
  trade in services sector, 202–3
currency

convertibility (hard currency), 64, 73, 141, 157, 205; enterprise-level currency conversion in foreign trade in Hungary, 49, 197–9; and East–West joint ventures, 200–1; establishing limited convertibility in Yugoslavia, 169–73; Finnish markka, 119 and Hungarian balance of paymets, 76; and use in clearing bilateral balances, 7–8, 69, 125 n3; convertibility of rouble, 62
roubles: clearing roubles, 110, 118, 147, 153 (*see also* bilateral clearing); inconvertibility of rouble, 31, 125 n6; transferable roubles, 6, 31, 37, 52, 113
upgrading Yugoslav national currency, 157–73
currency reform, in the Soviet Union, 61
Czechoslovakia, 7, 40, 41, 44
trade with Austria, 90, 95
trade with Yugoslavia, 7, 157, 160–4, 166

debt
and foreign trade performance of CMEA, 31, 33
Hungarian debt to the West, 29, 31, 37
rescheduling, 176
Soviet debt to the West, 70
developing countries, and Soviet-owned firms, 203
dual attachment, 9–10, 207
and impact on Yugoslav trade, 157–73
in the Soviet Union's import system, 140–56
dumping, 202
Durbin–Watson statistics, as used in Soviet import analysis, 150–5

East–West relations, 192–3, 207
joint ventures, 200–1

technology transfers, 194
enterprises
enterprise-level currency conversion in Hungary, 197–9
and Hungarian manufacturing, 45–54
and *perestroika*, 59
European Free Trade Area (EFTA), 80, 82, 83, 92, 97, 103
European Economic Community (EEC)
agricultural policy, 62
elimination of customs, 13–14
trade relations with Austria, 80, 82, 83, 92–4, 97
exchange rates, 114, 168
affected by trade between Centrally Planned Economies
between Austria and the FRG, 81
between Finland and the Soviet Union, 119, 120
between Hungary and the Soviet Union, 113
and 'double market' for international tourist services, 203
and market economies, 126–32, 136–7
export financing, in Austria's East–West trade, 104–6

Federal Republic of Germany (FRG), 40, 81
similarity to Austrian export procedures, 83, 90
trade with Czechoslovakia and the Soviet Union, 166
Finland, 7
abolition of clearing, 9–10, 13–16
currency clearing system, 7–8
government agencies, 116
hard-currency settlement of payments, 7
internal regulation of trade with socialist countries, 109–25
Licensing Office, 118
and purchasing of Soviet

Index

products, 129, 137
similarity to Austrian export procedures, 101
and trade with Soviet Union, 7, 53, 110, 116–20, 125, 147–8, 156 n11, 197
foreign-trading organizations (FTOs), 45–7, 55 n17

General Agreement on Tariffs and Trade (GATT)
conformity, 20
and Austrian customs regime, 92, 102–3
and customs authorisation procedure, 99
involvement in Soviet Union, 62
and trade liberalisation of Austria, 82
General System of Preferences (GSP), for Bulgaria, Rumania and Hungary in Austria, 92
German Democratic Republic (GDR), 7, 40, 77
trade imbalances, 77
trade with Austria, 90, 95
trade with Yugoslavia (bilateral clearing), 157, 159, 162
Germany, see Federal Republic of Germany
goods
'hard' goods, 16–18, 48, 65, 74, 157
'soft' goods, 16–18, 157
substitutes and complements, in relation to Soviet production, 140
Gorbachev, M.
'pre-crisis' of CMEA economies, 78
radical reform thesis, 195, 209
Gross Domestic Product
of CMEA countries, 30, 32
and growth of Hungarian economy, 32, 66

'hard' goods, see goods
Hewett, Ed, Hungarian GDP index, 54 n7

Hungarian Socialist Workers' Party, and economic reform, 29
Hungary, 7
agriculture, 23, 28
analysis of multiple trade-attachments, 45–51
co-dependency of reform and foreign trade policy-making, 51–4
convertible currency trade with Yugoslavia, 158, 159, 162
economic reform, 23–32, 122, 195
enterprise-level currency conversion in foreign trade, 197–9
foreign trade, 19, 23–57; Yugoslav trade, 7; Hungarian–Soviet trade, 35–7, 40–4, 45, 46, 50, 55 n10, 64–9; trade with Austria, 90, 92, 95
institutional obstacles to foreign trade decision-making, 33–44
macroeconomic and foreign trade performance, 32–3
market-type foreign trade practice, 9
monetary reform and investment from the West, 201
regulation of trade with socialist countries, 109–25

implicit subsidies, 74, 79 n7–9
import maximisation, and Hungarian–Soviet trade, 65, 78 n2
imports
of grain from CMEA to USSR, 148
see also trade
indicative planning, 60
inflation, in heavily-indebted Yugoslavia, 174–91
Institute for World Economics, Hungarian Academy of Sciences, survey of Hungarian enterprises, 45
integration, of Western Europe and

influence on trade, 92
inter-German trade, 90
international division of labour, 58, 162
International Monetary Fund (IMF)
  and abolition of clearing in Austria, 13
  and the Soviet Union, 62
  and interest rates in Yugoslavia, 178, 190 n14
investment
  in the East from West, 200–1
  and necessity of monetary reform, 200–1

Japan, and trade with Austria, 91, 100
joint ventures, 62, 200–1

Keynesian unemployment, 126–8
Kornai, János
  and discord between plan and market, 26
  and naiveté of NEM, 25–6

Laursen–Metzler effect, 129
least developed countries (LDCs), 7
limited convertibility, in Yugoslavia, 169–73

market economies (MEs), 126–39
  and East–East/East–West trade, 207–10
market mechanisms
  and exchange rates in Yugoslavia, 172
  relationship to trade systems, 9–10, 12
Marshall–Lerner condition in East–West trade, 130, 137 n1
Marxist–Leninist ideology, 29, 63
money, 200
  as means of communication, 204–6
  Monetary Policy, in Yugoslavia, 177, 188
  see also currency

most favoured nation (MFN) status
  Austria's MFN policy, 92, 99
  and *perestroika*, 63
  and the Soviet Union, 99

New Economic Mechanism (NEM), 112
  and reform in Hungary, 23–5
newly industrialised countries (NICs), 14
  and export-led growth, 2
  and settlements systems, 5–8, 13, 16–17

Organisation for Economic Cooperation and Development (OECD), 109, 137, 142
  Austrian trade relations, 82, 90
  Finnish trade relations, 13–15
  trade and settlements systems, 5–21
  Yugoslav trade relations, 14–15

perestroika
  domestic and international dimensions, 58–63
  resistance to, 62
Poland, 7, 41, 44, 77
  convertible currency trade with Yugoslavia, 158, 162
  and economic reform, 9, 195
  international competitiveness of services sector, 202–3
  market-type foreign trade practice, 9
  and production-inputs shortage, 77
  trade with Austria, 90, 95
politics of reform, 192–3, 195, 209
prices
  affected by trade between centrally planned and market economies, 132–6
  effects of clearing, 11
  intra-CMEA foreign-trade prices, 39, 46, 47, 53, 55 n12, 65, 76
  Soviet price reform, 61–2
  world market prices, 39, 48, 53, 55 n12, 76, 128, 140, 148

Index 215

purchasing power
  of Soviet Union on Western
    markets, 140, 141–2, 144, 148,
    155
  'natural' Soviet purchasing
    power, 147

regression analysis, of Soviet
  imports from the West, 145–55
Romania, 7, 35, 92
  and convertible currency trade
    with Yugoslavia, 158–9, 162
  CMEA trade relations, 7

selective crediting, 177
'soft' goods, see goods
Soviet Union, 21, 64, 75
  agriculture, 59, 60–1
  crude-oil exports, 11, 160
  economic growth, 58
  economic reform, 10, 59, 209–10
  international competitiveness of
    services sector, 202–3
  imports from West and CMEA
    countries, 140–56
  influence on European states'
    foreign policy, 192–3
  perestroika, 58–63, 195–6, 209–10
  structural investment policy, 59
  trade with Austria, 90, 95
  trade with Finland, 7, 53, 110,
    116–20, 125, 147–8, 156 n11,
    197
  trade with Hungary, 35–7, 40–4,
    45, 46, 50, 55 n10, 64–79
  trade with Yugoslavia, 7–8, 157,
    160–1, 166
  see also central planning
Stalinist economic policy, 210
Sweden, similarity to Austrian
  trade procedures, 101
Switzerland, similarity to Austrian
  trade procedures, 83, 90, 101

Trade, 1–4, 207–10
  reform in Hungary, 23–57
  Hungarian–Soviet trade, 35–7,
    40–4, 45, 46, 50, 55 n10, 64–79
  Fino–Soviet trade, 7, 53, 110,
    116–20, 125, 147–8, 156 n11,
    197
  'soft' and 'hard' goods, 16–19,
    157
  Yugoslav–Soviet trade, 7–8, 157,
    160–1, 166
Trade systems
  hard currency settlement and
    bilateral clearing, 5–21
  comparison of Hungarian and
    Finnish systems, 120–4
  in Yugoslavia, 157–73
  see also dual attachment

unemployment
  in Austria, 81
  Keynesian unemployment, 126–8
United Nations Centre for Trade
  and Development (UNCTAD)
  and Yugoslav trade, 159
United States, and influence on
  foreign policy of European
  states, 192–3

Vidierungsverfahren (countersigning
  procedure), in Austria, 91, 100

Walrasian equilibrium, 127
Warsaw Treaty, 7
World Bank, and the Soviet Union,
  62

Yamburg investment project, 71
Yugoslavia, 9–10, 35
  abolition of clearing, 14
  Associated Labour Act, 178, 189
    n6
  Banking System Act of 1986, 189
    n3
  bilateral clearing with Soviet
    Union, 7–8, 157, 160–1, 166
  dual systems of international
    settlement, 157–73
  capital gains of the productive
    sector of the economy, 183–4
  exchange imbalances of banks,
    178–83
  financial system's contact with
    the East, 188

inflation, 174–89, 190 n12
impact of settlement arrangements on international exchanges, 159–66
impact of settlement arrangements on internal economic development, 164–9
monetary policy, 177, 188
National Bank of Yugoslavia, 186, 190 n18
negative interest rates, 176–83

OECD trade, 7
proposals for improvement of alternative settlement systems, 169–72
seigniorage and capital losses in banking system, 185–7
Yugoslav Institute for Market Research (ZIT), surveys of Yugoslav trade with bilateral clearing countries, 165

SPRINGER NATURE

GPSR Compliance

The European Union's (EU) General Product Safety Regulation (GPSR) is a set of rules that requires consumer products to be safe and our obligations to ensure this.

If you have any concerns about our products, you can contact us on ProductSafety@springernature.com

In case Publisher is established outside the EU, the EU authorized representative is:

Springer Nature Customer Service Center GmbH
Europaplatz 3
69115 Heidelberg, Germany